# Russia's Economy in an Epoch of Turbulence

Over the course of the last thirty years, post-communist Russia has either been struggling with crises, discussing the lessons learned from past crises, or attempting to trace the contours of future crises. Based on the author's own experiences and his research over this long period, this book traces the logic of the development of the crises and the anti-crisis policies, and shows the continuity, or discontinuity, in determining particular solutions. It demonstrates how perceptions of the priorities for economic policy, and the problems of economic growth and the formation of a new model and its alternatives were formed and how they changed. It also outlines the evolution of ideas about the role of social politics and human capital sectors in addressing anti-crisis and modernization issues, and it discusses the changing views on the institutional and structural priorities for Russia's development. This is an important book on an economic subject of crucial global significance, by a leading participant.

**Vladimir Mau** was a leading participant in the formulation of economic reforms in Russia in the 1990s–2010s. In 1992–93, he was Advisor to the Chairman of the Russian government and, in 1997–2002, he was Head of the Working Centre for Economic Reforms of the Russian government. He is a leading expert in the fields of economic theory, the history of economic thought and the Russian national economy. He is the author of twenty-five monographs, books and textbooks published in Russia and the UK, as well as about 700 published papers. He is currently Rector of the Russian Presidential Academy of National Economy and Public Administration (RANEPA).

# BASEES/Routledge Series on Russian and East European Studies

*Series editor:* Richard Sakwa, Department of Politics and International Relations, University of Kent

*Editorial Committee:*
Roy Allison, St Antony's College, Oxford, Birgit Beumers, Department of Theatre, Film and Television Studies, University of Aberystwyth, Richard Connolly, Centre for Russian and East European Studies, University of Birmingham, Terry Cox, Department of Central and East European Studies, University of Glasgow, Peter Duncan, School of Slavonic and East European Studies, University College London, Zoe Knox, School of History, University of Leicester, Rosalind Marsh, Department of European Studies and Modern Languages, University of Bath, David Moon, Department of History, University of York, Hilary Pilkington, Department of Sociology, University of Manchester, Graham Timmins, Department of Politics, University of Birmingham, Stephen White, Department of Politics, University of Glasgow

*Founding Editorial Committee Member:*
George Blazyca, Centre for Contemporary European Studies, University of Paisley

This series is published on behalf of BASEES (the British Association for Slavonic and East European Studies). The series comprises original, high-quality, research-level work by both new and established scholars on all aspects of Russian, Soviet, post-Soviet and East European Studies in humanities and social science subjects.

For a full list of available titles please visit: https://www.routledge.com/BASEES-Routledge-Series-on-Russian-and-East-European-Studies/book-series/BASEES. Recently published titles:

116. **Rethinking the Russian Revolution as Historical Divide**
    *Edited by Matthias Neumann and Andy Willimott*

117. **Post-Soviet Armenia**
    The New National Elite and the New National Narrative
    *Irina Ghaplanyan*

118. **Russia's Economy in an Epoch of Turbulence**
    Crises and Lessons
    *Vladimir Mau*

119. **Oil and the Economy of Russia**
    From the Late-Tsarist to the Post-Soviet Period
    *Nat Moser*

120. **The South Caucasus – Security, Energy and Europeanization**
    *Edited by Meliha B. Altunisik and Oktay F. Tanrisever*

# Russia's Economy in an Epoch of Turbulence

Crises and Lessons

Vladimir Mau

LONDON AND NEW YORK

First published 2018 by Routledge

2 Park Square, Milton Park, Abingdon, Oxfordshire OX14 4RN
52 Vanderbilt Avenue, New York, NY 10017

*Routledge is an imprint of the Taylor & Francis Group, an informa business*

First issued in paperback 2019

Copyright © 2018 Vladimir Mau

The right of Vladimir Mau to be identified as author of this work has been asserted by him in accordance with sections 77 and 78 of the Copyright, Designs and Patents Act 1988.

All rights reserved. No part of this book may be reprinted or reproduced or utilised in any form or by any electronic, mechanical, or other means, now known or hereafter invented, including photocopying and recording, or in any information storage or retrieval system, without permission in writing from the publishers.

Notice:
Product or corporate names may be trademarks or registered trademarks, and are used only for identification and explanation without intent to infringe.

*British Library Cataloguing-in-Publication Data*
A catalogue record for this book is available from the British Library

*Library of Congress Cataloging-in-Publication Data*
Names: Mau, V.A. (Vladimir Aleksandrovich), author.
Title: Russia's economy in an epoch of turbulence : crises and lessons / Vladimir Mau.
Other titles: Krizisy i urok. English
Description: Abingdon, Oxon ; New York, NY : Routledge, 2018. | Series: BASEES/Routledge series on Russian and East European studies ; 118 | Includes bibliographical references and index.
Identifiers: LCCN 2017029588 | ISBN 9781138061712 (hardback) | ISBN 9781315162188 (ebook)
Subjects: LCSH: Russia (Federation) – Economic conditions – 1991. | Russia (Federation) – Economic policy – 1991. | Financial crises – Russia (Federation).
Classification: LCC HC340.12 .M383413 2018 | DDC 330.947 – dc23
LC record available at https://lccn.loc.gov/2017029588

ISBN: 978-1-138-06171-2 (hbk)
ISBN: 978-0-367-88846-6 (pbk)

Typeset in Times New Roman
by Florence Production Ltd, Stoodleigh, Devon, UK

**Dedicated to the memory of Yegor Gaidar**

# Contents

*List of figures* xi
*List of tables* xiii
*Preface* xv
*List of abbreviations* xix

Introduction: economic crises in the contemporary
history of Russia   1

**PART I**
**Crises and revolutions**   13

1  A breakdown in continuity: key aspects of a revolutionary
transformation   15

2  Post-communist Russia: characteristics of the revolutionary
transformations   29

**PART II**
**The 1998 crisis in Russia**   47

3  The background of the 1998 financial crisis in Russia   49

4  The chronicle of the financial crisis   53

5  The political nature of the financial crisis   63

6  Anti-crisis policies   73

7 Results of the 1998 financial crisis　83

**PART III**
**Challenges of the global crisis**　91

8 Global crisis: historical context and trends of economic development　93

9 Anti-crisis: labels, fears, traps　101

10 In quest of a new economic model　109

**PART IV**
**Global crisis in Russia**　119

11 The drama of 2008: from an economic miracle to an economic crisis　121

12 Economic policy of 2009: between crisis and modernization　127

13 Economic policy of 2010: in search of innovations　133

14 Economic policy of 2011: the global crisis and the search for a new growth model　147

15 Economic policy of 2012: between modernization and stagnation　155

16 Economic policy of 2013: reconstruction or acceleration?　161

17 Economic policy of 2014: a new frontier and old challenges　177

18 Economic policy of 2015: sanctions and anti-crisis agenda　187

19 New economic reality: lessons of stabilization and prospects of growth　209

Conclusion: medium-term economic policy priorities 225

Appendix 231

*References* 243
*Index (persons)* 251
*Index* 259

# Figures

| | | |
|---|---|---|
| 5.1 | The number of strikers and loss of working time, 1997–8 | 66 |
| 5.2 | Attitude to the work of the president and the government | 67 |
| 5.3 | Budget salary arrears. Data on eight sectors: industry, construction, transport, agriculture, education, health, science and art | 67 |
| 5.4 | Borrowing on the domestic market and the amount of repayment and servicing of domestic debt | 69 |
| 7.1 | Official and subjective living wage | 85 |
| 7.2 | Assessment of the financial condition of the family, the economic situation in the town (township) and in the country as bad and very bad (per cent) | 85 |
| 7.3 | Wage arrears and household income dynamics | 86 |
| 7.4 | Number of strikers and loss of working time, 1998–9 | 87 |
| 7.5 | Approval of the prime minister's activities, dynamics of real wages and nominal per capita income | 87 |
| 7.6 | Approval of the prime minister's activities and dynamics of real arrears on wages | 88 |
| 7.7 | Approval of the prime minister's activities and RTS-1 index dynamics | 88 |
| 7.8 | Approval of the prime minister's activities and the industrial production intensity index | 89 |
| 7.9 | Percentage of respondents who approved of the prime minister's activities | 89 |
| 10.1 | Gross domestic product, 2010, percentage change from 2007 | 109 |
| 11.1 | Dynamics of the RTS index | 122 |
| 11.2 | Dynamics of external debt, 2001–8 (external debt of the Russian Federation at the start of the period) | 124 |
| 11.3 | Structure of private bank deposits (data on deposits of private individuals attracted by credit institutions) | 125 |
| 13.1 | Gross domestic product | 133 |
| 13.2 | Surplus (deficit) of the federal budget | 134 |
| 13.3 | Urals oil price | 135 |
| 13.4 | National debt | 135 |
| 13.5 | External debt (year end) | 136 |
| 13.6 | Inflation | 137 |

xii  *Figures*

| | | |
|---|---|---|
| 13.7 | Agricultural production in all producers' categories | 137 |
| 13.8 | Net inflow–outflow of capital in the private sector according to the balance sheets | 138 |
| 13.9 | Foreign investments | 139 |
| 13.10 | Balance of payments, current account | 139 |
| 13.11 | Unemployment | 140 |
| 14.1a | Structural constraints of economic growth: 'scissors of competitiveness' in terms of GDP per capita | 150 |
| 14.1b | Structural constraints of economic growth: 'scissors of competitiveness' in terms of business environment | 151 |
| 14.2 | Structural constraints to economic growth (decline of Russia's able-bodied population) | 152 |
| 14.3 | The most significant institutional constraints to economic growth | 153 |
| 15.1 | Recovery of production and price competitiveness (January–September 2012/January–September 2008, per cent) | 157 |
| 16.1 | Growth rates of GDP, labour productivity and real wages | 164 |
| 16.2 | Growth rates of real disposable income and retail turnover (year on year) | 165 |
| 16.3 | Gross profit and mixed income, wages of employees | 165 |
| 16.4 | Gross operating surplus (per cent GDP, 2015) | 166 |
| 16.5 | GDP growth: USSR, USA, United Kingdom, France (1980–90; * produced national income) | 173 |
| 16.6 | National income, budget balance, external debt of the USSR (in actual prices, 1980–90) | 174 |
| 16.7 | Household debt servicing compared with disposable income | 176 |
| 18.1 | Interest rate and growth rate of rouble-denominated credits to non-financial organizations | 191 |
| 19.1 | The volume of bank deposits | 212 |
| 19.2 | The proportion of bank deposits in foreign exchange, per cent | 212 |
| 19.3 | The housing loan market indicators, RUB billion | 214 |
| 19.4 | The percentage of overdue loans in credits to individuals, per cent | 214 |
| 19.5 | The debt burden on the disposable income of the population in the Russian Federation and the United States, per cent | 215 |
| 19.6 | Dynamics of the share of product categories in total exports of Russia | 218 |
| 19.7 | The coefficient of the diversification of Russian exports | 218 |
| A.1 | Exchange rate dynamics of a number of national currencies against the US dollar | 239 |
| A.2 | The dynamics of the rouble and the currencies of a number of countries in 2008–9 (1 July 2008 = 100) | 239 |
| A.3 | The dynamics of the rouble and the currencies of a number of countries in 2014 (1 July 2014 = 100) | 240 |
| A.4 | Russia's external debt and international reserves | 240 |
| A.5 | Oil prices for 46 years, dollars/barrel | 241 |
| A.6 | Dynamics of wages and profit in GDP (1995–2016) | 241 |

# Tables

| | | |
|---|---|---|
| I.1 | Some indicators of socio-economic development (1991 = 100 per cent, where not otherwise specified) | 4 |
| 1.1 | The level of GDP per capita during periods of revolution | 19 |
| 2.1 | Policy rate of Central Bank and inflation, 1993–4 (per cent) | 39 |
| 2.2 | Financial results of privatization, 1992–2002 | 43 |
| 3.1 | The dynamics of internal debt and its servicing costs | 50 |
| 3.2 | The dynamics of Russia's external debt | 51 |
| 12.1 | Anti-crisis measures of 2009 | 129 |
| 13.1 | Inflation, consumer prices growth against the previous year | 136 |
| 14.1 | The level of economic development and quality of institutions | 153 |
| 14.2 | Doing Business rating | 154 |
| 15.1 | Results of growth adjustment: growth of industrial production | 156 |
| 17.1 | Spread between credit rate and refinancing rate in some countries (2013) | 183 |
| 18.1 | Capital outflow and dollarization of the Russian economy in 2014 | 190 |
| 19.1 | Changes in the breakdown of export and import products in Russia from 2014 to 2016, per cent of total | 216 |
| 19.2 | Dynamics of the cost of exports, 2012–16, US$ billion | 217 |
| A.1 | Main economic indicators for the Russian Federation, 2007–16 | 232 |
| A.2 | GDP growth rates by years of leading developed and developing countries in 1990–2016, per cent | 234 |
| A.3 | The increase in output of industrial production in 2009–16 over 2008, per cent | 236 |
| A.4 | The balanced financial result of the enterprises of the economy in January–September 2012–16, RUB billion | 237 |
| A.5 | The share of expenditures on the social spheres of transport, housing and communal services in the total amount of expenditures of the consolidated regional budgets in 2005–16, per cent | 238 |

# Preface

This book explores global crisis started in 2007–08 and its impact on Russia. The analysis is carried out in the context of the accumulated experience of large-scale (global, systemic or structural) crises of the past 100 years.

The specificity of Russian post-communist development is determined by the overlapping of several crisis processes that, with all their complexities, are not unprecedented and may be compared with some of the important episodes of global and domestic economic history of the twentieth century. Quite relevant for this analysis are the studies of two previous structural crises (which could be considered global as well): those of the 1930s and the 1970s. Each of these crises formed an economic model that was new for their time and new approaches to theoretical research. It is also important to notice specific characteristics of the radical transformations of socio-economic systems (revolutions) twice faced by Russia in the twentieth century. Also appropriate seems to be the experience of profound (systemic) economic transformations in Russia, forming a model of a state market economy (new economic policy; NEP) at the beginning of the 1920s and its destruction at the end of that decade. Sixty years later, Russia again attempted a complex transformation into a market economy (or market socialism, as it seemed at the beginning of transition) in the second half of the 1980s.

Of course, despite the importance of past experience, one should not rely on it as the only basis in the formulation of anti-crisis policy, as the very combination of past crises creates a new reality that requires new approaches to an economic policy agenda. Not to mention the fact that every structural (and global) crisis creates a new situation that makes a simple repetition of the anti-crisis policy of the past just impossible. Moreover, attempts to repeat past experience are counter-productive, as they only exacerbate the crisis.

That is why the author sought to combine the historical and problematic approaches in this book.

The Introduction presents an overview of the crises faced by the Russian economy since the collapse of the communist system in 1989–91.

Part I deals with the lessons of revolutionary crises and the transformations. A full-scale revolution is an exceptionally rare phenomenon; however, with all its uniqueness, revolutionary transformations have some logic and peculiarities.

Part II studies the development and lessons of the 1998 financial crisis in Russia, which completed the post-communist transformation and largely identified the socio-economic model of the country's development for the next decade and a half.

Part III examines the global crisis that began in 2008, in the context of the 1930s and 1970s crises.

Part IV concentrates on Russia's economic problems in the midst of the global crisis. The key thesis here is the juxtaposition of several crises, unfolding against the backdrop of the global crisis, but not identical to it. It also discusses key challenges of the post-crisis agenda for Russia and the world.

When writing this book, the author relied on his research studies over the past 20 years, above all reviews of the socio-economic development of Russia prepared at the Gaidar Institute for Economic Policy (Institute for the Economy in Transition before 2010), as well as articles from the journals *Voprosy Ekonomiki* (Economic Issues) and *Ekonomicheskaya Politika* (Economic Policy). Of course, much work had been done processing these materials in light of the challenges and realities of our time.

Using papers written during the events described as a basis, it is possible to trace the logic of crises' dynamics and anti-crisis policy and to show the continuity (or discontinuity) in decision-making. From chapter to chapter, the reader will see the formation and transformation of ideas about the priorities of economic policy, the issues of economic growth and the emergence of a new model and its alternatives. The reader will follow the evolution of attitudes to the role of social policy and human capital issues in addressing crisis and modernization tasks, as well as the perceptions of the institutional and structural priorities of the development of Russia.

I would like to thank the organizations that I have worked in during decades of crises and growth. They include the Russian Presidential Academy of National Economy and Public Administration (formerly the Academy of National Economy under the Russian Federation government), the Gaidar Institute for Economic Policy, as well as the Working Centre for Economic Reforms under the government of Russia. The research, expert and consulting activities of these organizations always formed the basis for their employees' individual research studies.

My thanks to my colleagues who have, for 25 years, shared their thoughts with me and who have given valuable pieces of advice when I was working on individual sections of this book. Many of them are working, or have in the past worked, in these organizations. They include Tatiana Drobyshevskaya, Serguei Drobyshevsky, Revold Entov, Hermann Gref, Georgy Idrisov, Pavel Kadochnikov, Mikhail Khromov, Alexei Kudrin, Olga Makarova, Tatiana Maleva, Alexsei Moiseyev, Vladimir Nazarov, Kirill Rogov, Carol Scott Leonard, Serguei Sinelnikov-Murylev, Irina Starodubrovskaya, Ilia Trunin, Pavel Trunin, Alexei Ulyukaev, Alexei Vedev, Ksenia Yudaeva.

I am grateful to E.T. Gaidar, who was one of the key figures in economic reform and anti-crisis policy in modern Russia. I have discussed many problems covered by this book with him.

When working on the manuscript, I appreciated the vitally important assistance of Valerian Anashvili, Natalia Demidova, Vladimir Gurevich, Maksim Kiselev, Yury Ponomarev, and Ksenia Zamanskaya.

The last but not the least is my gratitude to Richard Sakwa and Editorial Committee of BASEES/Routledge Series on Russian and East European Studies who supported publication of this book.

# Abbreviations

| | |
|---|---|
| BRICS | Brazil, Russia, India, China and South Africa |
| CDS | credit default swap |
| EU | European Union |
| FCS | Federal Customs Service of Russia |
| GDP | gross domestic product |
| GKO | government short-term commitment [*Gosudarstvennoye Kratkosrochnoye Obyazatyelstvo*] |
| IEA | Institute for Economic Analysis |
| IEP | Institute for Economic Policy |
| IET | Institute for the Economy in Transition |
| IFS | International Financial Statistics |
| IMF | International Monetary Fund |
| MICEX | Moscow Interbank Currency Exchange |
| OECD | Organisation for Economic Co-operation and Development |
| OFZ | federal loan obligations [*Obligatsyi Federal'novo Zaima*] |
| RAS | Russian Academy of Sciences |
| RBC | RosBusinessConsulting |
| RTS | Russian Trading System |
| SEZ | special economic zone |
| UNDP | United Nations Development Programme |
| VAT | value added tax |
| VTB | Vneshtorgbank |
| WTO | World Trade Organization |

# Introduction
Economic crises in the contemporary history of Russia

**Typology of crises**

Crises are an important topic on the economic agenda of today's Russia and an indispensable element of domestic economic and political discussions. During this country's quarter of a century of post-communist history, its people or its governments have been either struggling with crises, discussing lessons learned from past crises, or trying to see the contours of future crises.

The permanent role of crisis in Russian political and economic discourse should not come as a surprise. Economic crises are an important element of modern economic growth, which began about 300 years ago. In this regard, the famous question of Queen Elizabeth as to "Why no one saw the credit crunch coming?"[1] – reflects just an ordinary human wish. If crises could be predicted, they could be avoided.

Such a view is unusual for most people, especially in Russia. For roughly 60 years of the twentieth century – from the 1930s to the late 1980s – the term 'crisis' was not used in relation to the Soviet economy and was strongly associated with 'moribund capitalism'. This does not mean, however, that there were no economic crises in communist economies at all. They were just hidden, taking different forms from those in market economies (commodity shortage instead of inflation, excessive employment and low productivity instead of formal unemployment, etc.), but still one could observe a certain cyclicality in economic development, even in the Soviet economy.[2] Ultimately, it is this intellectual and political 'insensitivity' to crises, the unwillingness to accept them as a natural part of development, that played a cruel joke with the Soviet system, pushing it to the disastrous turn of the 1980s and 1990s.

Of course, the notion of 'crisis' is multifaceted and ambiguous. In this book, we do not intend to discuss its strict definition. We will be talking about the serious difficulties that were faced by the Russian economy and that required significant changes in the course of its economic policy. The signs of a crisis are significant disadvantageous changes in economic parameters and social dynamics: GDP (not necessarily a fall into a negative area, but also sharp braking), growing employment, high inflation (or deflation), high budget deficit and public debt, high interest rates and a number of other parameters. A crisis is not identical to an economic downturn, but negative GDP growth is important evidence of a crisis.

Since the late 1980s, Russia has experienced several crises of various depths and political consequences. One can conventionally identify the following crises that occurred in Russia over the past 25 years:

- transformational crisis, within which a radically new economic and political model is installed; its main feature is simultaneous changes in the political, economic, social and ideological foundations of the country, sometimes accompanied by changes in the state borders or the collapse of the state, when the crisis takes the form of a full-scale revolution;[3]
- systemic (structural) crisis, as the crisis of the current model of economic growth and economic regulation, requires the implementation of significant (albeit not necessarily radical) institutional changes; it is based on extensive technological advancements;[4]
- cyclic (investment) crisis, reflecting fluctuations in growth of GDP, investment and employment, is well known from the history of the nineteenth and twentieth centuries;
- financial crisis, which, in turn, could develop into a budget crisis, monetary crisis (currency crisis) or banking system crisis; these can occur together or predominantly in one financial area or another; in fact, in all these cases, we are talking about a macroeconomic destabilization;
- crisis of external shocks, which is related to circumstances external (exogenous) to the country – wars, with their economic consequences, a sharp change in the terms of trade, etc.

In practice, these crises, in varying combinations, overlap each other or predetermine one another. More precisely, systemic crises comprise crises of individual areas of economic life. Thus, transformational and structural crises always involve financial crisis, which often becomes their direct trigger. External shocks cause financial destabilization. The overlapping of crises determines the specificity of anti-crisis measures in each country at a given time. The overlapping of investment and financial crises significantly hinders escape from crisis, making the anti-crisis measures longer and more painful.

Post-communist Russia passed through all these crises, some of them more than once. However, with all the variety of economic problems during the 30 years (from the late 1980s), there are two fairly lengthy periods that can be characterized as crises: the 1990s transformation period and the contemporary global crisis that began in 2008 and is currently in full swing in Russia.

## The crisis of the 1990s

The first post-communist decade was a time of complex, multidimensional processes transforming Soviet socialism into a new market democracy (as it seemed at the beginning). The difficult, controversial nature of the transformation spawned fierce debates on the substance of the reforms, their effectiveness and adequacy, and on the availability of alternative solutions.

In the late 1980s, the USSR was confronted with four crises connected to four large-scale historical challenges. It is true that these processes fully defined the development of Russia in the 1990s. Although not internally connected to each other, in Russia they were closely entwined and greatly influenced each other.

*First*, the country faced the challenges of the post-industrial era. Emergence from an industrial society was accompanied by severe structural and macroeconomic crises experienced by the West in the 1970s. Thanks to a favourable external economic environment (sharp growth of oil prices), the USSR could delay the onset of structural adaptation, but it was so much the worse when this became absolutely inevitable.[5]

In the 1990s, fierce debates were held about the nature of the structural transformation of the Russian economy. The decline of a number of traditional sectors of the industrial economy is characterized by some authors as de-industrialization, although a deeper analysis of the running processes makes it possible to see the shoots of the service structures more attributable to a post-industrial economy (Table I.1). Telecommunication and electronic sectors grew rapidly.

The structure of the products of the chemical and metallurgy industries improved substantially. A marked increase could be seen in the numbers of educational institutions, students and postgraduates.

*Second*, Russian society faced post-communist transformation itself. The most complex transformation was that of property – privatization at the national level. However, this transition was not something specific to Russia only. At the same time, about twenty-five countries carried out post-communist transformations, and Russia was not a pioneer: a number of countries started this transition 2–3 years earlier, which offered the post-Soviet republics a certain experience, although not a very rich one.

*Third*, Russia faced a massive financial (or macroeconomic) crisis that was the result of populist economic policy (since the second half of the 1980s) as well as the political weakness of the post-communist state, which was unable to resist pressure from various interest groups (lobbyists). This led to the collapse of the fiscal and monetary systems, extremely high rates of inflation and the decline in production. However, the macroeconomic crisis and the ways to combat it had been well explored by the end of the twentieth century. In the 1940s–1980s, many countries in Europe, Asia and Latin America had to deal with similar problems, and Russia itself had a positive experience of overcoming a macroeconomic crisis (1922–3).

*And fourth*, the political, economic and structural changes faced by Russia at the turn of the 1980s–1990s were implemented under conditions of transformational crisis and full-scale social revolution. The systemic reforms that radically changed the social fabric of the country were carried out in the face of a weak state, which was the essential characteristic of the revolution.[6] By the beginning of the post-communist transformation, almost all government institutions had been destroyed, and their recovery was, in fact, the central political task of the first post-communist decade. Moreover, the economic reforms were advancing only in the

Table 1.1 Some indicators of socio-economic development (1991 = 100 per cent, where not otherwise specified)

| | 1992 | 1998 | 1999 | 2000 | 2005 | 2010 | 2012 |
|---|---|---|---|---|---|---|---|
| *Education* | | | | | | | |
| Number of higher-education institutions | 535 | 914 | 939 | 965 | 1,068 | 1,115 | 1,046 |
| Number of students in higher-educational institutions, thousand people | 2,638.0 | 3,597.9 | 4,073.0 | 4,741.4 | 7,064.6 | 7,049.8 | 6,075.4 |
| Specialists graduated from higher-educational institutions, thousand people | 425.3 | 500.8 | 554.8 | 635.1 | 1,151.7 | 1,467.9 | 1,397.3 |
| Teaching staff, thousand people (1993 = 100%) | – | 253.2 | 260.8 | 271.1 | 311.3 | 356.8 | 342.0 |
| *Production* | | | | | | | |
| Video tapes, million | 2.8 | 30.5 | 24.9 | 21.3 | – | – | – |
| The share of electric and BOF steel in total steel production, % | 50 | 72 | 72 | 73 | 80 | 91 (2009) | – |
| The share of steel obtained from continuous casting machines, % | 23 (1990) | 37 (1995) | 53 | 50 | 66 | 81 (2009) | – |
| Production of aluminium, including silumin | 99.4 | 111.4 | – | 120.6 | 137.1 | – | – |
| *Transport* | | | | | | | |
| Number of car owners (per 1,000 persons) | 68.4 | 120.4 | 126.2 | 130.5 | 168.4 | 228.4 | 257.5 |
| Paved roads, km/1,000 km$^2$ | 25 | 30 | 31 | 31 | 31 | 39 | 54 |

*Communications*

| | | | | | | | |
|---|---|---|---|---|---|---|---|
| Number of telephones of general telephone network (per 1,000 persons) | 0.1 | 5.1 | 9.3 | 22.3 | 862.6 | 1,663.7 | 1,826.9 |
| Number of home telephones (per 100 families) | 105 | 137.6 | 147.6 | 155.5 | 60.1 | 62.5 | 57.8 (2013) |
| Length of long-distance telephone channels | 245.6 (1990) | 295.8 (1995) | 351.1 | 1,222.7 | 16,017.8 | – | – |
| Share of digital channels in the total length of long-distance telephone channels, % | 1.5 | 56.9 | 69.1 | 76.9 | – | – | – |
| Number of subscriber devices of mobile radiotelephone (cellular) communication, thousand pieces | 6.0 | 747.2 | 1,370.6 | 3,263.2 | 123,549.3 | 237,689.2 | 261,887.8 |
| Cellular and zone communication channels, no. | 100 | 12,695 | 23,600 | 55,524 | – | – | – |
| Number of subscribers to cellular networks, million people | 0.27 (1996) | 0.63 | 1.08 | 3.4 | 123.8 | 237.7 | 252.3 |
| Number of Internet users, million people | 1 (1996) | 1.5 (1997) | 2.2 | 3.1 | 21.7 | 43.3 | 59.6 |

*Sources:* Federal State Statistics Service, Ministry of Telecom and Mass Communications of Russian Federation, VimpelCom (Beeline)

rebuilding of the institutions of state, resulting in a slower pace of change compared with most other post-communist countries. The revolutionary nature of the transformations was unique among the countries engaged in post-communist transition, but it was not completely new in the history of Europe.

Thus, the specificity of Russia's development in the 1990s was predetermined by the mere fact of the juxtaposition of four crises. None of them constituted anything unique, unknown in other countries' experiences or in the historical experience of Russia itself. The uniqueness lay in their overlapping in one country, at one time. This particular fact explained the specifics of the Russian transformation and has stumped many researchers in post-communism.

The first post-communist decade, or the decade of transformation, had two particularly acute phases when economic problems could blow up the political system.

It actually happened in 1991, when the USSR ceased to exist, having collapsed under the onslaught of mainly economic problems. Heavy liberalization reforms of 1992, accompanied by four-digit inflation, also led to serious political upheaval, but helped to create the basic conditions for the implementation of the anti-crisis policy in the future.

The second phase was the financial crisis of 1998, which was also fraught with political turmoil. However, despite the almost fourfold devaluation and inflation of up to 80 per cent in the fall of 1998, the crisis was quickly countered, and its results were used to restart economic growth.

By the end of the 1990s, at least three of the four aforementioned crises had shown signs of exhaustion.

First of all, *macroeconomic stabilization was carried out*. The crisis turned out to be quite long (about 10 years), but not unprecedented in economic history. Stabilization was carried out using a set of standard measures (liberalization, fiscal and monetary stabilization, privatization) that formed the basis for economic recovery. In this regard, the 1998 crisis became the final episode of the decade of post-communist transition.

By 2000, *the revolutionary transformation processes had been virtually exhausted*. The state institutions had been reinstated, and the macroeconomic stabilization had been synchronized with political stabilization. The analysis of the political parties' pre-election programmes for the state duma contest at the end of 1999 showed that the benchmarks of the major political forces, with all the differences between them, were converging.[7] A system of basic values had been formed, and these values ceased to be the subject of political struggle, at least for a certain period. For example, no one questioned private ownership as the basis of economic and political life (although the assessments of privatization remained controversial); no one, by this time, rejected tight fiscal and budgetary policy; all supported the policy of reducing the tax burden; and all were agreed on the need to shift the focus on to institutional reforms. Of course, the practical recommendations of political forces varied considerably, but these differences were no longer so deep that they could lead to the destruction of the political system. Authorities' ability to ensure basic macroeconomic stability serves as a vital economic and political characteristic of the end of revolution.

Thus, by the early 2000s, one could say that the challenges of the post-communist transformation had been exhausted. There are three basic characteristics that distinguish the communist system: a totalitarian political regime, absolute domination of state ownership in the economy, and commodity shortages as essential features of the economic and political life.[8] By the end of the 1990s, Russia had overcome all the three traits of communism.

However, this does not mean the formation of a new, efficient market economy in Russia. The structural and macroeconomic problems associated with the formation of the modern technological and institutional framework were not fully overcome. The failure to address these problems contributed to Russia's vulnerability in the face of global crises and external shocks.

In short, the dominant socio-economic problem for Russia after the completion of the post-communist transformation was the crisis in the industrial system and the formation of the foundations of modern (post-industrial) society. This process determined the nature of the crises to be faced by the country in the foreseeable future.

## Turbulent decade: 2008–?

The global crisis that started in 2008 coincided with the recovery of the Russian economy to the level that preceded the transformational crisis. In 2000–8, there was sustained economic growth that allowed the GDP to almost double within a decade. The average annual growth rate was about 7 per cent.

However, while the country was approaching the pre-crisis (1989) level, there occurred some signs of exhaustion of the current model of economic growth. This model was based on continuous advance growth in demand (due to the rapid rise in oil prices and the influx of petrodollars), along with a lag of growth in productivity and competitiveness. The institutional reforms initiated and successfully implemented in 2000–3 started gradually to roll back. The quality of institutions did not play a significant role when the financial capacity of the government was rapidly growing. Despite the undoubted macroeconomic success (reduction of sovereign debt to an insignificant level of about 2 per cent, formation of the Stabilization Fund, ensuring fiscal surpluses, lowering inflation) and political stability, it was obvious that the economy remained vulnerable to external currents and could not make a leap forward – the competitiveness in the 'Dutch disease' situation was declining.

The global crisis had a systemic (or structural) nature and was comparable, in scale and consequences, with two crises of the twentieth century – those of the 1930s and the 1970s.[9] This was a crisis of a special type that is not described by one or two parameters (for example, recession and rising unemployment), but is a multifaceted crisis covering various areas of socio-economic life, and it usually has important political consequences.

This crisis generated a big intellectual challenge. It requires a new agenda of economic and political analysis and has become a powerful stimulus for rethinking the existing economic and political doctrines, globally and for individual countries.

Of course, there may not be any direct analogues. Structural crises are unique – that is, the experience of overcoming each of them is of limited value in the new environment. And yet, there are a number of characteristics that allow us to attribute them to one class. That is, these crises can be compared with each other, their specific characteristics can be taken into account, but the anti-crisis policy recipes cannot be moved from one of them to another.

One can identify the following features inherent to system structural crises.

*First*, the crisis is associated with deep institutional and technological changes. These changes drive the economy to a new level of efficiency and productivity. The modernization of the technological base as the result of the latest achievements of science and technology is considered essential to successfully exit from the crisis. The formation of a new technological base will play the same fundamental role that was played by heavy engineering in the middle of the twentieth century and microelectronics and computer systems in the period after the 1970s. Technological innovation involves the transformation of demand for many industrial and consumer products, and particularly for investment and energy products. Naturally, this affects the prices of the majority of goods in the market and creates new equilibrium price levels, which changes political configurations.

*Second*, this crisis is inseparable from the financial crisis.

*Third*, the heart of the crisis is formed by the imbalances in the economic world. These imbalances are associated with deep technological shifts, that is, with the introduction of fundamentally new technologies (some economists call this a new technological paradigm). Therefore, the overcoming of the crisis involves the transformation of the productive base of the leading countries on the basis of these new technologies.

*Fourth*, geo-economic and geopolitical imbalances are accumulating. The most obvious example of this imbalance nowadays will be the change in the roles of the developed and emerging (developing) economies. Acquisition of a more balanced growth path (according to the parameters of savings and expenditures, exports and domestic consumption, income and expenditure) is the key challenge faced by many developed and developing countries in Europe, America and Asia.

*Fifth*, there is the formation of new foreign exchange configurations: a new world currency (or currencies). In the twentieth century, it was the fundamental change in the role of gold and the rise of the dollar; after the 1970s, it was the strengthening of the bi-currency nature of international payments. In the new circumstances, there occurs a new issue of the prospects for the dollar, euro, yuan, as well as the question of the role of regional reserve currencies.

*Sixth*, the crisis is long – it covers a period of about 10 years, which can be described as a turbulent decade. This means, on the one hand, that it can be divided into stages that are dominated by specific problems of a sectoral or regional nature, and, on the other hand, that no single characteristic can be considered the sole cause of the deepening crisis or the recovery. This also applies to recession (the crisis did not begin with a recession and is not limited thereto), fluctuations in the stock market and any other parameters.

*Seventh*, fighting the crisis is always accompanied by strong, not always adequate, anti-crisis measures being taken. On the one hand, this is due to the severity of the structural problems that require considerable economic and social sacrifices. On the other hand, the above-mentioned intellectual unreadiness for a structural crisis – that is, the attempts to solve new challenges using old methods – leads to the accumulation of additional difficulties and further aggravates the economic crisis, as well as the political one. Thus, a problem of *exit strategy* arises, and it takes time, not only to overcome the crisis, but also to deal with the consequences of anti-crisis policy (which also has its own price).

All these factors, taken together, explain the fundamental difference between a systemic crisis and a cyclical one. Cyclical crisis is healed by time, it does not assume policy changes and it disappears by itself after deflation of the bubble that occurred during the boom period. A systemic crisis requires substantial transformation of economic policies based on a new philosophy of economic life. In other words, structural problems here dominate over cyclical ones.

Russia's passage through today's global crisis can be broken down into several phases.

In the first phase, the most acute for the global economy (2008–9), the Russian economy developed in parallel with the rest of the developed world. Some problems were more severe than in other countries, others were milder.

Thanks to the responsible macroeconomic policies of the previous decade, the country managed to avoid the debt trap and preserve a balanced budget and significant foreign exchange reserves. This made it possible to mitigate the difficulties of the first phase of the crisis and to focus the anti-crisis policy on maintaining household demand. Major public investment projects (preparations for the APEC Summit in 2012, the 2014 Winter Olympics, construction of the Nord Stream gas pipeline) also helped to maintain economic growth. However, all this allowed the socio-economic situation to be mitigated, but did not keep the economy from falling: the decline of GDP in Russia in 2009 was the deepest among the G20 countries.

The main macroeconomic difference was the availability of budgetary balance and high inflation. This made it impossible to use monetary stimulation and significantly limited the possibility of budget stimulation. In fact, Russia faced the risk of stagflation, which required an anti-crisis programme different from those of other developed countries.

In the second phase (2010–13), when the situation seemed to have stabilized, and the oil prices and foreign exchange reserves had almost recovered to the pre-crisis level, the prevailing ideology was *business as usual*. In other words, an attempt was made to return to the economic growth model of 2000–8, which was based on stimulating demand.

However, government officials recognized the need for transition to a new growth model, which had been intensively discussed in 2011–12 in the framework of the "Strategy-2020" document.[10]

The third stage began in 2013, when the signs of slowdown occurred. For the first time since the beginning of the twenty-first century (except for the period

2009–11), the country's growth rate was below the world average. The slowdown was the result of several simultaneous factors: the lack of institutional and structural reforms for several years in a row, the reduction in investment activity (for both market and institutional reasons), the rise of geopolitical tensions and the deterioration of the external economic environment.

By early 2015, Russia was again under the influence of multiple crises – structural, cyclical and external shocks (the drop in oil prices and the imposition of financial sanctions).[11] Each of these problems can be solved within the framework of responsible economic policies. However, their coexistence creates serious difficulties, as not just diverse, but sometimes diametrically opposed, measures are needed to be taken to fight each of these crises.

The key crisis affecting the current situation in Russia is the global crisis, with the necessity to transform the current model of economic growth in Russia. This model had shown signs of exhaustion as early as 2008, as was noted by all economists. But, the short crisis recession of 2009 and the recovery of the fallen oil prices allowed the period of its existence to be extended for several years. Starting in 2012, the fall in economic growth once again recalled the necessity for structural and institutional reforms.[12] External shocks, no matter how important, play a secondary role, exacerbating the situation, but at the same time creating additional opportunities for anti-crisis manoeuvring and institutional renewal.

## Notes

1 See: Pierce 2008.
2 See: Ofer 1987.
3 See: Skocpol 1979; Tilly 1993; Starodubrovskaya and Mau 2001a.
4 Some economists consider the problem of the changing technological base using the logic of "major economic cycles" of N.D. Kondratiev – long waves covering 50–60-year periods (see: Kondratiev 1925).
5 The description of the Russian crisis as the crisis of industrial society is contained in the works of some researchers. See, for example: Bauman 1997; Rosser and Rosser 1997.
6 A detailed description of this conclusion may be found in: Starodubrovskaya and Mau 2001b: 288–92.
7 Arkhipov *et al.* 2000: 313–19.
8 The essential relationship, the indivisibility of the communist system and commodity shortages were clearly seen in the first years of the practical implementation of the communist experiment, and, by the end of the Soviet system, it was theorized by Janos Kornai (See: Brutskus 1922; Novozhilov 1926; Kornai 1980). This was in fact recognized by Stalin. His work *Economic Problems of Socialism in the USSR* states that one of the fundamental laws of the society built under his leadership is called "the law of the accelerated growth of the demand comparing with the possibilities to meet it" (Stalin 1997).
9 See: Mau 2010.
10 See: Mau and Kuzminov 2013.
11 If we consider the situation in detail, it will make sense to identify the following crisis phenomena in Russia in 2014–15, in addition to the global crisis: the crisis of Russia's economic growth model in the 2000s; the worsening geopolitical situation; the external shock from sanctions against Russia, primarily in the financial sector; the external shock

resulting from the fall in oil prices; the currency crisis resulting from the dual external shock (most notably, the fall in oil prices, but also the financial sanctions); the cyclic reduction associated with the decline in investment activity; and the demographic crisis in the form of a declining population of working age (see: Mau 2016).

12 The thesis of the primacy of structural reforms is shared by almost all experts. Following is a typical passage: "In order to overcome the recession and improve the long-term prospects, Russia will have to take steps of both counter-cyclical and structural policies. And, with regard to Russia, the structural measures are more important. The limitation of consistent structural reforms in the past have led to a gradual erosion of investor confidence" (The World Bank 2014: 5).

## References

Arkhipov, S., Anisimova, L., Batkibekov, S., Drobyshevsky, S., Drobyshevskaya, T., Izryadnova, O., Kadochnikov, P., Kochetkova, O., Lugovoi, O., Mau, V., Stupin, V., Trunin, I., Shardrin, A., Shatalov, S., Radygin, A., Bobylev, Yu., Logacheva, T., Serova, E., Khramova, I., Kralova, N., Tikhonova, T., Volovik, N., Leonova, N., Prikhodko, S., Ilyukhina, E., Mikhailov, L., Sycheva, L., Timofeev, E., Rozdetsvenskaia, I., Shishkin, S., Kolosnitsyn, I., and Sinelnikov, S. (2000). *Russian economy in 1999: Trends and prospects*. Issue 21. Moscow: IET.

Bauman, Z.A. (1997). "Post-Modern Revolution?" In Frentzel-Zagorska, J., *From a One-Party State to Democracy*, 1st edn. Amsterdam: Rodopi.

Brutskus, B.D. (1922). "Problemy narodnogo khoziaistva pri sotsialisticheskom stroie" [Problems of national economy under the socialist system], *Economist*, no. 1–3.

Kondratiev, N. (1925). "Bol'shiye tsikly konjunktury" [The major cycles of the conjuncture], *Voprosy konjunktury*, vol. 1, no. 1, pp. 28–79.

Kornai, J. (1980). *Economics of Shortage*, Vol. 2. Amsterdam: North Holland Publishing.

Mau, V. (2010). "Global crisis: Experience of the past and challenges of the future", *Herald of Europe*, no. 7, pp. 31–42.

Mau, V. (2016). "Between crises and sanctions: Economic policy of the Russian Federation", *Post-Soviet Affairs*, vol. 32, no. 4, pp. 350–77.

Mau, V. and Kuzminov, Ya. (eds) (2013). *Strategy-2020: New Model of Growth – New Social Policy*, 2 vols. Moscow: Delo.

Novozhilov, V. (1926). "Nedostatok tovarov" [Shortage of goods], *Finance Bulletin*, no. 2.

Ofer, G. (1987). "Soviet economic growth (1928–1985)", *Journal of Economic Literature*, vol. xxv, no. 4, pp. 1767–833.

Pierce, A. (2008). "The Queen asks why no one saw the credit crunch coming", *The Telegraph*, 5 November. Available at: www.telegraph.co.uk/news/uknews/theroyalfamily/3386353/The-Queen-asks-why-no-one-saw-the-credit-crunch-coming.html (accessed 27 July 2017).

Rosser, J.B. and Rosser, M.V. (1997). "Schumpeterian evolutionary dynamics and the collapse of Soviet-block socialism", *Review of Political Economy*, vol. 9, no. 2, pp. 211–23.

Skocpol, Th. (1979). *States and Social Revolutions*. Cambridge, UK: Cambridge University Press.

Stalin, I. (1997). *Sobraniye sochinenij* [Collected Works], Vol. 16. Moscow: Pisatel.

Starodubrovskaya, I., and Mau, V. (2001a). *Velikie Revolutsii ot Kromvelya do Putina* [Great Revolutions. From Cromwell to Putin]. Moscow: Vagrius.

Starodubrovskaya, I., and Mau, V. (2001b). *The Challenge of Revolution: Contemporary Russia in historical perspective.* Oxford, UK: Oxford University Press.

Tilly, Ch. (1993). *European Revolutions, 1492–1992.* Oxford, UK: Blackwell.

World Bank, The. (2014). *Confidence Crisis Exposes Economic Weakness. Russian Economic Report.* No. 31.

# Part I
# Crises and revolutions

# 1 A breakdown in continuity

## Key aspects of a revolutionary transformation

The transformation of a society can take many forms, and this shift in principal characteristics is often described as 'revolutionary'. However, a revolution can only be regarded as such depending on the results: they imply a qualitative change in the state of the society. Such a broad concept does little to help understand certain events that claim to be revolutionary. Not only the extent of the transformations, but also the mechanisms by which they are implemented, are significant.

Revolutions have traditionally been interpreted as violent changes of a regime and associated with the emergence of a new elite and new ideology. The experience of post-communist transit calls for a revision of this definition. A revolution is indeed a radical and systemic transformation of society. However, the role of violence and changes in the elite and the ideology need not be absolute. A far more important characteristic of a full-scale revolutionary transition is the fact that it is conducted under the conditions of a sharp decline in the power of the state. The political manifestation of this crisis involves a strong conflict of elites (and the main interest groups in general) and a lack of consensus among them in terms of basic values, key issues and the direction in which the country should develop. For economists, the weakness of the authorities is primarily evident in the financial crisis of the state, in its inability to collect taxes and balance its expenses with its income.

It is the weakness of the state authorities that is responsible for the spontaneous nature of the course of economic and social processes, which, in turn, makes great revolutions remarkably similar to one another, both in terms of the phases in which an economic and political crisis develops, as well as in terms of basic characteristics. Social progress suddenly becomes a result, not of an individual's deliberate actions (sometimes more, sometimes less effective, but always considered), but rather of various interests leading the country in different directions, which predefines the unstructured nature of ensuing events. Despite this, however, there are patterns that make great (large-scale) revolutions so similar to one another.

It is the spontaneity and unstructured nature, not violence, that are constitutive features of a revolution. Violence does, of course, play a certain role. Acute conflicts between major interest groups, an inability of the bulk of the society to share common values, to come to an understanding regarding fundamental issues of life in the country, make it impossible to avoid the use of force to impose a definite system of values – a system that cannot be agreed upon using conventional procedures (which are legitimate according to the country's level of development). However, the level of violence cannot be evaluated coherently, and certainly not in quantitative terms. Who can say how much violence is required for a transformation to be considered revolutionary? One can hardly agree with the statement that bloodier revolutions are more important. These reasons become even more unstable when we move from an agrarian society to analysing revolutionary events in the modern world. As the overall level of socio-economic development increases (and with it, the level of education, culture and material well-being), the role of violence generally decreases, because the people "have something to lose".

Revolution, of course, changes the elite. However, this should not be confused with the immediate physical elimination of representatives of the elite of the old regime (through execution, exile or dismissal). Two aspects must be taken into account. First, the radical nature of the renewal of the elite is often exaggerated by historians of revolutions.[1] When one looks at the statements of people present at the time of the events, one almost always finds complaints from many members about the old elite remaining in power. And, these complaints are characteristic even of such seemingly radical upheavals as the great French Revolution. The situation only changes with the passage of time.

A different aspect of the problem is of more importance. The change in the elite should not be equated with the individuals that represent that particular elite. A new elite is those people willing to act under new circumstances and play by new rules, with a new logic. Both members of the old elite and new individuals are capable of adapting to this. It cannot be said, for instance, that, because the Bishop of Autun was a member of the old elite, Talleyrand was not one of the most prominent representatives of the new regime. In the same way, Viktor Chernomyrdin's presence in the upper echelons of the Soviet nomenklatura (minister and member of the Central Committee of the Communist Party of the Soviet Union) does not detract from his role in the formation of new Russian capitalism. To put it briefly, individuals' roles are more important than their origins.

A similar line of reasoning can be applied to issues concerning the transformation of ownership. Arguments concerning a change of owner are undoubtedly important, but they should not be absolute. It is not the physical change of owner that is most important, but the change in the form of ownership. A good example of this is the English revolution (Civil War) in the mid seventeenth century. Most researchers consider it inconsequential and half-hearted, as it was not accompanied by a radical redistribution of ownership, and the aristocracy, for the most part, maintained its position. The researchers were particularly surprised by the tendency of the revolution's leaders to resell royalist estates back to their old owners after they had been confiscated. However, the fact was overlooked that, after the resale, it was a different type of property – private, freed from old feudal obligations, forming the basis for the forthcoming capitalist society and providing the necessary social basis for future economic growth. The situation developed in a similar way in the first years of post-communist Russia, where, after the initial phase of privatization, a significant portion of property fell under the control of company directors and was then gradually passed on to others.

The role of new ideology should not be exaggerated either. A revolution is undoubtedly connected with ideology; however, the relationship between the two is more complex than commonly thought. A revolution does not impose a new ideology on society. On the contrary, it happens when society (primarily the elite) absorbs a new ideology and new perceptions of the 'right' state order. Enlightenment and the ideology of 'natural order' and the 'spirit of the law' (*espirit de lois*) formed the basis of the French Revolution and the general framework of virtually all revolutionary and post-revolutionary governments. Crises in market democracy and assertions in the world of ideology of industrialism, monopolism and statism were characteristic features of the turn of the twentieth century. Modern post-communist transformations fit in perfectly with the system of economic and political beliefs and values that triumphed in the civilized world in the early 1980s. This system was based on liberalism and individualism, the symbol of which was the famous thesis on the "end of history" written by Francis Fukuyama.[2] In short, the dominant ideology of the era sets the general framework of the revolution as a whole, and of its economic dimensions in particular.

Therefore, we consider revolution as a systemic transformation of society with a weak state. It is a particular mechanism of social restructuring, passing through a systemic social crisis and adapting to new challenges of the era. Other mechanisms of adaptation are also possible: gradual reforms undertaken by the old regime, the conquest of a foreign state and, finally, a "revolution from above". However, the common feature of all these models of transformation that distinguishes them from a real revolution is the presence of a strong government controlling the nature and course of reforms. Real revolution is characterized by a chaotic struggle between interest groups with an indefinite political outcome. This is a struggle that makes all social life highly uncertain, both in the immediate future and in terms of the strategic outlook. This uncertainty created by political struggle largely determines the character of a revolutionary society, including the economic mechanisms of the revolutionary transformation.

## Revolution and modernization

The main objective of Russian policy in the twentieth century (both at the beginning and end of the century) was modernization, or, more precisely, to reduce the gap between it and the most developed countries and become aligned with them in terms of the level of socio-economic development, which is traditionally measured using the indicator of GDP per capita. This has been Russia's main challenge over the past three centuries. At least since the time of Peter the Great, the country has been attempting to modernize and overcome the gap that various observers estimate to be approximately 50 years behind countries such as France and Germany.

At the turn of the twentieth century, major efforts needed to be made to address the issue of increasing the pace of modernization. The defeat in the Crimean War

(1853–6) left no doubt that the issue of industrialization equated to Russia maintaining its position as an independent player in world politics. Alexander II began implementing a set of political reforms that were later followed by economic reforms (introduced mostly by his successors): these included budgetary, tax and monetary reforms, and external economic regulation. These efforts resulted in an increase in the pace of industrial growth, which, in the 1890s, came close to 10 per cent.

The mechanism of industrialization was clear and was based on two important factors. First, the source of funds for industrialization was the peasantry. Russia was the largest exporter of grain (45 per cent of the world market). Products of agriculture were the main export items and, accordingly, provided the country's main currency earnings. High taxes meant that huge amounts of money could be extorted from rural areas to be redistributed for the benefit of industry. "We shall eat less, but export more" – this quote from the minister of finance, Ivan Vyshnegradsky, expressed the essence of industrialization in Russia for decades to come, although no one else dared to state this so bluntly. It must also be noted that, at the time, Russian grain elevators were owned by the State Bank, which determined the nature of the country's fiscal and tax policy.

The fiscal factor in particular must be taken into account when we explain the reasons behind the long preservation of the *obshchinas* (communities) in Russia's rural areas.[3] Using the *obshchinas*, Minister of Finance Serguei Witte attempted to solve purely fiscal problems – to forcefully extract taxes from rural areas. Old institutions' ability to play a new role – that is, to be instrumental in modernization processes – should not be exaggerated.

A country will still have to pay to preserve ancient institutions, sometimes at a disproportionate rate. Returning to the example of the *obshchinas*, it can be assumed that, had this institution been eliminated earlier, it would have helped to speed up the development of capitalism in rural areas of Russia and might have prevented the revolution (or its development in the most disastrous manner). The government's desire to simplify the process of solving existing tax problems resulted in a systemic crisis and the collapse of the country in Revolution of 1917.

Second, the accelerated pace of industrialization, as many economists of the time believed, required the active involvement of the government to stimulate economic growth. Unlike countries that were pioneers of industrialization (England, Holland, France), Germany and Russia had to rely on the administrative resources of the state for modernisation. They were needed to compensate for the institutional failures of the underdeveloped country: the lack of reliable banks or credit histories of commercial companies, and the narrowness of the domestic market. The state became a source of financial resources and of demand for the products of industry. State-owned banks and the budget turned into key institutions ensuring economic growth. However, the main conditions of the accelerated modernization had to be provided by politics. Three of the first chairs of the Russian Council of Ministers – Sergei Witte, Pyotr Stolypin and Vladimir Kokovtsov – saw bright economic prospects for Russia, assuming that peace (both internal and external) was maintained for about 20 years.

*Table 1.1* The level of GDP per capita during periods of revolution

| Country | Year of revolution | GDP per capita (US$, 1990) |
| --- | --- | --- |
| England | 1640 | Approx. 1,200 |
| USA | 1774 | 1,287 (data from 1820) |
| France | 1789 | 1,218 (data from 1820) |
| Germany | 1848 | 1,476 (data from 1850) |
| Russia | 1905 | 1,218 (data from 1900) |
| Mexico | 1911 | 1,467 (data from 1913) |
| Russia | 1917 | 1,488 (data from 1913) |

*Source*: OECD 2016

With stable economic growth in peaceful conditions, it would be possible to solve the basic problems of industrialization and exit from the revolutionary "zone of turbulence".

These historical statistics show that revolutions took place in countries with a comparable GDP per capita. In other words, in England in the mid seventeenth century, France in the late eighteenth century, Germany in the mid nineteenth century, and Mexico and Russia in the early twentieth century, this indicator was approximately the same, which means that the structures of GDP and employment were also similar, as well as the literacy rate and other socio-economic characteristics of the society. Table 1.1 shows the comparability of the data, as well as the speed at which Russia exited from the "zone of turbulence" at the beginning of the twentieth century.

At the turn of the twentieth century, S. Witte highlighted the main areas for stimulating economic modernization. Being a subtle analyst, he stressed that, "there are in fact more capital assets in the country, but for various reasons they cannot all be placed in industrial enterprises".[4]

It was for this reason that it was suggested particular attention be paid to stimulating the transformation of savings into investments, and to do this by encouraging entrepreneurial activity and attracting foreign capital. After all, "the history of all modern wealthy countries shows that initially the development of their industries was, to a large extent, due to the inflow of foreign savings and the enterprises of foreign capitalists".[5] Russia's finance minister proposed removing restrictions that were in place when joint-stock companies, with Russian and foreign participation, were set up, and also called for regional and local authorities to stop creating obstacles to business activity:

> no matter how the legislative powers change the procedure for opening and operating factory businesses, they will always be highly dependent on numerous local authorities, from the rural police sergeant to the general governor, and these local influences will only be useful and beneficial when all government authorities embrace the fact that the development of industry is good from a state and national economic point of view and providing every possible kind of assistance is one of their official and moral obligations.[6]

In 1917, there was a breakdown in the revolution. Years of crisis and instability followed. However, after the restoration of the state and the economy, the post-revolutionary government was once again faced with the same issues of rapid industrialization. The Bolsheviks did, of course, take a more stringent approach to the challenges than the tsarist government. On the one hand, they saw themselves in a ring of hostile states and resolutely prepared for war, and, for this reason, industrialization had to be done in the shortest possible time. ("Either we do it, or they crush us", according to Joseph Stalin.)[7] On the other hand, the Bolsheviks' nightmare was the degeneration of the social basis of their power.

They were convinced, and rightly so, that organic economic growth would lead to the strengthening of the private sector, making it more competitive than state industry, and this would ultimately destroy the Bolshevik regime. This is why they sought to limit growth in the agricultural sector, ensuring the maximum expansion of urban industry and an increase in the number of urban workers, whose lives, unlike the peasants', were entirely dependent on state redistribution of funds. These two factors led to decisive steps for industrialization, which essentially was the same as at the turn of the twentieth century: transferral of funds out of Russia's rural areas, restoration of *obshchinas* (in the form of collective farms – *kholkhozs*) and the dominant role of the government. However, it was an unprecedentedly harsh form of industrialization, which cost millions of human lives. The revolution ended, and the country went back to resolving problems that had been abandoned in 1913. However, the new society that was built was extremely rigid and unable to respond well to the new challenges of the time. Therefore, when the country faced the challenges of the post-industrial era, its government and economic mechanisms were unable to react in an adequate manner. The country entered into the second revolution of the century.

The distinctive feature of Russia's post-communist transformation is that it involves the overlapping of several different, although interconnected, crises and, accordingly, several transformation processes. This refers, first, to the structural crisis of the industrial society faced with post-industrial challenges; second, the macroeconomic (financial) crisis; third, the post-communist transformation; and, finally, the revolutionary nature of this transformation.

This last factor sets Russia apart from most other post-communist countries, although it is not historically unique. The revolution in modern Russia can be viewed in the context of other major revolutions of the past, and this comparison is very useful, both in terms of achieving better understanding of the particular features of post-communist development in Russia, as well as gaining a good insight into other revolutions.[8]

Even with a cursory glance at the events in Russia over the last 25 years and comparison of them with the great revolutions of the past, one could place Russia's transformation in this particular category. This primarily has to do with the logic behind the development of the crisis in the communist system and the movement from one phase to another. The famous work by Crane Brinton, *The Anatomy of Revolution*[9] – written in the 1930s and dedicated to comparative analysis of the English, American, French and Russian (Bolshevik) revolutions –

had it been translated in time (in the late 1980s) and published in the USSR, could have become a reference guide for political forecasting. The similarity of the phases,[10] the specific characteristics of the political struggle, and the economic processes of the past and our present is remarkable and rather useful for understanding the nature and course of changes that are under way. Analogies, of course, do not prove anything. However, they do allow us to see a problem and raise a question about the mechanisms responsible for the occurrence of such analogies.

The impact of a revolution on the further development of a country's economic and political systems has been one of the most controversial and ideology-driven issues for more than 150 years. Researchers have expressed three possible principle viewpoints regarding this. First: a revolution becomes a catalyst for economic progress, freeing the economy from the shackles of the old regime. Seeing a revolution as an engine of history is in no way a Marxist innovation: this interpretation was expressed by French liberal historians in the early nineteenth century. Second: a revolution does not have much impact, because the main development trend is actually established under the old regime – an argument that goes back to De Tocqueville.[11] And finally, the third, conservative interpretation states that the revolution has a negative influence on the development of a country.[12]

One thing is certain: the nature of a post-revolutionary society, together with its social and political identity, is to a large extent dependent upon the development of the revolutionary transformation itself. This is where new interest groups and elite are formed and constituted, and this is where a new system of ownership is established.

Attention must be drawn to one aspect of the influence of a revolution on the further evolution of a country, associated with the level of social conflict. The fact that there are irreconcilable contradictions between the leading interest groups is the main source of instability and the inability of the authorities to implement any kind of consistent political and economic programme. However, it would be wrong to draw the conclusion that the most favourable result for the country's development is achieved when, after the revolution, a society is formed where the conflict between interest groups is as subdued as possible. These standpoints are characteristic of many historians and political scientists, especially those who adhere to Marxism.

A comparison of the English Civil War (revolution) and French Revolution provides the clearest example of this situation. The former is traditionally thought to be unfinished, half-hearted, because the landed aristocracy, which was in many ways linked with the old regime, was preserved. The French Revolution, on the other hand, resulted in a far more profound transformation of ownership, primarily land, and opened a wide field for the rapid political strengthening of the entrepreneurial classes, especially industrialists and bankers. For the actual course of events, substantial amendments must be made to this conclusion. It was in England, with its contradictory post-revolution social structure and acute conflict between leading interest groups, where fertile ground was created for the beginning of economic growth, which in turn led to the Industrial Revolution. The struggle between free-traders (industrialists) and protectionists (landowners) laid the foundations for the main economic and political confrontation, which held the elite in suspense for almost two centuries. Economic competition gave rise to political competition, which did not allow any social group to 'steamroll' the government and use political power to serve their own narrow self-interest.

In France, however, after the revolution, a mechanism emerged inhibiting economic growth: all the main groups were interested in protectionism. Peasants, industrialists and financiers were all in favour. This coalition stood the test of the restoration and the new revolution, as no government dared to enter into conflict with it.[13] The result was clear: France's economic backwardness compared with England continued until the 1850s.[14] This development of events is consistent with the conclusion we drew above that a change in the nature (form) of ownership is far more important than a change of owner. Similar examples could be taken from the history of various countries and revolutions, which allows us to formulate at least one highly important hypothesis: if the formation of a consensus on basic social values is the main prerequisite of a country exiting a revolution and achieving stability, then the absence of conflict in matters of economic policy becomes a source of stagnation and the preservation of economic backwardness.

## The economic problems of a revolution

The economic agenda of a revolution is based on a political crisis and the resulting increase in transaction costs. There are a number of factors that reduce incentives for entrepreneurship and restrict economic agents from assessing the prospects of their decisions. The first is uncertainty over the prospects of the new economic order, which is especially true with the redistribution of ownership, when new owners are not able to assess the reliability of their acquisitions. Second, early on in a revolution, there is a sharp break-up of the institutional structure of the society, that is, the rules of the game that economic agents were accustomed to. Third and finally, the weak state is unable to enforce laws and contracts, which means that entrepreneurs have to take additional measures to confirm the reliability of transactions. All of these problems are exacerbated during civil wars, which have accompanied all the great revolutions of the past. As a result, companies "tend to opt for a short-term strategy", and "the most profitable operations are trade, redistribution, or transactions on the black market".[15] Although trade and intermediary activity are more effective than production, losses are still incurred owing to the instability of the "rules of the game".

The increase in transaction costs was an important factor in the deterioration of the economic situation in all revolutions, starting with the English Revolution, when revolutionary processes were relatively straightforward, and ownership rights were more secure than in subsequent revolutions.

Naturally, in all subsequent revolutions, the problem of transaction costs had an even stronger impact on the development of events.

These problems were particularly acute in post-communist Russia. The low competitiveness of Russian companies is to a large extent associated with the inability of the state authorities to provide stability in the business environment and, particularly, provide law enforcement. Corruption in public administration and in the courts is a major obstacle to the development of the Russian economy. Companies are forced to pay 'law enforcement costs' (for justice administration and to obtain favourable settlements in government institutions), which not only increases expenditure, but also makes economic life significantly more uncertain.

The central point of a revolutionary economic crisis is the fiscal crisis, which remains in force throughout the entire period of the revolution. The financial crisis appears in this regard primarily as a crisis of the state budget – the inability of the state to finance its expenditures through conventional, legitimate means.

The issue of sources to replenish the treasury was always highly relevant for the last pre-revolutionary regime, and for successive governments of the revolution, and for the post-revolutionary government. The most acute conflicts of domestic and foreign policy are associated with the financing of a revolution. Not only indemnities, requisitions and new taxes, but also measures to redistribute ownership – nationalization, privatization, all possible types of confiscation – were predetermined primarily by the revolutionary government's need for money. In addition to this, the large-scale issue of paper money as a method of inflationary funding for the state budget was also a discovery of the two great revolutions of the eighteenth century (in America and France).

A revolution's financial crisis appears in the following forms:

First, we see a decline in tax collection and the government's inability to use state coercion to recover legitimate taxes. As a result, the authorities either turn a blind eye to the problem, resorting to unconventional methods of replenishing the treasury, or they even make formal decisions either to abolish taxes, as was the case in France in 1789–91, or to reduce taxes, in spite of the budget crisis, as happened in the USSR in 1990–91. The reasons behind these decisions mostly have to do with a weak government seeking political support. It is no surprise that, in post-communist Russia, the peaks of tax non-payment coincide with the times when the state authorities were at their weakest (August–September 1993 and winter 1995–6), when its ability to survive in the months that followed was clearly questioned.

Second, there is a marked increase in the role of government borrowing. In most cases, rather than conventional voluntary loans, loans turn out to be 'voluntary-compulsory' or openly compulsory loans. The latter often become the indemnity imposed on supporters of the old regime. The authorities tend to enter into individual agreements with taxpayers or major financiers, negotiating their contribution to the state budget. Although a revolutionary government may have no access to loans (as in revolutionary France or Bolshevik Russia), it is normally the case that revolutionaries (even in the radical phase) are able to conduct internal and external borrowing – although on a shrinking scale as the revolution advances. The USSR during perestroika and post-communist Russia had broad access to loans (primarily external loans), and debt during that period increased dramatically (almost fivefold from 1985 to 1997). Domestic debt also increased.

The third typical feature of a revolution is some form of default on government debt, as a way to break with the legacy of the past regimes. Typical examples of this are the refusal by the Directory in France, in 1797, to pay a substantial part of sovereign debt ("two-thirds bankruptcy") and the refusal of the Bolshevik (i.e. radical) government to pay for the debts of the former regimes. Russia defaulted on its internal debt in 1998, but continued to pay external debt scrupulously. A default in this type of situation essentially becomes a method of overcoming fiscal imbalances and a sign of the government's readiness to embark on the path to financial recovery.

The fourth feature is that the government's non-payment towards budget holders becomes widespread. This is especially true in the final phase of a revolution, when the government is strong enough to pursue a responsible financial course, but does not have sufficient political resources to formally balance the budget (i.e. to increase income to the level of budgetary obligations, or reduce obligations to the level of real income). Non-payments (arrears) were a serious problem in post-communist Russia, reaching almost 40 per cent of GDP. They affected all spheres of the country's economic life – in addition to budgetary non-payments, tax arrears also reached a considerable scale, as did delays in the payment of wages (in both state and private institutions) and debts between companies themselves.

As the revolution draws to an end and the political regime is consolidated, the measures of financial and economic stabilization begin to bear fruit, which is of benefit, not to the individuals who implemented the measures, but to the succeeding governments: the tax innovations of the Long Parliament and the Protectorate were well received by the government of the Restoration, and the results of the French Directory's stabilization were fully manifested under Napoleon Bonaparte. The weakening of the state and its inability to collect taxes and borrow money forced the authorities to resort (at least during times of peace) to 'unconventional' sources to replenish their income and primarily to the redistribution of ownership (property rights) and paper money issue.

These two economic mechanisms of a revolution are not alternatives, but, on the contrary, are closely related to one another.[16] As shown by the experience of the French assignats, redistributed ownership can serve as a method of providing paper money.

The inflationary mechanisms for financing a revolution are well documented in economics literature.[17] The logic of the actions of governments that resort to paper money issue is relatively simple. The revolution gets caught in a financial trap: the revenue base of the budget is broken down, and the expenditure of the revolutionary government increases sharply. The government rushes to the printing press, and the amount of money becomes more and more detached from the gold standard (or the commodity-resource base).

Money becomes worthless, prompting the government to instigate a standard set of compulsory actions: demanding that banknotes be accepted at their face value; prohibiting the use of metallic money, including as a measure of value (for price indexation); and banning the trading of basic consumer goods at market prices.

This is how standard the reactions to these measures are from economic agents who, even under the threat of the death penalty (as was the case in Jacobin France), refuse to accept these rules of play. High inflation leads to a gradual depletion of the issuing source of replenishment for the budget. The emission caused by the scarcity or absence of other sources of funding, primarily taxes, further undermines the tax base, and therefore the share of non-inflationary sources of the state budget steadily declines as the inflationary processes continue. Accordingly, the amount of paper money in circulation grows at an increasing rate, and its value begins to spiral downwards.

Inflationary financing of the budget was an important element in Russian economic policy of the 1990s: inflation was held back: it never turned into hyper-inflation and played a lesser role in solving problems of redistribution than actual privatization.

The redistribution of ownership is one of the most important mechanisms revolutionary governments can use to solve socio-economic and political problems. Following declarations by politicians or arguments from economists, researchers normally tend to see redistribution of ownership as a way of increasing the efficiency of the economic system and implementing new, more effective forms of economic management. This is exactly what is declared by revolutionary governments, regardless of whether they are talking about privatization (as in the revolutions of the seventeenth and eighteenth centuries and at the end of the twentieth century) or nationalization. However, one cannot speak of a real increase in efficiency before issues of political stabilization and the country's exit from the revolution are resolved. In the meantime, there are two other functions of the redistribution of property that come to the fore: the strengthening of the political base (through the transfer of ownership into the hands of political and social groups that support the government) and the acquisition of additional resources in the treasury.

In order to address these challenges, revolutionary governments of the past and present have used a similar set of mechanisms: first and foremost, the issue of securities provided by the redistribution of ownership, which the authorities have used to pay their debts. The results of these transactions are also clear. In conditions of political uncertainty, the recipients of these types of security gave preference to liquidity and sold the securities at a considerable discount. Ownership was concentrated in the hands of a small group of individuals, who received it at a low price. It is not surprising that among the new owners were members of the new political elite.

Our understanding of a revolution allows us to draw a number of important conclusions. First of all, it must be admitted that freedom from communism in most of the countries of Central and Eastern Europe can hardly be regarded as a series of revolutions in the strict sense of the word. In most cases, society and the elite were not split in terms of their attitude towards basic values. No matter how deep their internal conflicts were, they all sought to find a place in the united Europe. Accordingly, the authorities did not lose control of the socio-economic processes.

An understanding of a revolution as a specific mechanism of transformation in itself does not make it any easier to predict when the corresponding transformations will begin. The inability of experts to predict the near collapse of Soviet communism is rather typical of similar situations in the past.[18]

However, the same sentiment prevailed shortly before all great revolutions in history – from the English Revolution to the Bolshevik Revolution. It is not that no one expected change (it could almost be felt in the air), but no one was able to predict the mechanisms of change, their spontaneous nature, which could not be controlled by the authorities.

There is one feature that distinguishes the Russian transformation of the 1980s–1990s from other great revolutions of the past. We are essentially dealing with a full-scale revolution occurring in the context of a crisis of industrialism and a transition to a post-industrial society, in a country with a predominantly urban population with a high level of education and culture. With all the material problems, the level of wealth among Russians is incomparable with similar indicators of the revolutions of the past. This has a considerable impact on the modern Russian transformation, although it still cannot alter the basic characteristics of the revolutionary mechanism. We will examine the problems of the post-communist transformation in further detail throughout this book.

## Notes

1. This was noted by J. Goldstone (Goldstone 1991: 296).
2. See: Fukuyama 1989.
3. The possibility of using old institutions to address new challenges was noted by Alexander Gerschenkron (Gerschenkron 1962).
4. See: Witte 1900: 321.
5. Ibid., p. 323.
6. Ibid., p. 323.
7. See: Stalin 1951: 29.
8. This issue is examined in detail in the book by Starodubrovskaya and Mau 2001.
9. See: Brinton 1965.
10. The following main phases of the revolutionary process can be identified: the "rose period" (or "honeymoon"), when all forces are united in the task of overthrowing the old regime, and the extremely popular "moderate government" is in power; polarization, division of social and political forces leading to the collapse of the "moderate government"; the radical period, with the complete destruction of the old system, when going back is no longer possible; the Thermidorian phase (to use the famous term of the great French Revolution), laying the foundations for strengthening the state and stabilizing the system; post-Thermidorian stabilization and exit from the revolution.
11. See: De Tocqueville 1997.
12. For further details, see: Hirschmann 2010.
13. This situation is perhaps most eloquently expressed in the satirical sketches of F. Bastiat, above all in his pamphlet "A petition from the manufacturers of candles, tapers . . ." (Say and Bastiat 2000: 89–93).
14. For further details, see: Crouzet 1990, 1996.
15. See: North 1997: 92.
16. E. Burke was arguably the first to highlight this link. He sharply criticized the release of French assignats as a "violent outrage upon property and liberty", noting above all the redistributive function of assignats: "So violent an outrage upon credit, property, and liberty, as this compulsory paper currency, has seldom been exhibited by the alliance of bankruptcy and tyranny, at any time, or in any nation". Burke saw paper money as the source of future crises and the impossibility of the success of the French Revolution, unlike the English Revolution (Burke 1986: 226).

17  See, for example: Falkner 1919; Dalin 1983; Aftalion 1990.
18  The second edition of J. Dunn's *Modern Revolutions* refers to the impossibility of revolutionary transformation in communist countries. See: Dunn 1989: 2.

## References

Aftalion, F. (1990). *The French Revolution: An economic interpretation*. Cambridge, UK: Cambridge University Press.
Brinton, C. (1965). *The Anatomy of Revolution*. New York: Vintage Books.
Burke, E. (1986). *Reflections on the Revolution in France*. London: Penguin Books.
Crouzet, F. (1990). *Britain Ascendant: Comparative studies in Franco-British economic history*. Cambridge, UK: Cambridge University Press.
Crouzet, F. (1996). "France". In *The Industrial Revolution in National Context: Europe and the USA*, pp. 36–63. Eds M. Teich and R. Porter. Cambridge, UK: Cambridge University Press.
Dalin, S.A. (1983). *Inflyatsiya v epokhi sotsial'nykh revolyutsiy* [Inflation in the Period of Social Revolution]. Moscow: Nauka.
De Tocqueville, A. (1997). *Staryj poryadok i revolyutsiya* [The Old Regime and the Revolution]. Moscow: Moscow Philosophical Foundation.
Dunn, J. (1989). *Modern Revolutions*. 2nd edn. Cambridge, UK, and New York: Cambridge University Press.
Falkner, S.A. (1919). *Bumazhnye den'gi frantsuzskoj revolyutsii (1789–1797)* [Paper Money in the French Revolution (1789–1797)]. Moscow: Editorial and Publishing Department of VSNKh.
Fukuyama, F. (1989). "The end of history?", *The National Interest*, Summer 1989.
Gerschenkron, A. (1962). *Economic Backwardness in Historical Perspective: A book of essays*. Cambridge, MA: Belknap Press.
Goldstone, J.A. (1991). *Revolution and Rebellion in the Early Modern World*. Berkeley and Los Angeles, CA: University of California Press.
Hirschmann, A. (2010). *Ritorika reaktsii: izvrascheniye, tschetnost', opasnost'* [The Rhetoric of Reaction: Perversity, futility, jeopardy]. Moscow: HSE Publishing.
OECD. (2016). "Gross domestic product (GDP)." Available at: https://data.oecd.org/gdp/gross-domestic-product-gdp.htm (accessed October 2016].
North, D. (1997). *Instituty, institutsional'nye izmeneniya I funktsionirovanie ekonomiki* [Institutions, Institutional Change and Economic Performance]. Moscow: Economic Book Foundation Nachala.
Say, J.B. and Bastiat, F. (2000). Say, J.B., *Traktat po politicheskoj ekonomii* [A Treatise on Political Economy]. Bastiat, F., *Ekonomicheskiye sofizmy. Ekonomicheskiye garmonii* [Economic sophisms. Economic harmonies]. Moscow: Delo.
Stalin, I. (1951). *Sobraniye sochinenij* [Collected Works], Vol. 13. Moscow: Gospolitizdat.
Starodubrovskaya, I. and Mau, V. (2001). *Velikie Revolutsii ot Kromvelya do Putina* [Great Revolutions. From Cromwell to Putin]. Moscow: Vagrius.
Witte, S. (1900). "O polozhenii nashej promyshlennosti. Vsepoddaneyshij doklad ministra finansov. Fevral 1900" [On the condition of our industry. The most loyal report of the minister of finance. February 1900]. In S. Witte (2006). *Collected Works and Documentary Materials*, Vol. 4, Book 1. Moscow: Nauka.

# 2 Post-communist Russia

## Characteristics of the revolutionary transformations

One of the key problems with studying the socio-economic development of modern Russia is identifying the general and specific characteristics of its development over the past quarter of a century. This analysis would ultimately allow us to assess both the validity of the economic policy conducted in Russia after the collapse of communism and specific measures taken by the country's post-communist governments.

Existing studies of the logic of post-communist transformation show a fundamental similarity between the measures taken by a wide range of governments of different countries during the 1990s that generally led to the same results.[1] The paths to macroeconomic stability and growth in the majority of post-communist countries of Central and Eastern Europe were very similar. There was also similarity in the unresolved issues that prevented a number of other countries from escaping the grip of the crisis.

However, despite the similarities between the resolved and unresolved economic problems, the reasons for the different results of post-communist development obviously cannot be found by looking just at economics. What is most important is a set of social and political factors that have a significant impact on the transformations in different countries. Social and political challenges are what determine the specific characteristics of individual countries, whereas economics (and particularly macroeconomics) makes them comparable.

We can distinguish two groups of sociopolitical factors that have an impact on post-communist development in general, and the post-communist development of Russia in particular.

First is the stage of global trends, which essentially involves the transition from an industrial to a post-industrial society. The most important characteristic of the latter, as it seemed in the last quarter of the twentieth century, was economic and political liberalism – that is, a relative decrease in the role of direct state intervention in economic processes, an increase in the role of competition, and the shifting of economic processes outside the boundaries of nation states (globalization). The political result of this development is the transition of a significant number of countries from authoritarianism (totalitarianism) to democracy, which, in turn, becomes an independent factor of economic development in those countries and regions.[2]

Second, it important to consider the character and type of transformations conducted in a particular post-communist country – revolutionary or evolutionary. It is the revolutionary nature of Russia's development in the late 1980s and early 1990s that defines highly important features of the country's performance that are fundamentally different to those of most other post-communist states in Europe.[3] This last aspect of the problem is what we consider in greater detail in this chapter.

## A weak state

A weak state is a key characteristic of a society that is undergoing a revolutionary transformation. As we wrote in previous chapter, a systemic transformation under a weak state is the most general definition of a revolution.

The weakness of a state is manifested in various features of a revolutionary society. Among the most common universal traits of weak state authorities are the following: *First*, there is the constant fluctuation of economic policy, where the government is constantly seeking new ways of implementing its goals, although these goals are never very clearly defined. *Second*, there is the emergence of several power centres competing between themselves for a dominant role in society. *Third*, the absence of established political institutions, because the old institutions have been destroyed in the early stages of revolution and new ones are yet to be created, results in various spontaneously emerging organizations and institutions acting as political intermediaries. *Fourth*, there is a lack of any clear, well-established 'rules of the game', when procedures for the authorities to make decisions are not rigidly defined. And *fifth*, there is the inability of the government to collect taxes, which becomes an all-round economic facet of the political revolutionary crisis.

These characteristics were clearly present in the late USSR and Russia in the 1990s. Despite the formal power of the communist USSR, and the formal (constitutional) power of the executive authorities in Russia after 1993 (before this, all the power was clearly held by the legislative body), the opportunities for implementing all these vast powers were more than illusory.

The government in the USSR was, of course, extraordinarily stable and strong, and able to impose its interests on its own people. As a result, public opinion in the country was more inclined to overestimate the capabilities of the state, rather than underestimate them.[4]

And yet, state power at the end of the 1980s and in the early 1990s remained weak. This is especially evident in the relationship between political crises in the country and the dynamics of world oil prices. The most painful political and economic upheavals took place in the USSR and in Russia at a time when oil prices were at their lowest. This led to the authorities having far narrower possibilities for social manoeuvring.

Another factor of the crisis was the government's inability to collect taxes. Special analysis of this problem shows that a sharp decline in tax collection (the most noticeable increase in arrears) always happened at times when there was an acute political weakening of the central authority as a result of an aggravated political crisis.[5] In the 1990s, the most significant periods in this respect were August–October 1993 and from the end of 1995 to the beginning of 1996. In the first case, the conflict of the legislative and executive branches reached its peak, and the prospects of the regime seemed entirely uncertain to all economic and political subjects.[6] In the second case, after the communists' victory in the parliamentary elections in December 1995, and with the high probability of their winning in the presidential elections in 6 months' time, the economic subjects rightly judged that the existing government would not choose to be too rigid, and the new president would forgive disloyalty towards the "anti-popular regime".

Political instability is also the most important factor of instability in the legal framework for the functioning of the economy. As a result, the authorities become extremely vulnerable to various lobbyists and make decisions that soon have to be abandoned. Analysis shows that the stability of regulations adopted by executive authorities (presidential decrees and government resolutions) was directly linked to the level of stability of a country's political situation. At times of increased instability, there is a sharp rise in the vulnerability of the authorities towards interest groups, and a desire to purchase political support emerges, which reflects on the quality of the regulatory acts created. Decrees and regulations adopted during times when the authorities are weak differ in that they do not last for very long, as the authorities tend to cancel them quite soon.[7]

The problem of the polycentricity of power becomes evident. The central government was under constant pressure from the regional authorities, many of which openly ignored federal laws and the constitution. The weakening of the federal government was demonstrated by the gradual, but steady decline of the Federation's share in the consolidated budget. And, at times when the economic crisis worsened (e.g. in 1991–2, the middle of 1993 or September 1998), there was a sharp increase in pressure from separatist regions on the federal government (and therefore on the federal legislation).

The problem of the polycentricity of power is not limited to the struggle between the federal government and the regions. In the context of a weak government, leaders of the business elite and representatives of influential interest groups try to become special power centres. Representatives of such interest groups often tend to exaggerate their power and their capabilities, which was clearly demonstrated by the collapse of the so-called oligarchs – a group of major entrepreneurs (primarily bankers), who were very strong but lost their influence as a result of macroeconomic and political stabilization after the 1998 financial crisis. However, in the period of financial turmoil, the influence of the oligarchs on decision-making was significant and, as it turned out, did not entirely correspond to their real financial and economic weight.[8]

The weakness of the government in a period of systemic transformation manifests itself in various forms. However, the stages that a weak state goes through are of a universal nature: they can be traced through years of revolutions in different

32  *Crises and revolutions*

countries at different times.[9] Among the main features of economic development in the context of a weak state are the following:

- A severe financial crisis: This is only partly linked to the above-mentioned inability of the authorities to collect taxes. Another manifestation of this crisis is the weak government's inability to fulfil the financial obligations for which it has non-inflationary sources of funding. The inability to align income and expenses leads to the continued recurrence of the budgetary crisis, which has traditionally been solved by the printing press. However, this not only fails to ease the budget crisis, but, over time, further exacerbates the problem of budgetary obligations, as the government gets used to the inflation tax and neglects other sources of income. This results in significant underfunding of government.
- A sharp increase in transaction costs: This leads to a corresponding reduction in the competitiveness of domestic production. This is owing to the government's inability to ensure consistency of the rules of the game and guarantee that contracts will be fulfilled.
- Demonetization of the economy: This leads to a reduction in the ratio of money supply to GDP. Demonetization as a result of paper money issue is a fairly understandable and common phenomenon. However, historical experience shows that the amount of real money in circulation decreases even in countries that manage to avoid dependence on the printing press, which happens because money is withdrawn from circulation and hoarded.
- The weakness of the government: This has an inevitable impact on the nature of privatization – the solution of sociopolitical (power stabilization) and fiscal problems are moved to the forefront of the process, instead of privatization in favour of strategic owners.

All of the above reveals the most important feature of how the political process (primarily the development and implementation of economic policy) is conducted by a weak state. The key issue is not the formation of a political majority through existing political institutions (parliament, parties), which are weak, sometimes also poorly structured, and unstable. The most important thing is the interaction between representatives of power (the government) and leading interest groups that have real levers of political pressure and, in the early stages of transformation, de facto play the role of political parties.[10]

The weakness of state power had a direct impact on highly varied aspects of the functioning and development of post-communist Russia. First and foremost, it explains the very specific nature of the resolution of two of the main challenges that the country faced throughout the 1990s: macroeconomic stabilization and privatization. Authorities searching for social and political support without sufficient financial resources tend to resort to tools such as inflationary redistribution of financial resources and redistribution of ownership for means of production in order to buy political support. And, practice has shown (since the revolutions of the eighteenth century in the USA and France) that inflation and redistribution of ownership are usually linked to one another very closely.

## Delayed stabilization

In modern political and economic literature, there is a rather standard explanation for the stability of inflationary processes and, accordingly, the phenomenon of delayed stabilization. There are three fairly interconnected systems of explanations as to why a government may not be able to solve the problem of stabilization within a reasonable time.

First is a constant, fragile balance between interest groups, each of which attempts to shift the costs of disinflation to the others. If the influence of these groups is more or less the same, none of them will have a decisive impact on the balance of power in society, or on decisions to conduct a tight-money policy.[11]

The second concerns influential interest groups that benefited from inflation and, accordingly, are keen for the inflationary economic policy to continue. As inflation is a powerful mechanism for redistributing financial resources, the agents for whose benefit these resources are redistributed are not interested in financial stabilization.[12] Inflationists have considerable political influence: it is bought using a portion of the funds that are concentrated in their hands owing to inflation.

The third is the political support of *economics of populism*, that is, of soft budget constraints and inflationist (soft) monetary policy.[13]

What these three mechanisms have in common is that the state authorities are supposed to be weak – authorities that are heavily dependent on interest groups and the existing balance of social forces.

All three mechanisms of reproducing the inflationary cycle and, accordingly, delayed stabilization were evident in post-communist Russia.

Almost all social groups feared for a long time that the government would take decisive steps towards disinflation and financial stability: this was especially true in 1992, when virtually all interest groups joined together to counter the rigid stabilization rate. Soon, there was a split between inflationists and anti-inflationists, and the fragile balance of power between them became a factor of economic instability in the 1990s.

At the end of 1991 and the beginning of 1992, the policy of liberalization and stabilization hardly met any resistance at all, but, by the spring of 1992, there was sweeping resistance against stabilization. At first, the results of liberalization were poorly understood and not planned properly for economic agents: for decades, the Soviet economy had been operating with an 'economy of deficit' (shortages), and company bosses were not familiar with the equilibrium market and the problem of demand constraints. But soon, after encountering an unexpected and sharp decline in demand for their output and a non-payments crisis, they realized the consequences of liberalization and joined forces to demand more financial resources. It was a unique period in a socio-economic sense (spring–summer 1992), when the predominance of inflationism in the country was virtually unchallenged.

This could only be counteracted by splitting of the potentially different interests of various types of economic agent (enterprise), and this was done by privatization. Therefore, privatization at the starting point was a political phenomenon, as it was designed to consolidate political support for the liberalization and stabilization of the economy. In particular, Yegor Gaidar's government, in 1992, deemed it was possible to begin easing fiscal and monetary policy, thereby initiating the process of privatization. The political result of this decision was the clear formation, by the spring of 1993, of two main interest groups, committed to either inflationist or anti-inflationist policies. The problem of inflation became the dominant subject in the political struggle over economic reforms.

On the one hand, the ranks of the inflationists were clearly defined. The main elements of the economic policy they were upholding were: massive financial injections into the economy (monetary and fiscal easing), with a view to supporting economically weak, uncompetitive enterprises; efforts to "strengthen the controllability" of the economy by restoring power at the centre in relation to public-sector enterprises; tighter control over exports and imports; and blunt protectionism. Important components of this policy had to be large-scale dirigisme based on direct state interventions or through large monopolistic structures created 'from above' (corporations, industrial and financial groups).

The ranks of the supporters of this economic policy included a fairly diverse group of economic agents. Some of them directly benefited from inflation, making huge profits on the back of economic instability. For others, this policy meant a continuation of state financial support and protected them from imminent bankruptcy. Those interested in pursuing the policy of 'cheap money' were primarily weak state enterprises (although sometimes large in terms of the number of employees) that were unable to compete and were doomed to fail as a result of hard budget constraints. At that time, the inflationist course was also rather favourable to a significant number of banks: their economic well-being – and often their very existence – was largely due to monetary expansion budget subsidies to their clients. Finally, inflation was the source of high income from trading and intermediary activities, which explained the influence of this business sector in Russia's economic and political spectrum. In other words, inflationary policy enabled inefficient enterprises to survive, and banks and trading organizations to earn profits that were not comparable with the income of productive sectors.

There was also a gradual formation of ranks of supporters of macroeconomic stabilization. This required consistent liberalization of economic activity, a tight fiscal and monetary policy, and privatization. The essence of this policy can be defined as anti-inflationism. The number of supporters grew as the privatization process expanded, and a number of enterprises adapted to working in a real market environment, presenting active managers and skilled staff with a wide range of opportunities for economic and social growth. It is clear that those most interested in conducting a consistent anti-inflationary policy were economic structures that had already managed to realize their economic strength and had good opportunities to compete with domestic and, in some cases, even international producers. They were also ready to invest, and the key prerequisite for that was macroeconomic stability.

This reconfiguration of interests reflected a new, rather important trend in the country's political development and a new stage of post-communist reforms. Before, the dividing line between interests was whether an economic agent belonged to the public or the private sector, but now, belonging to a particular form of ownership had started to lose its criterial ('interest-forming') element. An important factor was the position of a particular economic agent in relation to flows of 'cheap money' (the only remaining shortage). This meant that both private and state-owned enterprises ended up on both sides of this 'economic barricade'.

The fact that there were two interest groups with fundamentally different expectations of the government's economic policy determined the instability of the macroeconomic policy that set apart the years 1992–6. During this period, important changes took place in Russia in these areas.

Approaching from a quantitative point of view, one can see that the original balance of social forces (interest groups) formed with a clear predominance of inflationists. The quantitative prevalence of inflationist-minded economic agents greatly complicated the stabilization efforts of the early post-communist years. The leaders of these enterprises had considerable political weight, with access to the central echelons of power. The number of people in employment and the burdening of the social sphere were among the main motivations to resolve the issues of financial support for certain economic agents, as the stance of the executive authorities was more than weak in a political sense and vulnerable in a social sense.

The lack of structural change in the economy only strengthened inflationists. During the first half of the 1990s, the position of the anti-inflationary forces remained rather weak, and their political prospects were quite bleak. Strong, consistent privatization strengthened their ranks, expanding the opportunities for entrepreneurial behaviour to emerge, as opposed to the 'political rent seeking' of state-owned or quasi-private structures of the traditional Soviet style. At the same time, the quantitative predominance of inflationists coupled with the unsustainable macroeconomic policies of the government contributed to certain negative transformations in the ranks of potential supporters of an open-market economy. Two kinds of process occurred in this respect.

First, the political activity of enterprises supporting the anti-inflationary policy became weaker. Hopes that inflation would stop quickly were not realized, and, consequently, those who were interested in fast, strong stabilization and built their market survival strategies around this adapted to function in conditions of prolonged high inflation.

Second, there was a merging between part of the new business layer and institutions of state power. The weak government sought support in new, economically strong, influential domestic business. For big business, this created a comfortable environment in which market survival was replaced by the ability to get state support. The state had to rely on the most powerful economic agents in exchange for its only resource – the provision of 'political rent'.

Alongside this, the social and political environment gradually changed the economic and political 'weights' of interest groups. Two of the most significant features of this transformation were the changes in the financial and banking sector, and also the transformation and stabilization of Russia's constitutional and legal framework.

The main beneficiaries of inflation were the banks. Unlike other sectors involved in inflation, primarily the Soviet industrial establishment, banks generally did not eat through the resources obtained through inflationary processes, but, on the contrary, accumulated them in cash or in kind to a considerable extent. As a result of this, towards the end of 1994 and the beginning of 1995, there were clear shifts in the banks' economic and political positions. Some banks, owing to inflation (or owing to their proximity to government structures), were able to save up significant capital that was sufficient to redirect their interests towards maximizing the volume (not the rate) of profit and creating a more stable environment for their work.

Low inflation and macroeconomic stabilization were attractive to major banks for a variety of reasons, in particular the following: First, favourable conditions were created for expansion in the banking services industry owing to the absorption of small banks that were unable to survive with the significant reduction in interest rates. Second, the expansion of banking capital into the production sphere that took place during privatization made financial institutions much more sensitive to the prospects of industrial development – at least in those sectors with which their capital was associated – and this required a reduction in inflation to a level suitable for investment. Of course, all of the above can in no way be interpreted as banks' sudden willingness to abandon the search for 'political rent'.

The reinforcement of the banking sector and the increase in anti-inflationist sentiments within the sector also contributed to the transformation in governmental policy. Even the formal changes in the government in 1994–7 showed the sharp decline of the role of the traditional Soviet economic establishment and an equally sharp increase in the influence of new private business and the politicians associated with it.

This conclusion was confirmed in the course of the 1998 financial crisis. The surge in inflation was short-lived, and almost all of the main political forces – both left and right – joined together to battle against inflation. The left-wing government of Prime Minister Eugeny Primakov (1998–9) took stabilization measures that were unprecedentedly strict from a social point of view. This was owing to concerns over political stability, which, if upset, could have unfavourable consequences for virtually the entire establishment.

## Constitutional problems of the Russian transformation

The formation of a new constitutional framework is an independent factor in reforming an economy and stabilizing political processes. In the context of a revolutionary transformation, the constitution plays a minor role because, in practice, the real relationship between social forces and interest groups is always dominant over written law.[14] However, the processes of forming a constitutional field can become important in a country achieving socio-economic stability, as evidenced by the modern experience of Russian constitutionalism.

Neither the constitutional system inherited by Russia from Soviet times, nor the ideas of desirable and effective constitutional and legal mechanisms, which were advanced compared with Soviet experience, matched the demands of the country's stable socio-economic development. This applied, for example, to the idea that the Soviet constitution corresponds to the democratic principles of organizing society and requires, not so much major transformation, but rather willingness from the authorities to apply it in practice.

Meanwhile, real life demonstrated that the constitution, which was not initially designed for practical use, was not functional in reality. When demands are made that it (the constitution) be fully functional in a deep crisis, and there is no sociopolitical consensus, it stalls and falters. And, in Russia, the lack of clarity of constitutional norms emerged painfully, in the economic sphere in particular.

There was also evidence of certain theoretical illusions reflecting the overall level of earlier ('pre-market)' ideas about the proper organization of government institutions. The most prominent example of this may be the understanding about the legal status of the Central Bank. One of the key illusions was the idea that taking the Central Bank out of the control of the executive authorities and subordinating it to legislative bodies would conform to the principles of market democracy and be a key factor in stabilizing the state's economic policy. However, one principle here was substituted with another: the independence of the monetary authorities was confused with their independence from the government.

Another example may be the sharp (almost unlimited) expansion of the legislators' budgetary powers. The essentially true principle of representative-government control of public finances was replaced by the prerogative of deputies to intervene in the process of developing and executing the budget, which meant that a budget could be continually reviewed, as late as at the stage of its execution.

The uncertainty about the powers of branches of the authorities gave rise to confusion, when decisions on the same issue could be made by the president, the prime minister and the chairman of the Supreme Soviet. Under the power conflicts at federal level, regional governments received instructions that contradicted one another.

Examples of this type of conflict were detailed in the literature of 1992–3. For instance, the issue of the legislative authorities' powers to make decisions regarding the allocation of resources from the federal budget to support individual sectors and industries remained unresolved. Or, another example: the results of a tender to develop oilfields under the Sakhalin-2 project, which were announced by the government, were subsequently disavowed by the Supreme Soviet as a result of pressure from the losing (but very wealthy) competitors. We emphasize that the problem in this respect was not about branches of authority exceeding or not exceeding their powers, but rather about the lack of clarity of these powers, and, consequently, the illegitimacy and unreliability of the decisions made under such circumstances. And this, in turn, did not help to stabilize the country's economic development.[15]

Other types of example were conflicting instructions from the government and the Supreme Soviet to the Central Bank: on the policy for interest rates, monetary issue and the category of banknotes, on the relationship with other CIS

(Commonwealth of Independent States) countries, or the stance in relation to individual regions where there were also authority bodies that overlapped each other. (The clearest example of this was in the Chelyabinsk Region, where, for some time, there were two governors who were supported in Moscow by different branches of the government.)

The very first steps toward implementing post-communist economic policy identified a number of critical issues related to the balance of power and the effectiveness of the decision-making mechanism for key economic and political issues.

First, the legislative process was extremely simplified, which meant that any decision (including financial decisions) could be adopted without any specific preliminary discussion or consultation procedures. The procedure for amending the Constitution was also quite simple, which resulted in frequent amendments being made to the Constitution in the period of 1992–3.

Second, there were no mechanisms to counter populism in the constitutional and legal field. The president's veto, in particular, was very weak: under the Constitution, legislators could override it with a simple majority vote – that is, essentially a revote for a bill.

Third, the Central Bank of Russia remained beyond the control of the executive authorities. Given the extremely populist attitude of the deputy corps, this situation had a negative impact on the possibility of the executive authorities conducting a consistent stabilization policy. The Supreme Soviet's intervention in monetary policy was virtually unlimited. It was under pressure from populist-minded deputies, to the degree that the Central Bank, throughout the year 1992 and part of 1993, was not able to raise the policy rates to a positive level. The policy rate only became positive in the final quarter of 1993 – that is, after the dissolution of the deputy corps (21 September 1993) and the actual annulment of the Constitution (Table 2.1). The leadership of the Supreme Soviet sought to intervene even in such issues of monetary regulation as the issue of notes of a certain denomination, which further aggravated the cash crisis.

Fourth, the tax system also encountered problems of a constitutional, legal and political nature, particularly in terms of the distribution of taxes between the federal and regional levels. The greatest impact was from the fact that the distribution of tax revenue was individualized, and there was constant bargaining between the federal centre and the regions regarding 'fair' proportions of distribution. Governors used all their power and influence to reduce the share of payments to the federal budget, and the federal authorities were too weak to resist the pressure. It was a chain reaction, where concessions to one region resulted in a squeeze on concessions to other regions.

Fifth, the lack of proper regulation of interfederal relations not only weakened the political position of the central government, but also undermined its position in such sensitive areas as the budget and taxes.

And finally, maintaining the transparency of the borders in the post-Sovet countries eroded the integrity of the Russian currency and customs space. Control of money flows was weak owing to the lack of legal regulation.

*Table 2.1* Policy rate of Central Bank and inflation, 1993–4 (per cent)*

|  | Policy rate | Consumption price index growth rate | Real interbank interest rate on loans for 1–3 months |
|---|---|---|---|
| *1993* | | | |
| January | 6.7 | 25.8 | –11.7 |
| February | 6.7 | 24.7 | –10.6 |
| March | 6.7 | 20.1 | –6.6 |
| April | 8.3 | 19.0 | –5.6 |
| May | 8.3 | 18.0 | –4.2 |
| June | 11.7 | 19.9 | –4.9 |
| July | 14.2 | 22.0 | –5.8 |
| August | 14.2 | 26.0 | –8.5 |
| September | 15.0 | 23.0 | –5.9 |
| October | 17.5 | 20.0 | –2.2 |
| November | 17.5 | 16.0 | 1.0 |
| December | 17.5 | 13.0 | 4.1 |
| *1994* | | | |
| January | 17.5 | 17.9 | 0.0 |
| February | 17.5 | 10.8 | 6.3 |
| March | 17.5 | 7.4 | 9.4 |

*Note*: * It must be noted that, throughout 1993, the monthly level of the policy rate was defined as 1/12 of the annual rate, not by compound interest rates, i.e. the annual rate was higher than the official rate. This was a simple psychological trick: high rates caused dissatisfaction among the economic elite, who needed time to become accustomed to such levels of payment for loans, and this arithmetic manipulation was intended to lessen this dissatisfaction somewhat.

*Source*: The Russian–European Centre for Economic Policy 1995.

Therefore, by mid 1993, the need to establish a new constitutional and legal space was clear. The task of bringing about a radical change in the Constitution was repeatedly raised by the president, who proposed that a special referendum be held. The need for a complete revision of the Constitution was generally not met with any objections from legislators, but they insisted on adopting the Constitution without a referendum, in a wording supported by the left-wing populist majority of the deputy corps. The situation, which had reached an impasse, was blown open by the conflict between the president and the Supreme Soviet from 21 September to 4 October 1993, the dissolution of the legislative body, the holding of new elections on 12 December and, most importantly, the constitutional referendum.

The new Constitution radically changed the principles for organizing the political space, including in the economic sphere. It was aimed at maximum stability of the institutions of government, minimizing dependence on populism.

Of course, there can never be absolute protection from populism, even in stable democracies. In post-communist Russia's constitution, the only real antidote to populism would be a major increase in the powers of the executive authorities (especially the president) over the parliament. Practice showed that the deputy corps was primarily and predominantly a medium of the populist origins among the branches of power, especially at times of crisis. This conclusion was confirmed by the unfolding of events from 1989 to 1993.

The key economic aspects of the new constitutional regime were the following.

The process of adopting legislation became more complicated, especially where it concerned financial and economic issues. Laws being considered in parliament now had to pass through several readings (normally three, and in the case of the federal budget even four). Adoption of laws related to the federal budget, taxes and fees, as well as financial, currency, credit and customs regulation and money issue required mandatory expert review from the government, and, unlike other draft laws, they had to be considered (and approved) in the Federation Council, the upper house. In order to avoid populism, it was forbidden to put economic issues to a referendum.

The Central Bank's main function was to protect and ensure the stability of the Russian Federation's currency – the rouble. It was a reaction to the problems of 1992–3, when the leadership of the Central Bank, partly under pressure from the Supreme Soviet, but more following its own ideas about the correct economic policy, concentrated its efforts on supporting output (enterprises), which only resulted in a build-up of the macroeconomic crisis. According to the Constitution of 1993, the Central Bank was proclaimed independent, although it was more connected with the executive authorities, as was manifested in the obligatory participation of the chairman of the Central Bank in government meetings. However, the Constitution declared that, "money emission shall be carried out exclusively by the Central Bank of the Russian Federation" and "independently of other State governmental bodies" (Article 75). In addition, the chairman of the Central Bank was appointed by the State Duma (lower house), as advised by the president, with de facto irremovability from office for 4 years. This created certain guarantees of stability and the independence of monetary authorities and, at the same time, meant that monetary policy had to be coordinated with the government.

There was still a significant problem concerning the financial and monetary policy that did not receive legal confirmation – prohibition of the budget deficit. In fact, constitutional prohibition of enacting the budget with a deficit is a fairly rare occurrence in global legal practice. In post-communist countries, the most logical solution to this issue was in Estonia. In Russia, constitutional prohibition of the budget deficit was not really raised or discussed.

Another important factor for macroeconomic stabilization was the more rigid division of powers between the centre and the constituent entities of the Federation, including a ban on the issue of banknotes other than those issued by the Central Bank. The fundamental position of the Constitution, along with decisive actions by the authorities, led to a suspension of the issuing activity that had begun in individual constituent entities of the Federation.

And finally, the mechanism of amendment of the Constitution became highly complicated. This was not only an economic problem, but it played a key role in improving the economic situation in the country. A simpler system of amending the Constitution would have made it vulnerable to the sentiments of legislators and created an environment of permanent instability, including in an economic sense.

In other words, despite all the shortcomings of the Constitution of 1993, its main advantage was that it formed clear rules of play in general, and in the financial and economic field in particular. The budget process became more manageable, and the Central Bank was separated from populist-minded legislators. All this had a positive impact in terms of enabling the executive authorities to conduct a responsible macroeconomic policy.

## Social and political dimension of privatization

A weak state in search of sociopolitical support inevitably resorts to the powerful mechanism of redistribution of ownership.

Among the main objectives of privatization are the following: first, a solution to the problem of the effective owner and the dynamization of economic reforms; second, the strengthening of the sociopolitical base of transition, as privatization could be a source of political support for the government; third, privatization can help to solve fiscal problems, providing money for the state budget. At various stages of Russia's development, the relevance of each of these objectives of privatization was different.

The USSR reform of enterprises in 1987–8 and its consistent implementation meant a step towards privatization in favour of their directors (general managers). They were practically independent from higher-level administrative authorities, and there was no dependence on owners because there were none. This reform by the Gorbachev government was very important in the revolutionizing of perestroika and was an attempt to expand the social base of the reformers by attracting directors and, to some extent, labour collectives (who were granted the right of appointing directors). At the same time, it was a step towards destabilization, because, in the society, there emerged an influential layer of economic structures that were not affected in their actions by either administrative or market limiters. It was all the more the case because soon, under the pressure of this interest group, new decisions began to be taken to increase its independence (and irresponsibility) through the development of various kinds of cooperative and leasehold (with a purchase option) source, which meant in practice an almost free transfer of ownership to the enterprise's management.[16]

As the crisis intensified, more and more attention was paid to privatization. The weakening allied authorities had no leverage to stabilize property relations and to regulate privatization processes giving them appropriate legal grounds. This was the legacy inherited at the end of 1991 by the Russian government, which had embarked on a path of radicalization of economic reforms. And that is why, in addition to the three main possible tasks mentioned above, privatization in Russia in 1991–2 had to address another issue: to ensure the minimum restoration of control over the economy by including property relations in at least some sort of legal field.

In virtually all of the main regulatory documents governing privatization processes in the Russian Federation,[17] it is typical to find at least a formal overlapping of all three above-mentioned objectives of privatization – economic (increasing efficiency), social and fiscal – although, of course, the specifics of the documents taken at various stages of the economic reform are different.

In the first Russian documents on the development of property rights still in the USSR there are regulations such as the allocation to enterprises of state and municipal property "under full economic jurisdiction" (which, in practice, meant the legalization of possible uncontrolled use of state property in private interests) and the entitlement to repurchase enterprises operating on a lease on preferential terms (the latter was a legal way for directors to purchase their enterprises). It was assumed that these measures would help to strengthen the political position of the Russian authorities in their conflict with the USSR government and stimulate transition of enterprises from USSR subordination to republican (Russian) control.

The initial period of the post-communist stage of development is characterized by a greater focus on the macroeconomic aspect of privatization. In the main provisions of the Programme of Privatization of State and Municipal Enterprises in the Russian Federation for 1992, of 29 December 1991, the objectives of privatization include: "promoting the general objectives of the policy of economic stabilization", "ensuring a major increase in economic efficiency of enterprises by transferring them to the most efficient owners" and "increasing budget revenues".

The fact that there are no sociopolitical goals of privatization mentioned in this document requires explanation. The formation of a system of private owners was evidently one of the most important policy objectives of the post-communist government. However, at the time, this problem was seen as strategic and was not considered to be a lever to strengthen the political position of the new regime. This understanding of the role of privatization came later, in the second half of 1992. At first, the Russian government tried to be beyond interest groups. On the contrary, the task of rapid macroeconomic stabilization and overcoming the financial crisis was seen as a key issue at this stage. The government was hoping for events to develop as they did in Poland, with rapid deceleration of inflation and a transition into a regime of economic growth. This is why the search for non-inflationary sources of funding, of the high-level government spending that was a typical feature of post-socialism, made the ability to attract budgetary funds from privatization extremely important.

However, the actual course of events went in a different direction, with the result that the mass privatization of 1992–5 was of a sociopolitical nature.[18] On the one hand, high inflation remained an important factor for the replenishment of budget revenues and temporarily eased budget problems. On the other hand, political instability, particularly in the run-up to the 1996 presidential elections, meant that an inflow of capital and, therefore, income for the budget from privatization could not be expected.[19]

By 1997, the situation had changed owing to the end of the period of high inflation. The government was faced with a severe budget crisis, and privatization

*Table 2.2* Financial results of privatization, 1992–2002

| Years | Federal revenues from privatization | | |
|---|---|---|---|
| | RUB billions | As a share of all budget revenues (%) | As a share of GDP (%) |
| 1992 | 19.0 | 0.6 | 0.1 |
| 1993 | 71.1 | 0.28 | 0.04 |
| 1994 | 117 | 0.14 | 0.02 |
| 1995 | 1,140 | 0.49 | 0.08 |
| 1996 | 898 | 0.32 | 0.04 |
| 1997 | 17,959.9 | 5.23 | 0.77 |
| 1998 | 14,977.8 | 4.60 | 0.57 |
| 1999 | 8,540.5 | 1.39 | 0.18 |
| 2000 | 31,324 | 2.77 | 0.43 |
| 2001 | 9,943.4 | 0.62 | 0.11 |
| 2002 | 13,413 | 0.61 | 0.12 |

*Sources*: State Statistics Committee of Russia 1994: 32, 1999: 290, 2002: 334.

began to be regarded as one of the most important sources for replenishing the treasury. The government resorted to selling its stake in a number of enterprises that were very attractive from a commercial point of view. The strengthening of the 'budgetary' nature of privatization can clearly be traced in Table 2.2.

However, it faced stiff resistance from business leaders, who were active participants in privatization and interested in understating the price of privatized objects. The long, drawn-out political conflicts that began resulted in political losses for both sides of this battle (business and the government).

In 1998 events took a new turn. The financial crisis led, on the one hand, to a sharp aggravation of the budget crisis and, consequently, to an increase in the significance of fiscal results for the government, and, on the other hand, to a drop in demand for privatized objects and, consequently, lower prices. Throughout the year, the government was torn between these two problems, without finding an effective way out of the situation. The slip into high inflation, the banking crisis and the collapse of Russia's credit rating once again delayed the obtaining of significant fiscal results from privatization.

In this chapter, we have discussed only some of the problems of post-communist transformation, namely those that are associated with the revolution. There are still a number of important issues that are vital to understanding the trends in Russia's development. Here is a brief outline of some of them.

There is a correlation between the level of socio-economic development and the stability of a democratic regime. In modern literature, there is convincing evidence of the connection between the level of economic development and the nature of the political regime in a given country.[20] If the assessment by S. Huntington is correct, the Soviet Union was on a path to democratic reform, being at the lower boundary of the 'band' of democratization, at least in terms of

GDP per capita. The decline in production and the increase in social polarization could not help but reflect on the nature of power, especially because the most acceptable solution to the problem of moving away from a revolution (and overcoming the accompanying economic crisis) did not favour democratic processes either.

## Notes

1 See: Fisher *et al.* 1996; Åslund 2002.
2 See: Huntington 1991.
3 For a detailed study of this thesis, see: Starodubrovskaya and Mau 2001.
4 The strength and rigidity of power in the USSR and the stability of the Soviet political system created a semblance of it being inviolable, not only among Russian social scientists (which is to be expected), but also among many Western analysts. Most researchers associated the possibility of radical shifts with poorly developed and middle-income countries of Asia and Africa, but not at all with the Soviet Union. This is exactly how the situation and its prospects for development were perceived by S. Huntington, for example when he highlighted the USSR and the US as the most consistent and stable types of country (see: Huntington 1968). This became a kind of methodological tradition, which was later reproduced in the works of many different authors – political scientists, economists and indeed also Sovietologists.
5 See: Mau 1997.
6 In August 1993, the leadership of the Supreme Soviet of Russian Federation openly called for the constituent members of the Federation (regional authorities) to stop paying taxes to the federal government. All this affected the possibilities of solving the problems of macroeconomic stabilization.
7 See: Mau 1999: 154–71.
8 See: Pappe 1997.
9 See: Ashley 1962; Aftalion 1990.
10 The importance of a significantly different political and economic model taking into account the factor of interest groups having dominance over state institutions is examined by A. Shleifer and D. Treisman (Shleifer and Treisman 2000: 6).
11 See: Drezen 1996.
12 See: Burdekin and Burkett 1996.
13 See: Dornbusch and Edwards 1991: 7–13.
14 These features of revolutions were noted by many revolutionary figures of the past, but Marxists (and Bolsheviks in particular) tended to absolutize this thesis (for further details, see: Mau 1999: 75–7).
15 See: Gaidar 1996: 259–60.
16 See: Åslund 1995: 225–6; Gaidar 1995: 149–51.
17 On Property in the USSR: USSR Law of 6 March 1990; On Enterprises in the USSR: USSR Law of 4 June 1990; On Property in Russia: Law of the RSFSR of 24 December 1990; On Privatization of State and Municipal Enterprises: Law of the RSFSR of 3 June 1991; Main Provisions of the Programme of Privatization of State and Municipal Enterprises in the Russian Federation for 1992 Approved by Decree of the President of the Russian Federation of 29 December 1991; State Programme of Privatization of State and Municipal Enterprises in the Russian Federation for 1992: Approved by Decree of the Supreme Soviet of the Russian Federation of 11 June 1992; State Programme of Privatization of State and Municipal Enterprises in the Russian Federation: Approved by Decree of the President of the Russian Federation of 24 December 1993.
18 This is seen clearly in two of the first versions of the State Privatization Programme – of 11 June 1992 and particularly 24 December 1993. The dominance of the social

problems of privatization and the sacrificing of fiscal problems for them was noted by many reformers, especially Ye. Gaidar: "a critical mass of private property had to be built as fast as possible. When choosing between the speed and quality of privatization, we consciously focused on speed" (Gaidar 1997).

19 Incidentally, this is why the low fiscal outcomes of loans-for-shares auctions at the end of 1995 must be explained, not only by the authorities' desire to gain the support of the financial community in the run-up to the elections, but also by a real, low demand for assets due to the threat of a communist victory in the presidential elections (the communists rejected privatization). A number of economists analysing Russian privatization note the inconsistency of its social, financial and economic aspects and characterize the situation from the standpoint of the problem of transaction costs. For example, S. Malle wrote that the sociopolitical struggle surrounding privatization in Russia "has a negative effect on the level of transaction costs. They become greater than they would have been had the transfer of property rights taken place on economic criteria alone" (Malle 1994: 55).

20 See: Lipset 1960; Huntington 1968; Vanhanen 1968.

# References

Aftalion, F. (1990). *The French Revolution: An economic interpretation*. Cambridge, UK: Cambridge University Press.

Ashley, M. (1962). *Financial and Commercial Policy under the Cromwellian Protectorate*. London: Frank Cass.

Åslund, A. (1995) *How Russia Became a Market Economy*. Washington, DC: The Brookings Institution.

Åslund, A. (2002). *Building Capitalism*. Cambridge, UK: Cambridge University Press.

Burdekin, R.C.K. and Burkett, P. (1996). *Distributional Conflict and Inflation*. London: Macmillan.

Dornbusch, R. and Edwards, S. (eds) (1991). *The Macroeconomics of Populism in Latin America*. Chicago, IL, and London: University of Chicago Press.

Drezen, A. (1996). "The political economy of delayed reform", *The Journal of Policy Reform*, no. 1, pp. 25–46.

Fisher, S., Sahay, R. and Vegh, C.A. (1996). "Stabilization and growth in transition economies. The early experience", *Journal of Economic Perspectives*, vol. 10, no. 2, pp. 45–66.

Gaidar, Ye. (1995). *Gosudarstvo i evolutsiya* [State and Evolution]. Moscow: Eurasia.

Gaidar, Ye. (1996). *Dni porazhenij i pobed* [Days of Defeat and Victory]. Moscow: Vagrius.

Gaidar, Ye. (1997). "Power and property: A Russian divorce", *Izvestia*, 1 October.

Huntington, S.P. (1968) *Political Order in Changing Societies*. New Haven, CT: Yale University Press.

Huntington, S.P. (1991) *The Third Wave: Democratization in the late twentieth century*. Norman, OK, and London: University of Oklahoma Press.

Lipset, S.M. (1960). *Political Man. The social basis of politics*. New York: Doubleday.

Malle, S. (1994) "Privatizatsiya v Rossii: osobennosti, tseli, deystvuyuschiye litsa" [Privatization in Russia: Peculiarities, goals, and agents], *Voprosy Ekonomiki*, no. 3.

Mau, V. (1997). "Stabilization, elections, and perspectives of economic growth", *Problems of Economic Transition*, vol. 40, no. 4, pp. 5–26.

Mau, V. (1999). *Ekonomicheskaia reforma: skvoz' prizmu konstitutsii I politiki* [Economic Reform: Through the Prism of the Constitution and Politics]. Moscow: Ad Marginem.

Pappe, Y.S. (ed.) (1997). *Finansovo-promyshlennye gruppy i konglomeraty v ekonomike i politike sovremennoi Rossii* [Financial and Industrial Groups and Conglomerates in the Economy and Politics of Modern Russia]. Moscow: Center for Political Technologies.

Russian–European Centre for Economic Policy, The. (1995). *An Overview of Russia's Economy*, no. 1, pp. 49–50, 204.

Shleifer, A. and Treisman, D. (2000). *Without a Map. Political tactics and economic reform in Russia*. Cambridge, MA, and London: MIT Press.

Starodubrovskaya, I. and Mau, V. (2001). *The Challenge of Revolution: Contemporary Russia in historical perspective*. Oxford, UK: Oxford University Press.

State Statistics Committee of Russia. (1994). *The Russian Federation in Figures in 1993*, p. 32.

State Statistics Committee of Russia. (1999). *Statistical Yearbook of Russia*, p. 290.

State Statistics Committee of Russia. (2002). *Statistical Yearbook of Russia*, p. 334.

Vanhanen, T. (1968). *Prospects for Democracy: A study of 172 countries*. London and New York: Routledge.

# Part II
# The 1998 crisis in Russia

# 3 The background of the 1998 financial crisis in Russia

The financial crisis, which peaked sharply in the summer of 1998, was caused by a number of fundamental factors that demonstrated the weakness of the Russian economy. These included primarily budget problems, that is, the inability of the Russian authorities in 1992–8 to bring government spending into line with revenues and, as a consequence, a large budget deficit with a rapid increase in public debt. An important factor was the deterioration of the balance of payments caused by the increased expenditure of the government and private borrowers on payments of foreign debt and the unfavourable terms of Russia's foreign trade (low oil prices). The vulnerability of the Russian banking system also contributed significantly to the development of the financial crisis. A notable factor that determined the length of the crisis and the manner in which it was expressed in Russia was the financial crisis that affected a number of Asian and Latin American countries. Of course, mistakes were also made by Russian authorities in conducting anti-crisis measures in 1997–8.

The main cause of the financial crisis was the failure by all Russian governments to adopt and implement a realistic budget. As a result, the positive trends of 1996–7 – the decline in inflation, stabilization of the exchange rate, lower interest rates and the start of economic growth – were entirely due to a tight monetary policy that was in contradiction to imbalances in public finances. The significant budget deficit led to an increase in government debt, which suppressed national savings and worsened the current account of the balance of payments. In other words, a weak fiscal policy was a key source of economic (and thus political) destabilization.

The budget crisis in post-communist Russia had a political origin. The political nature of the budget crisis reflected the government's inability either to increase tax collection to the level of its fiscal obligations or to reduce spending to the level of the tax revenues that the government was able to collect.

The state's real expenditure over the period from 1991 to 1997 decreased approximately two and a half times. Expenses on social needs were one-third lower. But, state revenue fell sharply, and the government was unable to maintain budgetary equilibrium.

In addition, sequestration during the implementation of the expenditure budget was conducted under pressure from various lobby groups (the agriculture and defence industries, banking and mineral resources sectors, etc.). Their activity led to an unsustainable expenditure structure that was unable to provide economic growth or social and political stability.

From 1995 onwards, domestic public debt began to increase rapidly, primarily thanks to borrowing on the financial market (Table 3.1). By the beginning of 1998, internal debt had increased to 18.7 per cent of GDP and, by the end of 1998, it had increased to 26.0 per cent of GDP (on an annualized basis).

The increase in domestic debt caused a corresponding increase in its servicing costs. From 1995 to 1996, they rose from 2.6 per cent to 4.8 per cent of GDP. In 1997 and the first 6 months of 1998, these costs decreased slightly, but nevertheless amounted to 3.6 per cent and 3.9 per cent of GDP, respectively.

In 1996–8, the widespread use of borrowing on the foreign financial markets also began. The dynamics of the foreign debt of the Russian Federation are shown in Table 3.2.

The overall sovereign debt was 49.8 per cent of GDP (on 1 January 1998), if compared with the situation in other countries, can be considered as relatively low.[1]

The particular situation with internal debt that had developed in Russia by 1997 was defined by its short-term nature and a significant portion of debt belonging to non-residents.

*Table 3.1* The dynamics of internal debt and its servicing costs

| Indicators | On 1 January 1994 | | On 1 January 1995 | | On 1 January 1996 | |
| --- | --- | --- | --- | --- | --- | --- |
| | RUB trillions | % of GDP | RUB trillions | % of GDP | RUB trillions | % of GDP |
| Internal debt, including: | 35.2 | 21.7 | 88.4 | 14.5 | 188 | 13.2 |
| – Debts on securities | 0.3 | 0.2 | 18.9 | 3.1 | 85.2 | 6.0 |
| – Debts to the Central Bank | 29.2 | 18.0 | 58.8 | 9.6 | 61.0 | 4.3 |
| – Domestic debt maintenance | 0.99 | 0.6 | 16.1 | 2.6 | 38.2 | 2.7 |

| | On 1 January 1997 | | On 1 January 1998 | | On 1 January 1999 | |
| --- | --- | --- | --- | --- | --- | --- |
| | RUB trillions | % of GDP | RUB trillions | % of GDP | RUB trillions | % of GDP |
| Internal debt, including: | 365.5 | 18.2 | 501 | 21.4 | 751 | 28.6 |
| – Debts on securities | 249 | 12.4 | 449 | 19.2 | 480 | 18.3 |
| – Debts to the Central Bank | 59.6 | 3.0 | 0.0 | 0.0 | 0.0 | 0.0 |
| – Domestic debt maintenance | 105.7 | 5.3 | 96.3 | 4.1 | 106.6 | 4.1 |

*Sources*: Ministry of Finance of the Russian Federation 2016a, Central Bank of the Russian Federation, Institute for the Economy in Transition (IET)

*Table 3.2* The dynamics of Russia's external debt

| Year | USSR debt, US$ billions | RF debt, US$ billions | Servicing, % of GDP |
|---|---|---|---|
| 1992 | 104.9 | 2.8 | 0.7 |
| 1993 | 103.7 | 9.0 | 0.3 |
| 1994 | 108.6 | 11.3 | 0.5 |
| 1995 | 103.0 | 17.4 | 0.9 |
| 1996 | 100.8 | 24.2 | 0.9 |
| 1997 | 97.8 | 33.0 | 0.7 |
| 1998 | 95.0 | 55.0 | 1.2 |

*Sources*: Ministry of Finance of the Russian Federation 2016b, State Statistics Committee, Institute for the Economy in Transition (IET)

The duration of the Russian Federation's domestic debt (the average time before the maturity of short-term state treasury bills, known as GKOs, and longer-term rouble-denominated bonds, known as OFZs, in circulation) increased in 1995 from 60 to 90 days; in 1996, to 150 days; and in 1997, to 250 days. And although, by August 1998, the figure was approximately 330 days, in the first 6 months of 1998, the money needed each month just to pay off previously issued bonds (excluding coupon payments on 2- and 3-year coupon securities and OFZs) reached 10–15 per cent of the monthly GDP.

The dynamics of the ratio between short-term internal debt and private bank deposits, characterizing the volume of domestic financial savings in Russia, demonstrates the rapid advance of internal debt, which continued until the autumn of 1997; in spring 1996, this ratio was greater than one.

This situation predetermined the decision to allow non-residents access to the domestic market of public debt. With the size of the state budget deficit at the time and the limited possibilities for external borrowing, there was no other choice. Either the public finance deficit had to be reduced, or the internal debt market had to be opened to non-residents.

From 1 January 1998, the Central Bank and the government of the Russian Federation announced the full liberalization of the market for non-residents (the guaranteed rate of return and restrictions on the period of repatriation of profit were cancelled). As a result, the share of non-residents in the GKO–OFZ market began to increase. According to data from the Russian Ministry of Finance, in April 1998, non-residents accounted for approximately 28 per cent of the market volume.

The substantial weakening of control over foreign capital and the corresponding decrease in the servicing costs of public debt led the government to believe that there were no problems with the provision of financing for the federal budget deficit, at least in the medium term. From this perspective, allowing non-residents access to the domestic debt market had a negative impact on economic policy, heightening the risk of choosing a soft fiscal policy, which did not intend a sharp decline in the budget deficit.

External borrowings were longer compared with securities placed on the domestic market. However, from 1999 onwards, Russia entered a period of paying off credit and loans provided earlier by international financial organizations and then, from 2001, bore the costs of repaying Eurobonds placed in 1997–8.

## Note

1  The value of Russian debt on 1 January 1998 was 7.6 per cent of GDP, i.e. 25.2 per cent of the total value. In the first 8 months of 1998, the Russian Federation's share of debt obligations in the total external debt, including the debt of the former USSR, amounted to 36.7 per cent.

## References

Ministry of Finance of the Russian Federation. (2016a). "Internal debt." Available at: http://minfin.ru/ru/perfomance/public_debt/internal/structure/total/ (accessed September 2016).

Ministry of Finance of Russian Federation. (2016b). "External debt." Available at: www.gks.ru/wps/wcm/connect/rosstat_main/rosstat/ru/statistics/publications/catalog/doc_11387 17651859 (acccessed November 2016).

# 4 The chronicle of the financial crisis

Four major stages can be seen in the development of the crisis processes: November–December 1997, January 1998, February–April 1998 and May–August 1998. Throughout this period, the risks of doing business in Russia increased steadily. The risks included currency convertibility, a change in the credit rating of the country and individual companies, loss of reputation, and a change in the taxation system that was not favourable to investors. Events developed according to the worst-case scenario.

The favourable situation in the Russian financial markets in September 1997 (the weighted average return on the GKO–OFZ market dropped to 20 per cent per annum, and the RTS-1 index was around 500 points) meant that Boris Yeltsin was able to declare that, starting in 1999, Russia would abandon the IMF's financial programmes. This announcement was also a form of preparation for the denomination of the rouble 1,000-fold, which symbolized currency stabilization above all. Meanwhile, at the end of 1997, Anatoly Chubais was named best finance minister by *Euromoney* magazine, which was considered a signal to foreign investors of the stability of the situation in Russia.

In early autumn 1997, the Russian economy was therefore demonstrating positive trends. However, financial stabilization and the rapid development of Russia's financial markets took place against a backdrop of worsening fundamental economic problems: the fiscal crisis, the deterioration of the balance of payments and the increasing instability of the banking system. The ratio of short-term treasuries held by non-residents and Central Bank international reserves caused serious concerns. After the political scandals that occurred as a result of the tender to sell stakes in JSC Svyazinvest in July 1997, investors' assesments of political stability and prospects of further reforms in Russia declined significantly.

On 27 October 1997, the Dow Jones Industrial Average fell by a record 554 points, and this date can be considered the beginning of the financial crisis in Russia, which destroyed the macroeconomic results achieved by 1997. The aggravation of the international financial crisis, which affected the developed markets and brought down the prices in several emerging markets, was only a trigger for the worsening situation in Russia.

In just the first week of the crisis, the weighted average yields on the treasuries market (government debt obligations) increased from 22 per cent to 28 per cent per annum. Trading volumes increased dramatically: the weekly turnover of the secondary market more than doubled. There was also a sharp decline in Russian Eurobond prices.

The Central Bank had to choose between bad and very bad decisions. One option was to protect the rouble from a sharp devaluation by increasing interest rates on the government debt market. Another option was to maintain interest rates at a relatively low level by conducting open-market operations. In November 1997, the Russian Central Bank chose the second option, increasing its GKO holdings.

It was only on 11 November 1997 that the Russian Central Bank raised the policy rate to 28 per cent from 21 per cent, which was clearly insufficient for a balanced public debt market. Interventions on the GKO market enabled the Bank of Russia to prevent a rate increase above 30 per cent, right up until the final week of November. However, the increased demand for foreign currency from non-residents who had sold their government bond packages led to a rapid decline in international reserves and jeopardized the stability of the exchange rate policy. During the course of November, the external reserves of the Central Bank fell from US$22.9 billion to US$16.8 billion. The November loss of reserves caused a dramatic increase in the ratio of short-term debt to international reserves – from 1.9 to 2.7.

The policy described represents an error that largely determined the further development of the crisis. The Bank of Russia should not have maintained the low level of interest rates on the GKO–OFZ market: they should have been allowed to rise until market equilibrium was reached. And, from 1 January 1998, full liberalization of the internal debt market for non-residents should not have been allowed – in particular, the guaranteed rate of return and regulation of the terms of profit repatriation should have been cancelled. With a timely and substantial increase in the Ct\entral Bank policy rate and a corresponding increase in interest rates on government securities, the attack on the Russian rouble could have been far less intense.

The policy of raising interest rates could have been coupled with a more rapid devaluation of the rouble. Although this would have served as a signal to investors of the increased risk of devaluation, with a sufficient level of foreign reserves and predicted behaviour of the exchange rate it could have helped to stabilize the currency market. This type of policy could be implemented by narrowing the currency corridor and increasing its slope. However, on 10 November 1997, when the time came for action, the Central Bank of Russia, having announced the targets for the exchange rate policy for 1998–2000 (extending the boundaries of the currency corridor), did not take advantage of the opportunities to accelerate the devaluation of the rouble. Thus, the Central Bank of Russia, having sent a negative signal about the increase in the exchange rate risk, continued to support the slow rates of decline of the rouble with currency interventions.

Obviously, the measures considered (raising interest rates, with an increase in the rate of the rouble devaluation) would have had a controversial effect on the financial situation. Some investors could consider the high level of interest to be sufficient compensation for the increased risk; more conservative investors would continue to withdraw their capital from Russia. Nevertheless, the most likely result of such a policy would be a new equilibrium on the Russian financial markets, with a moderate reduction in external reserves.

The government did not have a specific programme to reduce public spending and reduce the state budget deficit. An additional factor that worsened the situation on the financial markets involved the changes in the government that took place at the end of November 1997. These changes signified the definitive abandonment of the reform programme. Investors lost faith in the ability of the government to conduct a reasonable and consistent financial policy.

In the final week of November 1997, the Central Bank, having lost more than a quarter of its international reserves, gave up trying to maintain low interest rates and left the GKO–OFZ market. The weighted average yields on government debt rose to 40 per cent per annum.

At the end of 1997 and the beginning of 1998, the crisis grew worse in South East Asia. This led to large investment funds redistributing their investment quotas among different countries, another drop in prices on the securities' market and an increase in rates of return on the GKO–OFZ market.

In January 1998, there was a substantial decline in the prices of Russian securities of approximately 30 per cent. The total drop in the RTS-1 index, from 6 October 1997 to the end of January 1998, was 50.9 per cent. The decrease in the stock prices of Russian companies became a self-sustaining process. Having received orders for the sale of significant client packages and anticipating a drop in the level of market support, investment companies themselves sought to sell liquid assets, which worsened the crisis.

In early 1998, as a result of the outflow of portfolio investments from Russia, the increased pressure on the rouble led to rapid growth of the US dollar exchange rate and an increase in forward prices. The attempts in January by the Central Bank to help speed up the rouble devaluation led to a sharp rise in interest rates on the GKO market. The market extrapolated the increased pace in exchange rate growth and reacted to this with an increase in interest rates, offsetting the decline in foreign currency-denominated yields. This market reaction confirms the fact that conducting devaluation in a crisis of confidence, with a short government debt, high proportion of non-residents on the market and a low level of foreign exchange reserves is a difficult decision to implement.

In the second half of January 1998, the political situation became worse. There was a major redistribution of power in the government: Anatoly Chubais was placed in charge of the economy only, the financial sector came under the supervision of Viktor Chernomyrdin, and Boris Nemtsov lost control of the fuel and energy complex. The weakening of the position of the reformers lowered investors' expectations even further.

In February–April 1998, the markets entered a period of relative stability. These positive trends were, to a large extent, the result of several measures taken by the president and the government that clarified the short-term prospects of the economic policy. In particular, the president announced a tightening of the fiscal policy and called for a primary surplus of the federal budget to be achieved in 1998.

After the changes that were introduced, the government developed twelve key measures for socio-economic policy. The document defined the personal responsibility of all members of the government and representatives of the presidential administration for the implementation of measures in the field of budget recovery, normalization of the situation with the payment of wage arrears, and so on.

In February, the IMF decided to extend Russia's 3-year loan for another year. The executive director of the IMF, Michel Camdessus, said that Russia would receive another tranche of credit in the amount of US$700 million and, if all agreements were fulfilled, it would receive a loan until the year 2000. On 24 February, Russia and the UK fully agreed terms for the restructuring of Russia's debt within the framework of the Paris Club.

On 10 March 1998, despite all the fluctuations on the domestic financial markets, the ratings agency Fitch IBCA confirmed Russia's long-term credit rating for foreign currency borrowings at the level of BB+ and left the short-term rating at the same level as before – B. The next day, however, Moody's announced that it had downgraded the credit rating for foreign currency borrowings from Ba2 to Ba3 and for bank deposits in foreign currency to B1.

On 23 March 1998, the president dismissed the Russian Cabinet of ministers. Sergey Kiriyenko was appointed acting prime minister. The short-term response of the financial markets to the reformation of the government was positive; however, economic agents later became disoriented by the 5-week delay in appointing a prime minister and the political turmoil that followed.

With the arrival of the new government in May 1998, the main focus of economic policy became improving the budget. Analysis of the budget policy in the spring and early summer of 1998 shows that Sergey Kiriyenko's Cabinet succeeded in preventing the crisis from worsening.

The situation with tax revenues in the first quarter of 1998 developed somewhat better than it had in 1997. At the same time, the implementation of the expenditure side of both the federal and consolidated budgets in the first 6 months of 1998 was strikingly different from before. Practically all budget positions were cut, with the exception of servicing public debt and state administration expenses.

If we look at the reconstructed budget of Russia's enlarged (broad) government (including extra-budgetary funds) in the first 6 months of 1998, we see that the level of tax revenues in the first half of 1998 was lower than in 1997 (it decreased from 32.6 per cent to 30.7 per cent of GDP). Changes in the value of total revenues were even greater – 36.5 per cent against 33.4 per cent of GDP. A greater reduction in expenditure of the consolidated budget (from 43.2 per cent to 38.5 per cent of GDP) led to a decrease in the consolidated budget deficit of 1.6 per cent of GDP.

The culminating stage of the financial crisis in Russia had a political nature. Fiscal difficulties, short domestic debt, a high proportion of foreign investors and an emerging banking crisis were directly connected to political instability, and pressure grew on foreign exchange reserves. Even with a correct and consistent policy to recover the budget and observe investors' rights, and so on, it was highly likely that problems would continue to worsen.

In mid May, immediately after the approval of Sergey Kiriyenko's Cabinet, there was a sharp drop in quotations for government securities. The turnover of the secondary market increased, the RTS-1 stock index fell by 40 per cent, and pressure increased on the rouble exchange rate. Foreign exchange reserves in May decreased by US$1.4 billion (almost 10 per cent).

The State Duma passed, and the president signed, a law on the specifics of managing shares of RAO UES of Russia and shares of other electric power joint-stock companies under federal ownership. The law violated the rights of the owners, as it limited the proportion of foreign investors (no more than 25 per cent of the shares).

In May, at a government meeting, the Central Bank governor Sergey Dubinin, warned of the threat of a crisis in the financial system and the catastrophic build-up of public debt. The shock that this statement caused was heightened by a lack of transparent statistics to characterize the monetary and foreign exchange policy. The first warning signs of the beginning of the banking crisis began to appear: external management was introduced at Tokobank, which held significant loans from Western banks. On 26 May, it was announced that the sale of Rosneft had been cancelled (owing to falling share prices), which deprived the budget of US$2.1 billion and sent a negative signal to investors.

Despite the expansion of the crisis in the Russian financial markets, the government reacted slowly. It was only at the end of May 1998 that it began to develop anti-crisis measures. On 17–19 May, statements were made by the government (on its commitment to macroeconomic stability), the Central Bank (on the immutability of the monetary policy and the inadmissibility of monetary issue as a method of financing the budget), the Ministry of Finance (on the plan for fiscal austerity) and the Federal Commission for Securities (on ensuring investors' rights). On 29 May, the government issued a statement about immediate measures to stabilize the financial market and about the fiscal policy in 1998. A few days after his appointment as head of the tax service, Boris Fedorov outlined the main methods of inproving tax collection in Russia. A certain level of optimism began to appear in the financial markets after Anatoly Chubais's visit to Washington on 29–30 May, during which the prospects of a large package of financial aid to Russia were discussed. At the beginning of June, the yields on government obligations decreased to 51 per cent and then, in the second week, to 46 per cent.

Nevertheless, the government did not undertake systematic action to withstand the crisis, and this led to an increased lack of confidence among investors. A further negative factor was the fact that, in June, the Russian government was slow to conduct negotiations with the IMF about the allocation of a large package of financial aid.

In the second half of June, the mass withdrawal of investor funds from the financial markets led to a new increase in interest rates on GKOs – to 50 per cent. The reduction in the stock index in June was 20 per cent. This dramatically increased pressure on the rouble exchange rate and required large-scale intervention by the Central Bank.

Despite the unfavourable situation, on 10 June, Russia placed 5-year bonds in the amount of US$1.25 billion at an interest rate of 11.75 per cent. On 24 June, a new Russian loan was placed for US$2.5 billion, now at a rate of 12.75 per cent. The high cost of borrowing served as a negative signal to investors and reduced the quotations of other traded Eurobonds.

On 17 June, Boris Yeltsin appointed Anatoly Chubais as the president's special representative for negotiations with international financial organizations with the rank of deputy prime minister, which was welcomed by financial markets. On 23 June, the IMF Board of Directors approved the allocation of another credit tranche of US$670 million. The IMF also made a statement that supported the measures of Russian government to prevent a sharp devaluation of the Rouble.

In June 1998, the government developed anti-crisis programme, which included a reduction in gas and electricity prices, a change in tax legislation (transition to levying VAT based on shipments, prospects of flat income tax, a reduction in profit tax, an increase in excises, limiting the number of current accounts held by companies, the introduction of sales tax, etc.), and sales of state-owned stakes in major Russian corporations (in particular, 5 per cent of shares in RAO Gazprom and state-owned shares in JSC Svyazinvest). Kiriyenko presented anti-crisis draft laws to the State Duma at the beginning of July 1998.

During these days, the weighted average yield on the government securities market reached 126 per cent per annum. On 8 July, the Ministry of Finance cancelled auction bids for the placement of GKOs and OFZs. On 13 July, the Russian government announced its intention to offer GKO holders the option of converting them into medium- or long-term bonds, denominated in US dollars and maturing in 2005 and 2018. The situation improved after an announcement on 13 July: the IMF, the World Bank and the Japanese government would provide US$22.6 billion of financial aid to Russia, of which US$5.6 billion would be provided immediately after the meeting of the IMF Board of Directors.

From 13 to 19 July, the weighted average yield of GKOs dropped to 53 per cent. During that week, the RTS-1 index rose by 34 per cent. However, on 15 July, an auction bid for the placement of GKOs failed to take place yet again, and the state debt was serviced at the expense of the federal budget. On 20 July, it was announced that the issue of state securities would be suspended for a period of 1 year.

Many of the draft laws that were part of the anti-crisis package proposed by the government in June–July were rejected by the State Duma. As the adoption of these laws was an integral part of Russia's negotiations with the IMF, it could be assumed that there would be a certain reduction in the amount of expected financial support. Nevertheless, as a result of negotiations between Anatoly Chubais and the management of the IMF, the amount of the first tranche was only moderately reduced: from US$5.6 billion to US$4.8 billion. On 21 July, the IMF decided to allocate a new package of aid to Russia.

Despite the reduction in the amount of the first tranche, the financial markets reacted positively. The yield of government obligations decreased to 45 per cent. Therefore, further development was largely dependent upon clear signals to the market about the next steps that the Russian government would take to normalize the situation. However, the government did not take any measures to demonstrate that it had a coherent plan.

The government believed that the temporary stabilization of the market in the last week of July was a sustainable trend and waited 1 week before conducting a meeting, on 27 July, between Prime Minister Sergey Kiriyenko and major investors to explain to them the government's action plan to repay and service government debts in the short term. However, the government failed to clearly demonstrate – about the growth in tax revenue, and the increase in the level of international reserves – that Russia would be able to cope with its obligations before the end of 1998.

Aside from the increasingly evident political weakness of the government, which was not capable of carrying a package of anti-crisis draft laws through the State Duma, there were a number of additional factors that, by early August, caused a sudden change in the development of the situation and sent it spiralling out of control.

First, there was the deterioration of the situation in the world financial markets. Second was the seasonal decline in the share of risky assets in the portfolios of major institutional investors just before the summer holidays. The most important reason for this was aggravation of the banking crisis. It was triggered by the worsening of the situation in the financial markets amid the tight monetary policy pursued in the first 6 months of 1998. The drop in prices of Russian government foreign currency securities, which served as collateral for loans issued to Russian banks by their foreign counterparts, played an important role in exacerbating the liquidity crisis. As a result of the drop, there were additional deposit requirements for Russian banks to maintain collaterals (margin calls). In order to deliver these funds, the banks sold the GKO–OFZs in their portfolios, as well as corporate shares, and converted the proceeds obtained into foreign exchange, which caused additional anxiety in the financial markets, including in the market for Russian securities denominated in foreign currencies. The first banks that were unable to meet their obligations to foreign credit institutions were SBS-Agro and Imperial.

As a result, between the time of obtaining the IMF loan and the first days of August, the financial situation deteriorated sharply. The yield on government obligations increased to 56 per cent, and the rate of decline of the stock market increased. From the time the stabilization loan was issued by the IMF to 17 August, the RTS-1 index fell by almost 30 per cent. The volume of international reserves began to decrease rapidly. On 23 July, they amounted to US$19.5 billion, but, by 31 July, it had dropped to US$18.4 billion, and by 7 August to US$16.3 billion.

Along with the fundamental causes, there were two other factors that prevented Russia from avoiding a deep devaluation of the rouble in August: the lack of support of the government's anti-crisis programme from the State Duma and the insufficient level of aid from the IMF. By mid August, the situation could potentially have been rectified by urgent help from the G7 in the amount of US$10–15 billion. However, it would not have been realistic to expect to receive these funds. The only possible way out was the devaluation of the rouble.

The government's plan, which was unveiled on 17 August, included three groups of measures: the introduction of a floating exchange rate for the rouble, with its devaluation before the end of the year to approximately RUB9 to US$1; the introduction of a 3-month moratorium on the repayment of foreign debts of Russian banks; and forced restructuring of debts on GKO–OFZs.

On 15–16 August, the government's plan was agreed with the IMF. The announcement on 17 August 1998 of the programme, without a scheme for the restructuring of the internal public debt, caused a negative reaction in the financial markets. In just 1 week, the stock market dropped by 29 per cent. The Russian government waited for 1 week before announcing the restructuring scheme. The total amount of Russia's frozen internal debt was RUB265.3 billion (US$42.2 billion at the exchange rate of 14 August 1998). OFZs worth approximately RUB75 billion, with maturities in 2000–1, remained in circulation. Kiriyenko's government's programme was not implemented in its original form. On 23 August, the government resigned, and Viktor Chernomyrdin was appointed acting prime minister. This decision had serious economic and political consequences. The resignation and the declaration of a shift in the economic course practically cancelled the agreement with the IMF, both in terms of the expanded lending programme, as well as the stabilization loan (taking into account the IMF-supported measures according to the announcement made on 17 August). The political crisis dramatically increased the uncertainty of forthcoming economic performance.

These factors caused a new wave of panic in the financial and commodity markets. On 26 August, after having wasted considerable reserves on supporting the rouble at low dollar prices, the Russian Central Bank suspended trading on MICEX indefinitely. From 28 August, trading was suspended on regional currency exchanges. The Central Bank was then unable to keep the rouble from falling owing to the decrease in the level of foreign exchange reserves (US$12.46 billion on 1 September). The threefold devaluation of the rouble and the sharp increase in the velocity of money determined the rapid growth of consumer prices. In August, prices increased by 3.7 per cent and, in September, by 38.4 per cent.

The inflation rates then began to slow down. This was largely owing to the Central Bank's monetary policy. In August, there was virtually no change in the monetary base, despite the fact that the Central Bank had spent US$5.95 billion of its reserves. It was evident that foreign exchange interventions had been sterilized as a result of transactions with government bonds on the open market and the issuance of stabilization loans to commercial banks.

In September, the monetary base increased by 9.5 per cent, with a slowdown in the reduction of external reserves. The inflationary impact of the printing press was, to a large extent, offset by the reduction in the monetary multiplier owing to the withdrawal of private deposits from commercial banks.

Eurobonds were traded at 20–30 per cent of their nominal value (70–85 per cent before the crisis).

In September 1998, the dollar exchange rate in the System of Electronic Lot Trading demonstrated considerable fluctuations. On 31 August, the dollar exchange rate was 7,905 RUB/US$, but, on 9 September, it rose to 20,825 RUB/US$. The need to reduce the estimated losses on forward contracts for delivery in mid September determined the subsequent decline in the dollar exchange rate to 8.67 RUB/US$. After this exchange rate level was fixed on 15 September, dollar quotations rose once again to 16 RUB/US$. At the end of September, the US dollar exchange rate had risen by 102.4 per cent. After the August drop in prices, in September 1998, the decline in the prices of Russian stocks slowed down somewhat. In August, the RTS-1 index decreased by 56.2 per cent, but, in September, this figure was 33.2 per cent. From the beginning of 1998, the RTS-1 index fell by 89 per cent and, from the beginning of October 1997, by 92.3 per cent.

On the rouble interbank loan market, interest rates on overnight loans in mid September reached 450 per cent per annum, and those on 3-day loans reached 130 per cent per annum. Loan reimbursements were provided for by the high yield of currency operations. In September, the volume of transactions was ten times lower than in August. This was the most acute phase of the crisis, after which the situation gradually began to stabilize. A new stage had begun in the economic life of the country – and that was a new stage in the Russian anti-crisis performance.

# 5 The political nature of the financial crisis

## The budget deficit as a political and constitutional problem

The most important macroeconomic problem of Russia's post-communist economy, after decreasing inflation, was the budget deficit. The excess of state expenditure over income had been steadily reproduced year on year. The inability to cover expenditure through tax revenues made it necessary to borrow funds on the domestic and foreign financial markets. The budget deficit was replicated owing to the continuous decline in tax revenues. Experience from 1996–8 showed that attempts to strengthen political and administrative pressure on companies to force them to pay taxes delivered only short-term results. We can distinguish three groups of causes underlying the crisis of the budget revenue, and they were mostly political.

First, the political instability in Russia limited the willingness and the ability of the authorities to collect taxes. The most dramatic increases in tax arrears occurred in the moments of dramatic weakening of the political positions of the federal government, and improvements in tax collection occurred when it looked consolidated.[1]

Second, the non-balanced budget had a dampening impact on the economic situation, including the level of tax revenue. Poor tax collection and a lack of revenue to meet public-sector needs resulted in budget arrears to and evasion of the tax basis (tax non-payments).[2]

The third cause was the principal inability of a state (especially a democratic state) to collect taxes above a certain level. Of course, this level can only be measured roughly. However, world practice shows that there is some link between the level of a country's economic development and the tax pressure on the economy. This issue is particularly important for understanding of the nature of 1998 financial crisis in Russia, and that is why we will consider it in more detail. One can observe a direct correlation between the level of economic development of a country and the budget's share in GDP.[3] The more developed democratic countries can redistribute a greater share of their product through the budget, but this is more because of the opportunity rather than the necessity for such redistribution. The United States, being one of the leaders in terms of economic development, redistributes a much smaller share of GDP through the budget than, for example, France or Spain, or the countries with strong social democratic traditions (Sweden, Norway).

However, all other things being equal, the countries noticeably lagging behind are characterized by a smaller share of the fiscal burden.

This scheme is greatly distorted if the analysis takes the political factor into account. This regularity applies to countries with more or less democratic regimes. Authoritarian regimes concentrate a much larger share of resources in the hands of the state than is possible under democratic rule. That was the way of transition in communist countries, and that is why they all, having embarked on the path of market democracy, faced the problem of reducing the budget load.

Russia's budget problems, therefore, become more understandable. In terms of the level of economic development, Russia was one of the outsiders among the democratic states, whereas the country's budget load was quite high.[4]

Here, in fact, lies the problem in defining the essence of the budget crisis and the method of overcoming it. The budget crisis in democratic, post-communist Russia was of a political nature not because the government lacked the political will to combat tax evasion and tax arrears; the political character of the budget crisis just reflected the lack of capacity to extract bigger revenue from the country or to reduce spending to an acceptable level.

Incorrect understanding of the budget crisis predetermined the actions taken to overcome it. During 1996–8, the focus was on improving tax collection, either by strengthening tax administration or by upgrading the taxation system and tax legislation. The issue was considered by the government; it was put forward as a criterion by the representatives of international financial institutions when granting loans to Russia from the IMF and the World Bank; and it attracted the attention of the heads and analysts of leading investment banks.

The authorities made various organizational and political efforts to improve tax collection. The role of tax administration extended, its head was promoted to the rank of minister and then deputy prime minister. An enormous amount of effort went into the development and promotion of the tax code, which, however, was not adopted by the State Duma by that time. Evasive techniques were used in order to expand the roles of taxes that, for technical reasons, were better to collect. The latter was especially evident in the thesis of Prime Minister Sergey Kiriyenko about the desirability of strengthening taxation of consumers while at the same time easing the tax burden of manufacturers, which actually meant simply switching the focus from direct to indirect taxes. The measures taken gave a very limited (approximately 1 percentage point of GDP) and short-term result; the tax collection rate fell once again to the same level or below. Although the task of preventing a further sharp decline in budget income was resolved, it was impossible to ensure a substantial and stable increment of revenues to a level that could match the expenditure commitments of the state.

The key point of balancing the budget had to lie in restructuring and improving the effectiveness of expenditure, and also reducing it – a very painful matter, both politically and socially. During the period under review, the government made quite strong attempts to put things in order in terms of spending the funds of the federal and local budgets, and, in June–July 1998, Sergey Kiriyenko's Cabinet even developed and approved a special programme for that purpose. However, the measures taken in this area were more about putting the costs in order and were an attempt at identifying and eliminating unreasonable expenditure, whereas the problem was more complex as well as more distinct: the state had to abandon a part of its obligations, which politically was almost impossible to implement.

The particular features of the Russian constitutional system got in the way of accomplishing this task. The mechanism for establishing government institutions stipulated in the 1993 Constitution prevented such a solution. A strong presidential republic was being formed to limit the populist and lobbying activity of the legislative bodies. However, independence from the Duma did not defend the government against populism: it put many deputies in a comfortable and politically strong position when parliament did not bear responsibility for the results of the socio-economic course that was being taken. This was especially painful when the federal budget was under consideration in the Duma.

Furthermore, the opposition majority of the Duma of the Second Convocation (1996–9) had no desire to share responsibility with the government for the social consequences of the budget policy. Economic instability was an important factor in political instability and created favourable conditions for the opposition in the forthcoming (in 1995 and 1996) parliamentary and presidential elections.

Another problem was the oppressive impact of the budget deficit on the status of the tax system. The budget imbalance greatly increased the level of arrears, including payments to the budget.

## Consolidation of power, political conflicts and financial crisis

Aggravation of the financial crisis was also associated with the crisis of the socio-political base of the macroeconomic stabilization policy of 1995–7. The influential interest groups providing support for this policy included export-oriented industries and banks.[5] The stability of the rouble created favourable conditions for their businesses. However, in 1997, the situation began to change.

First, the fall in world prices for energy and metals gave rise to exporters' interest in a decreasing rouble exchange rate; thus, they joined the pro-inflation forces. Second, the oil lobby increased pressure in favour of reducing excise duties, which could not help but have a negative impact on the federal budget and, consequently, on macroeconomic stability.

In such circumstances, devaluation would have become practically inevitable, had it not been for the situation occurring in the banking system. The significant foreign exchange liabilities of leading Russian commercial banks put them on the brink of bankruptcy in the event of rouble devaluation, which was an important factor impeding devaluation. The real situation proved to be even more difficult, as the banking and oil and gas businesses in post-communist Russia were closely interwoven.

Finally, an important factor of the internal instability was the growing struggle between various factions of the Russian business elite, in which the government was involved. The budget crisis in 1997 forced the Cabinet to pay closer attention to tax collection, on the one hand, and the fiscal results of privatization, on the other.

The formation of the new Cabinet in March 1997, with prime minister Viktor Chernomyrdin and Anatoliy Chubais as his first deputy and minister of finance, generated some hope, which was reflected both in the reduction of strike activity and in positive shifts in the polls (Figures 5.1 and 5.2).

The fight for tax discipline complicated relations between the government and the leading export-oriented and politically influential companies, most notably Gazprom and the oil companies. It was primarily these companies, which made significant contributions to the federal budget, that were ordered to maintain fiscal discipline and repay debts to the state. Steps were taken to increase state control over Gazprom: despite its natural-resource monopoly status and the blocking stake of the state, the organization was fully controlled by its top management (which formally signed a trust contract to manage the state-owned stake). Gazprom, as well as other energy-exporting companies, was required to implement modern forms of accounting to improve the transparency of its work. The naturally negative reaction to such actions by the government, actions that were thought to be unconventional and unfavourable, was greatly strengthened by two groups of factors. First, the high level of arrears, and especially non-payments of budget organizations, gave the energy companies reason to argue that tax arrears were the result of non-payments for the supply of relevant energy resources (this primarily concerned Gazprom and the national electricity company – RAO UES of Russia). Second, the efforts to improve tax collection coincided with the decline in world oil prices, which further complicated the position of relevant companies and gave them a reason to accuse the government of deliberately undermining the oil industry. Of course, the increased transparency could partially

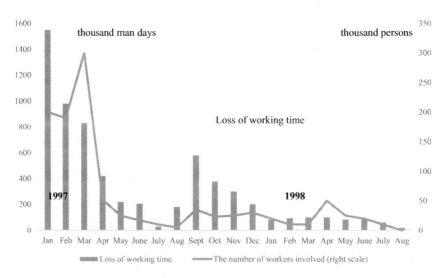

*Figure 5.1* The number of strikers and loss of working time, 1997–8
*Source*: Rosstat 2016b

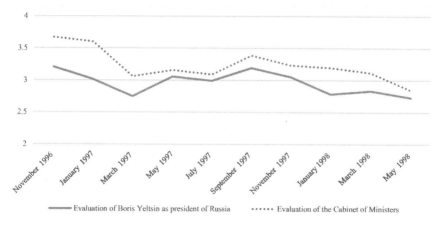

*Figure 5.2* Attitude to the work of the president and the government
*Source*: Russian Public Opinion Research Centre

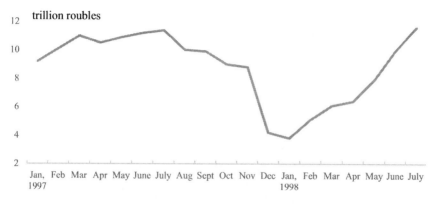

*Figure 5.3* Budget salary arrears. Data on eight sectors: industry, construction, transport, agriculture, education, health, science and art
*Source*: Rosstat 2016a

reduce costs and increase efficiency, but it would strongly oppose the interests of the owners and managers of these firms.

In 1997, the attitude of the authorities toward privatization was revised when the fiscal tasks came to the fore. It was considerably different from the preceding approach, when privatization was considered mainly as a tool to strengthen the political base of the post-communist government. The attempt by the government to maximize revenue from the privatization of large, very attractive companies caused extreme discontent among the banking elite. A major disagreement was caused by the results of privatization of such big companies as Svyazinvest (telecommunications) and Norilsk Nickel (non-ferrous metals), as well as the prospects for the privatization of Rosneft (oil).

All these events resulted in a growing political struggle inside the Cabinet. From December 1997, the government found itself weakened, and the adoption of practically any significant decision was blocked. The most typical example is the story of the decision to confiscate the property of some major oil companies that had failed to pay taxes. The decision was taken by the first deputy prime minister, Anatoly Chubais, and cancelled by Prime Minister Viktor Chernomyrdin (December 1997).

However, at the beginning of 1998, the situation was getting worse. The worsening financial situation and political scandals in the government reduced its public support. In 1998, the budget arrears began to increase again, which primarily concerned military and social workers (Figure 5.3). Accordingly, strike activity increased, as well as a level of dissatisfaction by the government.

These events resulted in the resignation of Viktor Chernomyrdin's Cabinet in March 1998.

## The financial crisis and Kiriyenko's government

The reasons for the resignation of Viktor Chernomyrdin and his Cabinet came down to at least the following three arguments, which are quite closely related.

First, the excessive politicization of the Cabinet made it unable to focus adequately on addressing the economic challenges. This reproach was put into words directly by Boris Yeltsin, when he explained his decision regarding the resignation of the government. This was particularly a signal for Chernomyrdin who was clearly intending to take part in the next presidential elections scheduled for 2000.

Second, the socio-economic situation deteriorated, which was reflected in the slowing down of the increase in production that had recently occurred, as well as in the renewal of the budget arrears on salaries and pensions.

Third, the effectiveness of the work of the government decreased dramatically, which was associated with the exacerbation of the internal political struggle. It became clear that the Cabinet, which contained two potential candidates for the presidency (Viktor Chernomyrdin and first deputy prime minister Boris Nemtsov), could not provide an efficient policy.

The situation was quite clear, and fundamental restructuring of the government was inevitable. However, the question remained open: should that reorganization be done by replacing the prime minister or, on the contrary, by strengthening its positions by dismissing other members of the Cabinet? The approach based on teamwork and professionalism (or the technocratic approach) outweighed the factor of political significance. This had both advantages and disadvantages, which soon emerged in full.

The new government was supposed to stabilize the situation in the country and mitigate the impact of the global ("Asian") financial crisis on the Russian economy. The main tasks of the Cabinet of new prime minister Sergey Kiriyenko were as follows:

- to prevent (or slow down) the devaluation of the rouble;
- to prevent a default on public debt;
- to overcome the crisis of payments and repay the state's debts to state-funded organizations;
- to implement an industrial policy with a view to maintaining the economic growth that had occurred in 1997.

It is easy to see the contradictions in these tasks. In the face of the deepening financial crisis, the main efforts were focused on addressing macroeconomic problems, which, in turn, created the basis for a reasonable industrial policy.

The task of preventing devaluation seemed highly important. This approach caused many objections, as the falling oil prices and, consequently, the worsening of trade and payment balances were putting devaluation on the agenda. However, the governments of Viktor Chernomyrdin and Sergey Kiriyenko focused on preventing it. The reasons were in the sociopolitical sphere: devaluation would lead to a dramatic rise in inflation, primarily affecting consumer goods, and would cause the collapse of the banking system. Both could have predictable negative social consequences. In addition, the Russian budget's dependence on external borrowings would undermine the confidence of international financial circles in the Russian market. But, finally, devaluation would lead to a sharp rise in the servicing of external debt, with a high probability of default. The political effects of this could include, not only a huge rise in social unrest, but even a change of political regime.

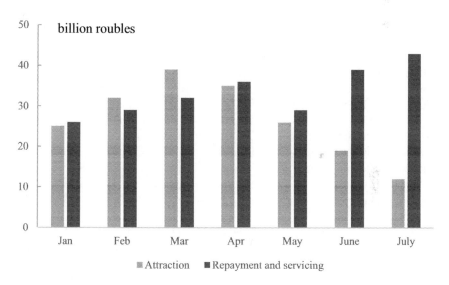

*Figure 5.4* Borrowing on the domestic market and the amount of repayment and servicing of domestic debt

Source: Author's calculations

The reorganization of the government coincided with the transition of the financial crisis in Russia to a whole new phase. In March–April 1998, the federal budget revenues began consistently to lag behind what was needed to service and repair the domestic debt, and the income from GKOs (short-term treasury bonds) finally ceased to be a source of additional budget resources – that is, a new placement of GKOs would entirely go on covering payments on previous loans (Figure 5.4).

The government developed a programme to stabilize the financial situation and restore investors' confidence. The major components of the programme included improving tax collection, strengthening control over infrastructural monopolies and getting additional financial resources from privatization. The government reckoned on the possibility of obtaining additional resources from international financial organizations, whose support would be an important factor of restoring confidence in Russia from foreign and domestic debt holders.

Thus, it was an attempt to return to the policy of the previous Cabinet of spring–summer 1997, associated primarily with the names of Boris Nemtsov and Anatoly Chubais, who was appointed the special representative of the president in negotiations with international financial institutions.

However, the real situation evolved differently in 1997. Not only did the government fail to increase tax collection, but, on the contrary, the federal budget revenue in May faced a sharp decline. The government also failed to implement major privatization projects, which resulted in new losses for the federal budget. Combating natural-resource monopolies was not as successful as in the previous year, and investors continued to flee the country. These differences led to a number of objective and subjective factors.

The external factors included the continuing global crisis and further deterioration of the economic situation in Asia. The attitudes towards emerging markets deteriorated, and Russia was only one link in the chain of this crisis. More problems were created by the rumours about a likely rise in the rates of the United States Federal Reserve, and, although they remained nothing more than rumours, portfolio investors became increasingly inclined to opt for less risky investments in North America and Europe.

The new prime minister could not ensure the stability of the actions and statements of the team members. The relationship between the Ministry of Finance and the Central Bank remained extremely tense. The statements of the heads of both departments were often contradictory and led to further macroeconomic destabilization: they communicated signals that strengthened the doubts of the world's financial community about the competence of the Russian authorities.

Sergey Kiriyenko failed to achieve at least an outward appearance of correctness and coherence of actions. When, upon the receipt of a loan from the IMF on 20 July, the Central Bank froze the accounts of the Ministry of Finance, and the latter announced its intention to borrow, on the domestic market and within one day, an amount exceeding the monthly tax revenue of the federal budget, the political crisis became apparent to investors. It was the failure of the political leadership to ensure the stability and consistency of economic policy.

The government's political weakness was also seen in vulnerability from the side of the oil lobby. The need to collect taxes was combined with the desire to help the management of the oil companies in a situation of the ongoing decline in world oil prices. The attempt to link the payment of taxes with access to exports sparked sharp resistance from the oil sector lobby.

Being politically weakened, the government failed to urge the natural monopolies to increase their transparency and to repay their debts to the state. The pressure, as usual, started from Gazprom, all the more so as its political weight decreased after the resignation of Viktor Chernomyrdin. Gazprom had to pay, but the Cabinet was not able to either change the leadership of the company or get consent for its restructuring. It was another factor that further reduced the level of confidence in the Cabinet.

All of this affected the government's ability to use privatization to make fiscal gains. Of course, financial crisis considerably reduced the likelihood of attracting money from privatization. This restriction was accompanied by an additional factor – the fight by the participants in the deals for a reduction in the price of objects to be privatized. The steps taken by them included their refusal to file applications for tenders (investment competitions) and attempts to oust potential competitors. The best example of the latter was the decision on the possibility of seizing Gazprom's property at the very moment when its head was negotiating with foreign partners about the establishment of a consortium for the acquisition of Rosneft.

In the early summer of 1998, the first signs of default appeared in the financial markets. A number of Russian regions failed to pay their debts. Regional payments on agricultural bonds became overdue. Although, officially, the federal government had nothing to do with these payments, the defaulted regional debt contributed to political destabilization. The steps taken in response by the federal government to limit foreign borrowing by the regions aggravated its relationship with the national political elites.

Finally, the relationship between the executive and legislative branches remained difficult. To overcome the crisis, they had to pool their efforts together to adopt a set of anti-crisis legislation. However, the relationship with the Duma, which was very tense owing to the fact that Sergey Kiriyenko was approved as prime minister under strong pressure from the Kremlin, also continued to worsen. Relations with the Upper House, the Council of Federation, which represented regional elites, were uneasy owing to the inability of the executives to pay regional transfers and the attempts to impose financial restrictions on the regional authorities to borrow money. The inability of the authorities to develop and approve an anti-crisis package challenged the prospects of further assistance from international financial organizations.

## Notes

1 To read more, see: Gaidar 1998a: 297–302.
2 Re the relationship between the imbalance of the budget and the level of non-payments, see: Gaidar 1998a: 1032–3.

3  The World Bank 1996: 114.
4  The World Bank 1997: 240–1; Illarionov 1997: 257–60.
5  See: Gaidar 1998: 157–65.

## References

Gaidar, Ye. (ed.) (1998). *Ekonomika perekhodnogo perioda: ocherki ekonomicheskoj politiki postkommunisticheskoj Rossii. 1992–1997* [Economics of Transition: Essays on the economic policies of post-communist Russia. 1992–1997]. Moscow: IET.

Illarionov, A. (ed.) (1997). *Rossiya v menyajuschemsya mire* [Russia in the Changing World]. Moscow: IEA.

Rosstat. (2016a). "Budget salary arrears. Data on eight sectors: Industry, construction, transport, agriculture, education, health, science and art." Available at: www.gks.ru/bgd/regl/B03_36/IssWWW.exe/Stg/d020/i020420r.htm (accessed October 2016).

Rosstat. (2016b). "The number of strikes." Available at: www.fedstat.ru/indicator/33477 (accessed October 2016).

World Bank, The. (1996). *From Plan to Market*. Washington, DC: Oxford University Press.

World Bank, The. (1997). *The State in a Changing World*. Washington, DC: Oxford University Press.

# 6 Anti-crisis policies

## First steps

The acute phase of the financial crisis had several important economic and social consequences that formed new conditions for the anti-crisis policies.

One can distinguish the following economic effects of the August 1998 crisis:

- A decrease in confidence among foreign and domestic investors towards the government, the Central Bank and the Ministry of Finance meant loss of the opportunity to borrow money on both the external and domestic markets, as well as the outflow of foreign investments and bleaker prospects for economic growth.
- The closure of both external and internal sources of financing of the federal budget deficit meant a return to direct Central Bank financing of the Russian government, which would be followed by an increase in inflation.
- The crisis in the domestic banking sector, which was caused in part by the losses in the financial markets,[1] led to the worsening of the non-payments crisis. The collapse of the Russian stock market, which reflected the real attractiveness of portfolio investments in the Russian corporate sector (from 1 October 1997[2] to October 1998, the RTS index fell by 90 per cent), meant even fewer opportunities for Russian companies to attract funding.

The social and political consequences of the devaluation of 17 August 1998 were also fairly obvious:

- First, owing to the inflationary spike, the level of social discontent had risen significantly, and the people who suffered the most belonged to those layers and groups who were supporters of the existing economic and political system: the new middle class (particularily the fast-growing service industry), small businesses and residents of major cities in general.
- Second, the president's political position had weakened. Insisting on approval of Sergey Kiriyenko as prime minister, Boris Yeltsin had actually taken over that responsibility from the new Cabinet. The devaluation and default came as a powerful blow to the president, and the dismissal of the Cabinet and interweaving of the political crisis with the financial crisis lowered the level

of trust in Yeltsin once again and strengthened the political positions of those forces who advocated change in the constitutional system and re-election of the president. It reinforced the position of the legislative branch, and the appointment of Minister of Foreign Affairs Evgeny Primakov as prime minister, supported by the Duma, made him a strong, legitimate political figure.
- Third, there was a notable reconfiguration of interest groups. Owing to the bankruptcy of many large banks and the reduction in the financial opportunities of energy exports, the political role of the richest businessmen ('the oligarchs') – mainly those who were associated with the banking and energy businesses – had weakened dramatically. The lobbies of the military, industrial and agricultural sectors seemed to be strengthened.

## The economic and political alternatives

Evgeny Primakov's government, which was formed in September 1998, clearly expressed its strong desire to significantly change the economic course of the country. Representatives of the executive authorities had not made such statements since at least 1992. Now, in September 1998, they started to openly talk about such milestone changes. It was quite understandable.

First, Primakov's government was formed with the active support and participation of left-wing political forces and factions (primarily communist and agrarian). Of course, the representatives of the Communist Party and the agrarians had been a part of previous governments on a number of occasions, but they had occupied minor posts in the Cabinets. This time, the prominent, iconic left-wing figures took key positions, which enabled them to have a decisive influence on the Cabinet. Most of them were either members of or were close to the Communist Party and belonged to the traditional Soviet establishment. The typical representatives of this stratum in the new government were Deputy Prime Ministers Yuri Maslyukov, Vadim Gustov and Gennady Kulik, as well as the Central Bank governor, Viktor Gerashchenko.

Second, the need for a strong swing was dictated by the magnitude and depth of the economic crisis. The explosion of August 1998 was not only a financial phenomenon – it inevitably led to serious social and political disruption. The increase in prices and the loss of savings, the dramatic increase in unemployment, which in particular affected the social groups most actively included in the market economy, the crisis in the consumer market, shrinking demand and the deterioration of conditions for entrepreneurial activities – all these developments had struck the country, and that seemed quite unexpected to many. The requirement to change course had become a general consensus, although various sociopolitical forces attached totally different meanings to this concept.

However, the following questions remained unanswered: What exactly should this swing consist of, and what should replace the previous course? As the analysis shows, the real options for the government were very limited and fairly obvious. They flowed logically from the practical experience of the implementation of economic policies in the post-communist period, especially during 1995–8.

Thus, Primakov's government was, from the very beginning, faced with a tough political choice, which could not be avoided, and no compromise could be made between the alternative options. One way was to return to the practice of 1992–4, with its combination of soft money and weak fiscal policies. Another way was to maintain a tight monetary policy and rouble stabilization, followed by radical budgetary reforms that could ensure a balance between the budget revenues and expenditures, that is, to achieve consistency in the actions of the Ministry of Finance and the Central Bank. This choice was completely political.

The first option was inflationary. The increase in the money supply would result in rising prices and the depreciation of the rouble. It was expected that this would help to resolve social problems, overcome the crisis of payments, replenish the working capital of enterprises and increase demand for domestic goods. Taking into account the strengthened Communist Party influence on the government, the most probable reaction to the rise in prices could be attempts to freeze them, as well as the introduction of a fixed exchange rate.

The second option was stabilization policy. This assumes that a rigid budget balance and macroeconomic stability can be achieved, which are the basic prerequisites for economic growth to be restored. It involves resolute measures to ensure the state budget surplus, restrictive monetary policies (including the introduction of a currency board regime) and a more coherent liberalization of economic life. The structural and budgetary reforms following on from these steps should create the conditions for economic agents to adapt to the competition and find their niches in the market.

Both options were announced in the first few weeks after the start of the full-scale financial crisis. The scholars in the Russian Academy of Sciences (RAS) Economic Department, headed by Dmitry Lvov, consistently supported the inflationary and dirigiste ideas; they published an open letter to the government outlining their views and specific proposals. The opposite course – that of rigid stabilization – was formulated in the policy proposals of a group of economists led by Yegor Gaidar.[3] The choice between the inflationary and stabilizing options was largely political. The lack of sources of foreign and domestic funding after the resignation of Kiriyenko's government prompted a choice in favour of the inflationary path of development.

The main political aspect of choosing between the inflationary and stabilizing options was the choice of the social strata and groups that would pay the prime cost for the future course of economic policies. These two models were fundamentally different.

The inflationary option was mostly favourable to banks. The growth of the Russian banking sector was due largely to the inflation of 1992–4, and, in this case, when many banks were in a desperate situation, they could be rescued by resources from the Central Bank – by 'cheap money'. Strong losses would be incurred by those enterprises that were in line with the market competition, both exporters and manufacturers competitive in the domestic market. The lack of financial and monetary stability deteriorated their business, preventing them from making investment activity and from developing their companies. Inflation strongly affects major cities that were industrial centres. The state of affairs after 17 August 1998 showed that it was the big cities (especially Moscow) that were the most vulnerable to sharp price increases and disruption of commodity flows.[4]

## Economic programme of the Primakov government

Primakov's government did not make a clear choice between the two options that the economic course could take. It was expected to turn towards inflationism and populism, the likelihood of which was clear from the dominance of agrarians and communists, and numerous statements of politicians and economists supporting this government. The prime minister promised to pay – within months, if not weeks – the debts to public-sector employees and pensioners, resolve the problem of non-payments, ensure the stability of the rouble and restore stability. The top authorities talked almost every day about the need to start a 'controlled money printing', revise the results of privatization, nationalize various sectors of the economy, introduce a fixed exchange rate, prohibit the holding of foreign currency, and so on.

The inflationary way had some natural preconditions that were partly connected to the left-wing (communist) basis of the new Cabinet. The significant budget deficit forced the government to use the printing presses.

The proposals to switch on the printing presses also included certain institutional ideas that caused serious concerns regarding the adequacy of the Cabinet's assessment of the situation and the possible actions of the authorities.[5]

If the new government had begun to act strictly in accordance with these expectations, the events that followed would have been easy to predict. The model proposed by the advisers from the Duma and the Academy of Sciences was not unique; it had been tested for decades in dozens of countries, particularly in Latin America. This model was referred to as populist and was examined in detail.

The economics of populism during its practical implementation includes four main phases that are repeated consistently, albeit with some variations, in different countries.

In the first phase, the government attempts to speed up industrial growth by pumping resources from export sectors to the sectors of 'national pride' (usually mechanical engineering), with a simultaneous increase in the money supply. In response to these measures, the economy really starts to grow, and people's welfare improves. It appears as if the government is taking major strides, and the country is on the brink of an economic miracle. The popularity of the authorities increases significantly.

During the second phase, the economy starts to face imbalances. It turns out that the increase in the level of production and welfare is accompanied by the deterioration of some macroeconomic indicators: a rise in the deficit of trade and payment balances, shrinking foreign currency reserves and increasing external debt. For a while, however, these negative shifts are only visible to professional economists (and, if a country has been excluded from the real market economy for a long time, not to all of them). The budget difficulties increase, but there is normally little focus on 'temporary problems' in a situation where there is a clear increase in the pace of industrial growth.

In the third phase, commodity shortages in the public sector grow rapidly, and inflation of free prices accelerates. Attempts to freeze prices lead to greater commodity shortages, and the inevitable devaluation of the national currency results in an inflation explosion. Tax collection worsens, and the budget collapses. No matter what the government does, living standards begin to decline, and production shrinks.

During the fourth phase, the government collapses, and the new authorities (often military or emergency bodies) take radical measures to stabilize the socio-economic situation.[6]

The idea of what was expected from Russia's new government, both domestically and abroad, was clearly described by Primakov himself when he spoke to foreign entrepreneurs participating in the Davos Forum session in Moscow:

> Predictions were recently made for us: nationalization as the basic path for the government to follow – it didn't happen, annulment of the results of privatization – it didn't happen, a fixed exchange rate of the rouble – it didn't happen, we are not fixing the rate, it is floating. They predicted uncontrolled emission – it didn't happen, they predicted a ban on dollar circulation in the country – it didn't happen, they predicted the suspension of imports – it didn't happen . . . they predicted the support of national production to the detriment of foreign investments – it didn't happen, they said we wouldn't pay the debts – it didn't happen.

This list is illustrative because these outcomes were exactly what were expected: the reason for this was the mentality of the traditional Soviet establishment, which had come into power along with Primakov, and the rhetoric and traditions of communist forces in post-communist Russia. In reality, Primakov's government acted more cautiously than expected.

The programmes created by Primakov's Cabinet, and the economic ideas of the prime minister himself, underwent significant changes during the period of his rule. In the early stages, policy documents were dominated by an openly inflationary and dirigiste mood. Things were called by their proper names, and unsecured emission could be spoken about without reserve. Later on, there were a lot of technical details, specific decisions, but the issues of emission and budget deficit were carefully avoided.

It was expected at the beginning that the government would base its policy on the proposals from the RAS Department of Economics. Authors of these proposals were included in a special task force formed by the government to develop its the economic programme. First deputy paime minister Yuri Maslyukov held regular consultations with them during the first month of the new Cabinet.

The "Programme of academicians" was a document embodying the ideas of populism, inflationism and dirigism in the most coherent and rigid manner. It was quite a coherent and consistent system of measures that could be easily formalized into official regulatory documents. The authors of the programme believed that the reasons for the crisis were the viciousness of all the economic policies conducted after 1991, particularly the liberalization of the economic policy, and the exaggeration of the role of macroeconomic regulation compared with institutional changes.

The programme involved using significant cash infusions to solve social problems, increasing demand as a factor in overcoming the recession, mending the payment system and combatting the banking crisis. It was even suggested that it would be advisable to maintain the 'automatic' switching printing press to prevent non-payments in the future. The printing press was seen as a universal tool to resolve almost all economic problems. Proposals were also made to introduce strict control over foreign currency circulation.

The programme was criticized from the very beginning, not so much for its open inflationism, but rather for the fact that it was clearly detached from real economic processes. Many of its measures had the potential to lead to abuse, on the part of both the government (through granting cheap loans) and business. The idea of automatic money provision in case of non-payment meant that virtually any entrepreneur could gain unlimited access to 'cheap money', and full deposit insurance meant that a banker could raise funds with any interest rates and then file for bankruptcy.

By early October 1998, the government had prepared its own version of an economic programme. This document was developed by the Ministry of Economy and was not confirmed officially. The document caused a highly negative reaction among the public, including the mass media, which resulted in its being disavowed by Primakov. However, this programme deserves special consideration, because it was the most consistent and specific.

The programme was very close to the "Programme of academicians". It was also focused on the active use of the printing press to resolve economic and social problems in the shortest possible time, and a much stricter policy of state intervention in the economy, including measures to ban the dollar on domestic markets, not only as a means of money accumulation, but also as a means of saving. It was anticipated that there would be large-scale state regulation of prices and tariffs ("for production of basic industries, food and non-food essential goods", etc.), protectionism and state support of import-substituting industries.

There was also a new sentiment. The government clearly began to fear its own inflationary intentions and, even more so, the overall inflation expectations. The Central Bank was in no hurry to start printing money. The lessons of the past had not gone unnoticed. Viktor Gerashchenko, the governor of the Central Bank, did not want to take responsibility for the promotion of inflation and therefore insisted that the Duma took relevant decisions in monetary policy. The government tried to place greater emphasis on its administrative capacities. The idea of tightening control over foreign currency was worded very clearly. Along with the informal publication of the programme, the governor of the Sverdlovsk region, Eduard Rossel, put forward a proposal to ban circulation of the dollar in Russia. At that time, similar moods prevailed among the part of the political elite that was closely linked to the government. Relying on the Central Bank, foreign exchange control and other forms of state intervention replaces ideas of unlimited inflationism and covers them, to a certain extent.

The slogan of a 'strong state' became one of the most popular at that time. Its active supporters believed that the weak state was the result of implementation of market ideology that ignored the problems of 'market failures'. This implies that, in order to restore the economic and political power of the state, it had to be acknowledged that the previous doctrine was incorrect, and it would be important to extend the state's regulation.

By the end of October, the government policy paper had become more moderate and less specific in details. It contained a huge amount of segmentary measures, in social and industrial areas, tax policy and inter-budgetary relations. However, the essence of the economic policy was outlined with apparent reluctance. In analysis of the causes of the crisis, less was said about the incorrect course of the past and more about the role of the budget crisis and the problems of overcoming it. Yuri Maslyukov even said that the new government intended to do all the things that had been planned, but not implemented, by its predecessors (a statement made at a meeting with the participants of the Davos Forum in Moscow on 4 December 1998).

The core idea disappeared from the programme. There was no more reliance on the printing press. On the contrary, there was an awareness of the danger of inflationist policy, which was reflected in the noted problem of "the critical gap between the need to expand the money supply and the possibility of inflationary-safe emission", and it was recognized that there was "a risk of hyperinflation". The hopes for a 'strong and wise state' were also reduced to ritualistic words about the need to "strengthen the state system as an essential resource to enhance the productivity of the economy". As a result, the prime minister renamed the programme as a document "On the measures to . . .", thereby emphasizing that it involved fragmentary measures.

A very specific aspect of all the programmes discussed by this time was the microeconomic concept of growth. First and foremost, minimal importance is given to the protection of private property, which goes virtually unmentioned in most documents. For example, it is worth noting that the first version of the programme contained no mentions of 'private property', or 'private' at all, and thirteen out of fourteen references to property concerned various forms of public ownership. The concept of privatization was entirely absent. In addition to this, the government constantly demonstrated its preference for direct investment as opposed to portfolio investment.

Besides this work on the basic government programme, a strategic role was certainly played by two other documents: the concept of tax reform and the draft federal budget for 1999.

Thus, by the end of 1998, the government had become aware of the danger of a populist economic policy, but it had not been able to find an adequate replacement for the original populist programme.

Evgeny Primakov adopted the tactic of avoiding tough decisions. The political mandate given to the prime minister, and the support of the legislative branch and a large part of society, meant that Primakov was able to use such tactics. However, the real economic processes had increasingly narrowed the margin for manoeuvre.

## Contours of the anti-crisis economic policy

The government policy can be characterized both by specific actions in the economic sphere and by the adopted legal acts. The actions of Primakov's Cabinet can be divided into two groups. On the one hand are the traditional measures of a Soviet economic establishment focused on finding a compromise between the leading interest groups and those traditional of the Soviet system: agricultural and machine-building lobbies. On the other hand, there were actions aimed at correcting the decisions taken by previous Cabinets, especially by Kiriyenko's government, mainly related to fiscal matters and streamlining financial flows. These groups had points of intersection. The government cancelled those regulations that were not in line with the policy of establishing a balance of forces between the interest groups, but accepted those that were of benefit to them. Examples of the latter could be the confirmation of tax reduction, permission to sell goods below their prime cost and similar measures, which could support the real sector. When analysing the fiscal policy, one can see two approaches and two groups of decisions that had very different effects on the prospects of economic development: decisions undermining the budget revenue base and related especially to actions in the field of fiscal policy, and the budget for 1999, which had to be based on the principles of minimum inflationary financing of the deficit. The conflict between these two approaches was largely attributable to the evolution of the macroeconomic views of the Cabinet – from inflationism in September–October 1998 to an awareness of the need to tighten budget in November–December. This conflict was rooted in the Cabinet's desire to avoid drastic actions, to ensure maximum political support, even for unpopular decisions. After all, ensuring political support was the imperative of Primakov's actions and an important factor in his decision-making in economic policy.

The decisions and actions of the government fell into two groups and, respectively, into two phases in its practical work. First, the populism of the first 3 months and, second, the development of a prudent budget for 1999.

In seeking political support, the government concluded individual agreements with major taxpayers concerning the timing and mechanisms for fulfilment of their obligations on payments to the budget. The first such agreement was signed with Gazprom, and it was announced that the government was ready for other agreements. Moreover, according to a statement from the tax authorities, Gazprom was allowed to connect its budget payments with the volume of indebtedness due to it from public organizations. The government also recommended launching large-scale offsets of enterprises' debts due to budgets of all levels.

As a measure to stabilize the exchange rate of the rouble, on 11 September, the Central Bank decided to restore the practice of the compulsory sale of 50 per cent of businesses' foreign currency revenues. In the short term, this measure had some positive effect. It created additional stimulus to understate the foreign currency revenues transferred to Russia.

The government's decisions in agribusiness and food security were inconsistant, but similar in terms of implications for the budget. On the one hand, steps were taken to support agriculture and the related industry sectors. First of all, the government, in accordance with a communist tradition of the past 4 decades, restructured the fiscal debts in agriculture for 5 years at 5 per cent per annum (i.e. it was virtually written off). This sent a message that not paying taxes to the state was possible and was economically justified behaviour, and the good-faith payers once again realized that their behaviour was irrational. On the other hand, the government started the reduction of import duties, which had been raised by Kiriyenko's Cabinet. The duties were lowered for many food items, especially for meat and dairy products.[7] These decisions could be explained by the typical Soviet fear of food shortages, the loss of competitiveness of import products as a result of devaluation, the pressure on the part of food import-related interest groups, and the difficulties in ensuring the increased fee within the Customs Union.

The new policy lines assumed strengthening of the union with Belarus. Having visited Minsk during the first official visit, Yevgeniy Primakov expressed his willingness to take into account the positive experience of this country and to pursuit further integration.

Among other decisions of a largely symbolic value made by the government, one can name the restoration of state guarantees for certain economic activities, and the urgent appeal to Western governments for the provision of humanitarian food aid.

## Notes

1 The package of T-Bills in the assets of Russian banks at the time of default reached about RUB40 billion (excluding Sberbank of Russia). According to various estimates, Russian banks hedging exchange risks of foreign investors lost US$15–22 billion owing to the runaway devaluation of the rouble.
2 The maximum historical value of the RTS index as of 16 October 1997 amounted to 571.66.
3 See: Scholars of the Department of Economics of the RAS (1998).
4 It is worth mentioning that the main political disasters in this country in the twentieth century were directly related to the disruption of trade flows and its impact on the situation in capitals and major cities. The collapse of the monarchy was a direct result of the fact that, in 1916, the governors started to strictly limit the outflows of food to other provinces, and, after that, the problem of food supply in the cities was dramatically exacerbated by the transport crisis. In 1927–8, the dismantling of the NEP market system ("the great turn") was associated with the fact that the peasantry, in the face of the growing commodity shortages and real depreciation of the *chervonets* (the former gold-backed currency of the Russian Empire and the Soviet Union), lost interest in supplying goods to the general public and to the industrial cities. Finally, in 1990–91, it was the commodity shortages and lack of real currency that led to the rapid disintegration of the country and the food crisis.

5   Characteristic proposals were made by the chairman of the State Duma, Gennady Seleznyov, as to the measures that would need to be taken in economic policy within a matter of days. These essentially strategic points were put forward almost immediately after the appointment of Primakov, whose candidature was actively supported by the chairman of the Duma: "The activities of the currency exchange must be suspended, and the Central Bank must set a fixed exchange rate for the US dollar at the rate of 7 roubles per dollar ... Negotiations must be conducted with the financial institutions of the West and a request made to temporarily suspend the circulation of foreign currency credit cards in order to prevent foreign currency from flowing abroad. Foreign exchange offices must be temporarily prohibited from selling foreign currency to the public. These offices should only buy dollars ... The foreign currency available in commercial banks should be used exclusively for the purchase of food and other necessities, medicines" (*Kommersant*, 11 September 1998, p. 2). In addition there were also proposals from the new government leaders to renationalize the unprofitable enterprises of the military industrial complex, which were not in line with the government's basic operational logic in the face of the fiscal crisis. (A typical feature of the Cabinet's doctrinal principles was that it focused on the nationalization of unprofitable enterprises, rather than export-oriented companies.)
6   Dornbusch and Edwards 1991: 7–13.
7   See: Government RF 1998.

# References

Dornbusch, R. and Edwards, S. (eds) (1991). *The Macroeconomics of Populism in Latin America*. Chicago, IL, and London: University of Chicago Press.

Government RF (1998). Resolution of the Government of the Russian Federation, dated 21 October 1998, no. 1226.

Scholars of the Department of Economics of the RAS (1998). "Open letter of scholars of the Department of Economics of the RAS to the president of the Russian Federation, the Federal Assembly and the government of the Russian Federation", *Economics & Life*, no. 37.

# 7 Results of the 1998 financial crisis

## Economic results

After the 1998 crisis, a number of macroeconomic and institutional indicators improved, and, one year after the default, the situation in Russia had become more stable. This was largely owing to the decisions of 17 August 1998, supplemented by the responsible macroeconomic policies of the successive governments.

Among the main positive outcomes, one can note the following:

- The rouble exchange rate was no longer overvalued. Thus, one of the main causes of the destabilization of the macroeconomic situation disappeared. The rouble became quite stable, and its dynamics became predictable.
- The problem of the short-term rouble debt was almost solved. The ratio of short-term debt to liquid reserves became quite satisfactory.
- The budget deficit reached a minimum level.
- In June 1999, the bank-restructuring process began. The surviving banks were healthier, more robust financial and credit institutions than those that had dominated the Russian banking system before August 1998; they were more interested in working with the real sector than in financial speculation.
- Thanks to the August 1998 default, government borrowing – the pump that was drawing money out of the real sector – had disappeared. Although it was too early to talk about full-scale financing of firms by credit institutions, short-term loans were already available to enterprises.
- Capital flight decreased by about half – from US$3 billion to US$1.2–1.5 billion a month, with half of that amount spent on buying foreign currency.
- The corporate equities market was the fastest growing among all developing markets in the first half of 1999 (more than 60 per cent every quarter). That is, the recovery of the market happened much faster than expected. The growth meant increased investor confidence in Russia, despite the decisions taken in August (and partly even thanks to them).
- Inflation fell quickly.
- Production in the country revived significantly. Industrial growth in the first half of 1999 totalled about 6 per cent.
- There were significant, positive trade and payments balances.

- Direct foreign investments began to increase, surpassing the level of 1998 (US$648 million in Q1 1999, against US$546 million on average per quarter in 1998), but still below the level of 1997 (US$1.6 billion on average per quarter). However, a sharp rise in investment was unlikely before the new presidential elections and until political stabilization had been achieved.
- A set of legislative initiatives introduced during Primakov's time in office and approved under Prime Minister Sergey Stepashin was, in fact, a set of measures developed in July 1998.

The macroeconomic stabilization, together with the rouble devaluation, had intensified the process of import substitution. As a result, the drop in industrial production was lower than predicted, based on the inertial evaluation of production dynamics.[1]

Between November 1998 and January 1999, some industries started to grow. In January 1999, compared with January 1998, engineering production had increased by 2.3 per cent, forestry and wood processing by 5.8 per cent, industrial construction materials by 2 per cent, glass and porcelain–faience by 2.6 per cent, and microbiologicals by 0.4 per cent.

At the end of 1998, the government had largely succeeded in ensuring macroeconomic stability (most importantly preventing an increase in the rate of inflation) and had managed to significantly normalize the payment and settlement system.

## Sociopolitical results

The government paid a high price for achieving budgetary balance. Public spending depreciated nearly two times. Such a reduction in expenditure was painful from a sociopolitical and economic point of view. Since the beginning of 1999, the wave of strikes had subsided, and the level of public confidence in the head of the government had risen. Let us take a closer look at the reasons for this.

Consider household incomes. It is interesting to note the high negative correlation of the official and subjective statistics on incomes: the correlation coefficient of the official and subjective living wage amounted to –0.72, and the correlation coefficient of the official and subjective per capita income was –0.85[2] (see Figure 7.1).

As can be seen from Figure 7.1, starting in January 1999, the subjective living wage remained below the official level. This is probably owing to a number of factors.

First, the promised catastrophe (paralysis of the financial system, hyperinflation, return to the times of total deficit, rationing of goods) had not come about.

Figure 7.2 shows that, according to the Russian Public Opinion Research Centre, after peaking in early autumn 1998 (i.e. immediately after the crisis), the percentage of respondents who evaluated the economic situation, both in their locality and in Russia, as bad and very bad had generally tended to decline.[3]

Second, having personal savings in dollars, which had been prevalent, became 'more expensive' after the devaluation, despite the 1998 trend for the growth of

*Effects of the 1998 financial crisis* 85

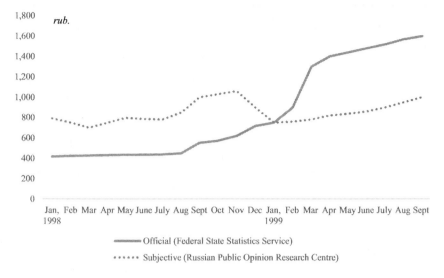

*Figure 7.1* Official and subjective living wage
*Source*: Russian Public Opinion Research Centre, Federal State Statistics Service

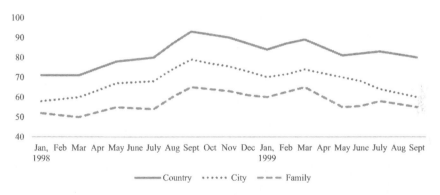

*Figure 7.2* Assessment of the financial condition of the family, the economic situation in the town (township) and in the country as bad and very bad (per cent)
*Source*: Russian Public Opinion Research Centre, Federal State Statistics Service

other types of saving. In addition, their subjective value increased in the opinion of their owners.

Third, the growth of production and the reduction in the share of barter (the increased monetization of the economy), which became one of the consequences of the devaluation of the national currency in the second half of 1998, had led to an increase in real income due to more stable payment of wages in cash and a decrease in wage arrears.

So, the reduction in real wage arrears was almost fully explained by the increase in industrial production (normalized R-square is equal to 0.97, negative correlation).

86  *The 1998 crisis in Russia*

The coefficient of correlation between the index of the intensity of industrial production and the amount of the subjective average annual income per capita was positive and reached 0.73 (Figure 7.3).

However, owing to the particular calculation methodology used, the official statistics do not record the growth of real payments to households. Figure 7.3 shows that, as early as autumn 1998, the reduction in the real value of wage arrears had been accompanied by rising incomes declared as actually received by the respondents of the Russian Public Opinion Research Centre, whereas, according to the Federal State Statistics Service, medium per capita income began to grow only in the spring of 1999.

A similar conclusion can be drawn from the dynamics of the strike movement (Figure 7.4). After the peak in the autumn of 1998, in line with the reduction in real wage arrears, as well as the growth of real income and the growth of production, the number of participants of strikes and the loss of working time started to decrease.

The percentage of respondents who favoured the prime minister's activities in 1998, especially in the second half of the year, was largely determined by the level and dynamics of real wages (negative correlation coefficient: more than 0.8). In 1999, this relationship weakened. In contrast, in 1998, the prime minister's rating hardly depended at all on the level of nominal per capita income. However, from the beginning of 1999, the positive relationship began to increase (Figure 7.5).

The level of confidence in the prime minister was closely (negatively) linked to the dynamics of real wage arrears throughout 1998 and during the period

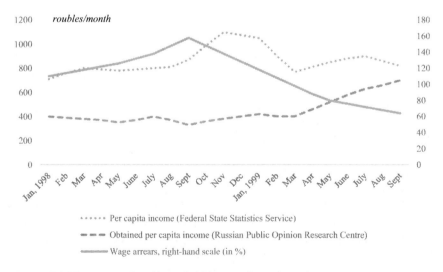

*Figure 7.3* Wage arrears* and household income dynamics

*Note*: *Real wage arrears at the end of the month (December 1997 = 100 per cent)

*Source*: Russian Public Opinion Research Centre, Federal State Statistics Service

*Effects of the 1998 financial crisis* 87

between January and May 1999. From June 1999 onwards, no statistically significant relationship was recorded (Figure 7.6).

In other words, after the summer of 1999, the approval of the prime minister had essentially ceased to depend on the real state of affairs in the economy and transformed into a purely political phenomenon. A similar conclusion can be drawn

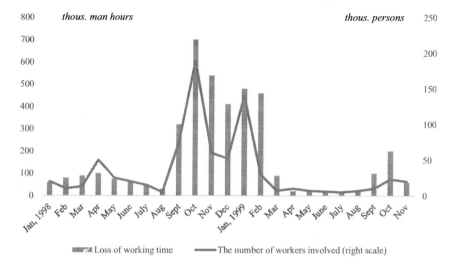

*Figure 7.4* Number of strikers and loss of working time, 1998–9
*Source*: Russian Public Opinion Research Centre, Federal State Statistics Service

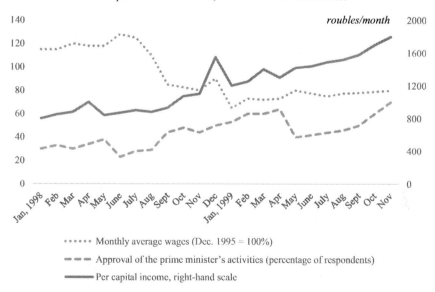

*Figure 7.5* Approval of the prime minister's activities, dynamics of real wages and nominal per capita income
*Source*: Russian Public Opinion Research Centre, Federal State Statistics Service

88  *The 1998 crisis in Russia*

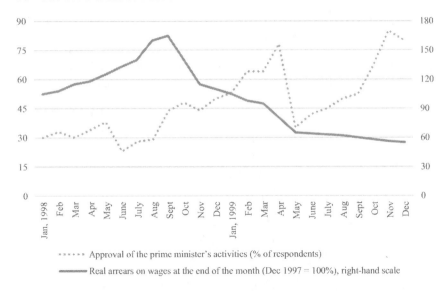

*Figure 7.6* Approval of the prime minister's activities and dynamics of real arrears on wages

*Source*: Russian Public Opinion Research Centre, Federal State Statistics Service

from the analysis of the correlation between the prime minister and the stock market index. From September 1998 to May 1999, one could see an extremely strong positive ties (correlation coefficient of about 0.8) between the approval of the prime minister (Primakov's Cabinet) and the stock market index. At the same time, in the periods from January to August 1998 and from June to December 1999, no

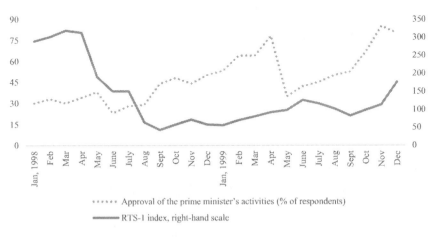

*Figure 7.7* Approval of the prime minister's activities and RTS-1 index dynamics
*Source*: Russian Public Opinion Research Centre, Federal State Statistics Service

*Effects of the 1998 financial crisis* 89

statistically significant dependence was registered. The situation is similar with regard to the level of trust in the head of government and the intensity of industrial growth (Figures 7.7 and 7.8).

The increase of trust in the government (Figure 7.9) signalled the end of the crisis. The country entered into a new stage of development.

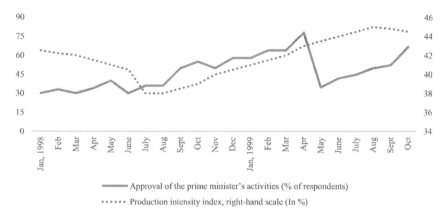

*Figure 7.8* Approval of the prime minister's activities and the industrial production intensity index

*Source*: Russian Public Opinion Research Centre, Federal State Statistics Service

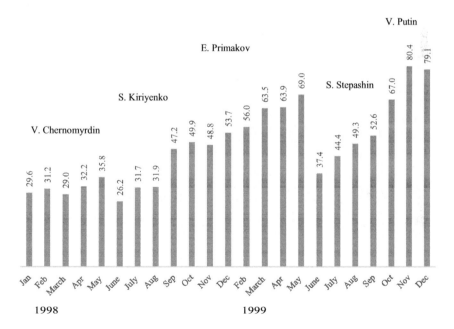

*Figure 7.9* Percentage of respondents who approved of the prime minister's activities

*Source*: Russian Public Opinion Research Centre, Federal State Statistics Service

## Notes

1 Centre for Economic Conjuncture 1998a, 1998b, 1998c.
2 Subjective living wage: assessment of the living wage by respondents; subjective per capita income: the income declared by respondents as really received in the previous month per family member (according to the Russian Public Opinion Research Centre).
3 However, the proportion of respondents who considered the financial condition of their families poor or very poor is lower than the proportion of those who are sceptical as regards the country's situation.

## References

Centre for Economic Conjuncture (1998a). Business activity of basic industrial enterprises of Russia in November 1998. Moscow: Center for Economic Conjuncture, 1998.

Centre for Economic Conjuncture (1998b). Industrial production dynamics. Preliminary results of 1998. Conjunctural assessment for 1999 (according to the reporting data for January-November 1998). Moscow: Center for Economic Conjuncture, 1998.

Centre for Economic Conjuncture (1998c). Industrial production intensity indices (January 1990–October 1998). Moscow: Centre for Economic Conjuncture, 1998.

# Part III
# Challenges of the global crisis

# 8 Global crisis

## Historical context and trends of economic development

The global crisis that began in 2008 can be fairly compared with the largest economic shocks of the past, of which the most significant are:

- The first global economic crisis of 1857–8. It was global by the standards of those times, covering the countries with a prevailing capitalist system. It is sometimes called 'Marx's favourite crisis', because this event was crucial for building the economic model of the 'inevitable demise of capitalism'. Ten years later, the first volume of *Das Kapital* was published.
- The first large-scale financial crisis of 1907, which was overcome thanks to focused actions. However, the anti-crisis measures were implemented, not so much by governments, but rather by John Pierpont Morgan and a group of financiers close to him. The previous reactions to crises was generally passive: the main economic agents preferred to wait until everything resolved itself. In fact, it was in 1907 that the concept of an opportunity to create and carry out coordinated anti-crisis activities appeared. This important ideological shift predetermined the direction of theoretical and applied economic science in the twentieth century. An important political consequence of the crisis was the establishment of the US Federal Reserve System in 1913.
- The crisis of the 1930s, or the Great Depression. Its experience and analysis put the foundation of the modern model of state regulation of the economy and economic thought as such. It was a systemic global crisis that went far beyond a strictly economic framework. Keynesianism, generated by this crisis, offered a universal formula that promised an end to global economic catastrophes.
- The crisis of the 1970s, which brought to the world the unprecedented phenomenon of *stagflation*, that is, the combination of high unemployment and high inflation. There was even a new aggregate measure of economic hardship, which was the sum of the unemployment and inflation rates. The way out of this crisis was associated with deregulation and rejection of economic populism – first in most developed economies, and later in many developing countries, including post-communist states.

Structural crises are unique. It is virtually impossible to use the experience of overcoming each one of them in a new context. And yet, there are a number of qualities that allow them to be attributed to one class; in other words, these crises can be compared, their specific characteristics should be taken into account, but the anti-crisis policy formulas effective in one case cannot be applied in another. One can distinguish the following features of systemic (or structural) crises:

*First*, this crisis is both cyclical and structural. It involves fundamental institutional and technological changes, that is, a transformation of the technological base (which some economists term the 'technological paradigms'). These changes raise the economy to a whole new level of efficiency and labour productivity. A renewal of the technological base, during which the latest technical and scientific innovations are applied, is the main precondition for emerging from the crisis.[1]

*Second*, a financial crisis is a significant component of any structural crisis. The combination of a financial crisis and an economic crisis (decline in production and employment) renders the crisis even more difficult to overcome and creates the need for a variety of structural and institutional reforms to steer the economy back on to a trajectory of sustainable growth.

*Third*, the consequence of a structural crisis is the formation of a new growth model: this involves modernization of both the developed and developing economies and, in turn, the creation of new technological drivers. The emergence of new industries and sectors, and their geographical relocation throughout the world, is creating a new global reality that poses new challenges that require the adoption of new instruments of economic policy. This trend is captured well in a formula: 'the new normal'.[2]

*Fourth*, There are significant geopolitical and geo-economic shifts, new balances of power (involving countries and regions) on a global scale. In the early stages of the present crisis, it was assumed that this would result in the consolidation of a bipolar world based on confrontation between the United States and China, sometimes referred to as the "G2", the "Big Two"[3] or "Chimerica".[4] However, we are gradually but ever more distinctly beginning to see the formation of a multipolar world, which assumes two or three key economic centres, but resembles a return to the well-known nineteenth-century model of the 'concert of nations', where nations balance each other's interests.

*Fifth*, in the course of a structural crisis, the model of socio-economic process regulation changes. The 1930s marked the transition to the industrial society and the establishment of the ideology and practice of the 'big government', accompanied by the growth of taxes, budget expenditures, public ownership and planning, and, in some cases, public pricing. In contrast, the crisis of the 1970s resulted in large-scale liberalization and deregulation, a reduction in taxation, and privatization – in short, what was required for the transition to a post-industrial stage. At the beginning of the current crisis, it seemed that the world was again returning to a model of state domination of the economy (crass Keynesianism). However, this trend has not been proven in practice. The role of state regulation does really increase, but this applies primarily to regulation of financial markets at national and global levels. It is true that a significant anomaly currently exists in that, whereas financial activity operates on a global scale, regulatory mechanisms have remained national. In the absence of global governance, there is need for a mechanism to regulate global finance.

*Sixth*, a structural systemic crisis creates the need for a new global financial architecture. Following the crisis of the 1930s, the world adopted a single reserve currency – the US dollar. After the 1970s, a dual system based on the dollar and the euro was adopted. What type of currency system will evolve in the aftermath of the present crisis is not yet clear. If there is a consolidation of regional groupings in the global balance of power, this might be accompanied by a strengthening of the Chinese yuan or of regional reserve currencies. A proliferation of reserve currencies could contribute to the emergence of a multipolar world and encourage increased accountability by the corresponding monetary authorities (to the extent that the reserve currencies would compete with each other). The prospects of cryptocurrencies as a modern form of private money are also should be considered.

*Seventh*, a new mainstream economic doctrine emerges from the structural crisis, similar to Keynesianism and neo-liberalism in the twentieth century.

All the above suggests important implications concerning the prospects for overcoming the systemic crisis and related mechanisms.

First, this crisis creates a large-scale intellectual challenge, requiring a deep re-understanding of its causes, mechanisms and ways to overcome it. As generals who are always preparing to fight a past war, politicians and economists are preparing to fight the past crises. This can work for a certain time, as long as they have to deal with economic cycles, that is, with repeated challenges of economic dynamics. This is why the first response to a systemic crisis entails recourse to the methods of the past. In relation to the 1930s, it was the desire of George Hoover's government (primarily the secretary of the treasury, Andrew Mellon) not to interfere with the natural course of events, to strictly balance the budget and strengthen the monetary system based on the gold standard. As the preceding 100 years' experience demonstrated, crises would usually disappear in about one year, and no special social policy for this was required. Similarly, in the 1970s, with the onset of the crisis, the authorities tried to use the traditional methods of Keynesian regulation (budget stimulation in the face of slowing growth and even state control of prices undertaken by the Republican administration of Richard Nixon), but this resulted in abrupt inflation and the onset of stagflation processes.

Structural crises cannot be dealt with by application of the economic policies of preceding decades. Too many new problems arise, and it is unclear from the outset what mechanisms are driving the crisis, what is its scale, how long it will last, and how it can be overcome. In the twentieth century, it usually took around 10 years to overcome a systemic crisis. This fact was indicated by Paul Volcker, when in July 1979, in the middle of a previous systemic crisis, he was appointed chairman of the Federal Reserve System: "We're face to face with economic difficulties really unique to our experience. And we've lost that euphoria that we had 15 years ago, that we knew all the answers to managing the economy".[5]

In 2008, the world faced a serious intellectual challenge: it is impossible to remain in the outdated economic paradigm of the previous decades. New financial market instruments appear and the states are not always able to regulate them.

The debate on combating the crisis revolves around the traditional twentieth-century dilemmas: Keynesianism versus monetarism, dirigisme versus liberalism. Each argument in favour of the thought that the responsibility for what happened lies in the market is opposed with a no less compelling counter-argument proving the guilt of the state. Anti-crisis economic policies also use these models, and, in practice, the Keynesian methods of budget-stimulating demand and monetary methods to promote supply via a soft monetary policy were applied simultaneously.

Second, a structural crisis cannot be considered merely as a recession, as an increase in unemployment or as a run on the banks. It consists of various episodes and waves that affect individual sectors, countries and regions. This determines its duration, which is approximately a decade, which can be described as turbulent. Moreover, the statistical data do not accurately or even adequately describe the economic processes at work. The mere fact of technological renewal may distort (to a significant degree) the dynamics of the output, as the traditional statistical methods at first fail to adequately describe the emergence of new sectors in the economy.

Problems also arise with employment statistics. During a cyclical crisis, one of the most important indicators of its being overcome is employment growth, but, in a structural crisis, this criterion can only be applied at the very end. Technological renewal assumes new demands on labour resources – that is, significant structural changes in the labour market. This means that, during the emergence from a systemic crisis, employment recovery may be delayed, and there will be high unemployment even as the economy grows. Or as in the current demographic situation in several developed countries (when population in working age is reducing) it could be zero growth rate with stable employment. There arises a kind of conflict between the new economy and the old statistical methods, and some time is required to resolve it.

Third, it is impossible to overcome a structural crisis and launch economic growth only by macroeconomic instruments, however important the budgetary and monetary problems might be. As we see from the experience of 2008–17, macroeconomic measures could mitigate the crisis but not provide sustainable economic growth. Of course, a responsible macroeconomic policy should not lose sight of the importance of structural and institutional solutions, ensuring the modernization of the national socio-economic system.

Structural crises can be described as innovative. They entail the appearance (before, during or after the crisis) of new economic and political institutions, the emergence of a new generation of politicians, businessmen and experts, and the creation of a new technological base. Such a crisis comes to an end when the shifts and transformations described above take place, or, in other words, after the problems created by the crisis have been resolved.

When applied to current structural crisis these key problems include:

- growth rates, and primarily the likelihood of a long period of low growth rates (secular stagnation);
- new challenges in macroeconomic policy involving widespread use of non-traditional instruments (particularly in the area of money circulation);

- theory and institutions of the welfare state that are relevant to the demographic and political realities of the twenty-first century;
- the prospects for globalization or de-globalization;
- the prospects for re-industrialization and new technological challenges;
- the role of inequality as a factor of economic growth.

These problems involve rethinking the theoretical foundations of economic policy and practical recommendations. During the 1980s–2000s, the key issue was to ensure economic growth and macroeconomic stability, and the main obstacles to achieving this goal were considered high inflation and excessive state intervention. This understanding of the challenges and risks was summarized in the so-called "Washington Consensus", a set of basic recommendations primarily for developing countries.[6] We do not deny the importance of macroeconomic stability, but today, economists and politicians are faced with the challenge of finding additional tools to regulate economic development that would avoid a prolonged stagnation against the backdrop of low inflation.

The tasks of structural modernization in a period of crisis are raised, not only by emerging economies, but also by the most developed states. The elites of most countries realize the danger of ignoring innovation challenges. It is no coincidence that the US administrations continually rise the problem of the fundamental upgrading of the country, and this means not only upgrading technology, but also social and economic institutions. According to Larry Summers:

> this new American economy will be in different, and better, shape than it was before the bust. It will be "more export-oriented" and "less consumption-oriented"; "more environmentally-oriented" and "less energy-production-oriented"; "more bio- and software- and civil-engineering-oriented and less financial-engineering-oriented"; and, finally, "more middle-class-oriented" and "less oriented to income growth that is disproportionate towards a very small share of the population".[7]

When addressing the causes of the current global crisis, one should specify both the fundamental problems of modern development and the special problems of various economies.

The unprecedented economic growth rate in previous two decades was a separate factor of the crisis. In the course of such recovery, there will inevitably be contradictions that go unnoticed owing to the increase in prosperity. But even if they are noticed, it is difficult to intervene and correct something: after all, why should you take any restrictive or corrective measures when everything is going so well? During such boom periods, whenever someone starts to express cautions or doubts about whether the course being taken is correct, confident voices say: "This time things will be different".[8]

An important role in the onset the crisis was played by the rapid spread of financial innovations. As a result, financial derivatives, such as CDSs, reached the level of US$60 trillion by the beginning of the 2010s – that is, four times higher than the US GDP. Thus, the crisis has become a kind of revolt of financial innovations against their own creators – an unpleasant, but not entirely new, phenomenon in financial history. When global crisis began, it became clear that the situation with Barings Bank, bankrupted in 1995 solely by the actions of Nick Leeson, a young trader in the Singapore branch of the bank, had been a harbinger of the crisis, a message to the financial world that was not understood.

One of the major, deep-seated problems that led to the crisis was the domination of the interests of capitalization over the interests of improving the effectiveness productivity factors (or productivity growth), which emerged in the last quarter of the century. Market capitalization rather than sustainability of business, and not the amount of dividends, was the foremost interest of shareholders. Their attention was focused on this indicator, and they used it to judge the effectiveness of management. Parametres of productivity and modernization took a back seat. More precisely, these last two factors played a role, but only if they did not contradict the growth of capitalization. This meant striving for maximum concentration of production in the hands of a few global players, the impossibility of closing inefficient enterprises and, on the contrary, the willingness to include them in large holdings as a factor in market expansion and capitalization.

The motivation of managers of large companies increasingly resembled the motives of the 'red directors' in Soviet times. The need to constantly report to the party and administrative authorities in order to fulfil planning targets (in roubles or in pieces) made it impossible to upgrade production, to switch to better quality products, as this would lead to a reduction in the release of older products that was unacceptable from a political and administrative point of view.

This motivation of modern management resulted in the growth of monopolies (as a result of mergers and acquisitions), a suspension of improvement in productivity and, ultimately, the discouragement of innovation.

Changing the motivation of shareholders and managers to pay greater attention to the long-term and qualitative aspects of the development of firms is the main issue of regulation raised by the current crisis.

## Notes

1. Some economists consider the problem of changing the technological base in the logic of "big cycles of conjuncture" of N.D. Kondratiev – long waves covering 50–60-year periods (see: Kondratiev 1925). This is an interesting and potentially useful hypothesis, but it has not been proven, nor can it be in the absence of sufficient statistical data. Kondratiev himself considered his conclusions to be only a hypothesis.
2. See: Ulyukaev 2009; El-Erian 2010.
3. See: Brzezinski 2009.
4. Chimerica = China + America; see: Ferguson 2008.
5. Paul Volcker's speech on taking the post of the FED president, July 1979.
6. See: Williamson 1990.
7. See: Freeland 2009.
8. The trap of believing that *"this time things will be different"* was comprehensively considered through the example of various crises, starting with fourteenth-century England, in a book by Reinhart and Rogoff (2009). Originally, it was an article (Reinhart and Rogoff 2008).

# References

Brzezinski, Z. (2009). "The group of two that could change the world", *The Financial Times*, 14 January. Available at: www.ft.com/content/d99369b8-e178-11dd-afa0-0000779fd2ac (accessed 1 August 2017).

El-Erian, M. (2010). *Navigating the New Normal in Industrial Countries*. Washington, DC: Per Jacobson Foundation.

Ferguson, N. (2008). *The Ascent of Money: A financial history of the world*. New York: Penguin.

Freeland, Ch. (2009). "Lunch with the FT: Larry Summers", *The Financial Times*, 11 July. Available at: www.ft.com/content/6ac06592-6ce0-11de-af56-00144feabdc0 (accessed 1 August 2017).

Kondratiev, N. (1925). "Bol'shiye tsikly konjunktury" [The major cycles of the conjuncture], *Voprosy konjunktury*, vol. 1, no. 1, pp. 28–79.

Reinhart, C.M. and Rogoff, K.S. (2008). "This time is different: A panoramic view of eight centuries of financial crises." Working paper 13882, National Bureau of Economic Research. Available at: www.nber.org/papers/w13882.pdf (accessed 1 August 2017).

Reinhart, C.M. and Rogoff, K.S. (2009). *This Time Is Different: Eight centuries of financial folly*. Princeton, NJ: Princeton University Press.

Ulyukaev, A. (2009). "Rossiya i novaya ekonomicheskaya realnost'" [Russia and new macroeconomic reality]. In *X International Scientific Conference on Development of Economy and Society*. Moscow: Higher School of Economics Publishing House.

Williamson, J. (1990). "What Washington means by policy reform". In J. Williamson (ed.). *Latin American Readjustment: How Much Has Happened*, 1st edn. Washington, DC: Peterson Institute for International Economics.

# 9 Anti-crisis
## Labels, fears, traps

The global crisis that broke out in 2008 shocked the world's economic and political elites. Nobody expected that it would be so extensive, or that it would develop so rapidly. The initial reaction to the crisis was quite chaotic, as the governments of developed countries attempted to stop it from spreading. Most attention was focused on solving two groups of problems: first, to prevent the collapse of the financial system; second, to prevent or at least ease the recession, to avoid a major decline in output and employment.

Developed countries, fearing the collapse of the banking system and deflationary shock, launched aggressive measures to support and stimulate production activity. The most important measures included: providing liquidity; extending guarantees on individuals' bank deposits; the acquisition of some banks by the state; the reduction of policy rates of central banks; and the adoption of 'incentive plans' (budget spending to spur demand in the real sector). Many governments pushed depreciation of their national currencies against the US dollar (see Figure A.1), which should have helped to preserve their international reserves and become an additional factor in boosting domestic production.

Ideologically and conceptually, in 2008, this policy led to the renaissance of Keynesianism, developing as rapidly as the crisis itself. The suddenness and scale of the latter entailed anti-crisis measures taken by governments, most of which dropped their economic doctrines and political traditions that had, until very recently, seemed eternal and immutable.

> This was the year when political labels lost all meaning. With governments of all persuasions nationalizing banks and pumping money into the economy what now distinguishes left from right, liberal from conservative, socialist from capitalist, Keynesian from monetarist?[1]

The phrase "We are all Keynesians now", which *Time* magazine put on the front page on 31 December 1965, attributing it to Milton Friedman, and which was modified 5 years later by Richard Nixon, re-emerged. Just like half a century ago, in 2008–10 the name Keynes was written on the banners of state interventionism, without regard to what the great economist wrote and actually thought. Richard Nixon, who uttered this phrase, used this reputed name when introducing the state regulation of prices, although Keynes himself would hardly put his name to the economic policies of the American administration of the time. Strong-minded politicians took a sceptical and mocking view of this "collective shift to Keynesianism": Peer Steinbrueck, Germany's finance minister (2005–9) and a social democrat, described the actions of the EU partners as a *crass Keynesianism*.

The discussion on the contemporary crisis somehow revolved around historical precedents and even genetic fears generated by them. First of all is the Great Depression, with prolonged deflation and a two-digit unemployment rate, which was only overcome after World War II. Less frequently mentioned is the crisis of the 1970s, which saw the emergence of a new phenomenon – stagflation.

Judging by the measures adopted by the governments of developed countries, they are most afraid of deflation, which requires decades to overcome. In addition to the Great Depression of the 1930s, this was demonstrated by Japan in the 1990s.

The deflationary and stagflation models of the crisis are actually alternatives and they, therefore, assume fundamentally different mechanisms for addressing the crisis.

In order to counteract deflation, demand has to be stimulated, meaning an active fiscal policy, fiscal expansionism. This requires a reduction in interest rates and taxes, along with an increase in budget expenses.

In the case of stagflation, the measures must be the opposite: first of all, the money supply must be monitored, that is, by tightening the fiscal policy and raising interest rates. After a decade of economic crisis in the 1970s, the way out was found only when Paul Volcker, the FRS chairman, introduced unprecedentedly harsh measures, after having sharply increased the policy rate. As a result, unemployment exceeded 10 per cent, and interest rates exceeded 20 per cent. A fierce recession broke out in the United States, which cost Jimmy Carter his presidency, but the country came out of it with an updated and dynamic economy.

It is important to understand that the formula for treating an illness depends on the nature of the disease, and treatments that are different and sometimes completely opposite may be required.

The experience of both crises was useful for understanding the 2008 crisis. Strictly speaking, the developed countries have adopted policies that they considered unacceptable in emerging markets in the 1980s and 1990s (in the post-communist countries in particular).[2]

Powerful financial infusions carried out by the United States and the European Union can really prevent the deterioration of their economic situation to a politically unacceptable level. However, when trying to apply these measures in developing countries, one has to exercise extreme caution. This is because monetary authorities of the United States have two distinguishing features.

First, they have the printing press for the global reserve currency, and this status is not doubted by anybody. Moreover, most countries in the world that hold their reserves in dollars are interested in maintaining the dollar's relative stability.

Second, it is because of the special status of the dollar that firms and households in the United States do not have alternative instruments for hedging currency risks – it is unlikely that they would rush to change dollars to euros or yen, even if they doubted the correctness of the policies of the monetary authorities.

The reaction to the financial expansion in most developing countries would be completely different, especially in Russia.

In the current crisis, it is quite acceptable to combine deflation in one part of the world and stagflation in another. It is the latter risk that is one of the most serious for Russia.

Thus, the world faces two crisis models simultaneousely, requiring opposite approaches. The fight against deflation in the Western world would push inflation into the outside world, to the developing economies. And the latter, trying to copy the Western recipes to fight the crisis, were at risk of being trapped in stagflation.

From the beginning of the global crisis in 2008, one could expect the growth of economic populism as a result of monetary expansion. Populism did emerge, 10 years later, but it was not traditional left-wing fiscal populism, well known from the twentieth century, but predominantly right-wing populism in the developed countries.

Populism is usually defined as political activity the slogans of which are popular with the general public but, as a rule, have no real (material or economic) grounds for practical implementation.[3] The real goals of populist politicians (primarily the struggle for power) are disguised as socially attractive ideas.

Populism is directly associated with the aforementioned conflict between short-term and long-term economic objectives. At best, populist measures yield the promised positive shifts for a short period of time, causing a loss of long-term stability, with a dear price to be paid for its recovery. In the political domain, populism often leads to the destruction of democratic institutions: populists can retain power on the wave of short-term achievements, but, afterwards, if the situation worsens, they abandon democratic procedures (directly or through manipulation) while promising prosperity after defeating internal and external enemies.

Populism became widespread during the twentieth century and became either a source of degradation for many countries (Argentina) or a roadblock along the path of economic progress.[4] Two varieties of populism clearly emerged at that time: political and economic (fiscal). The former could exist without the latter, but the latter was always associated with the former. Political populism is a tool in the struggle for power, but its economic implications are ambiguous. A party rising on a wave of populist slogans and retaining power can pursue any economic policy, whether populist or responsible. In some cases, throughout the twentieth century, political populism was accompanied by economic populism – that is, irresponsible fiscal and monetary policies, property manipulations, and so on. This led to economic crises that took a long time to be overcome. Most populist regimes in Latin America combined economic and political populism, from Juan Peron in the mid twentieth century to Hugo Chavez and Nicolas Maduro in Venezuela in the early twenty-first century.[5] At the same time, there have been cases where politicians rose to power backed by populist slogans and reputation but managed to pursue a responsible and well-balanced economic course (e.g. Lula da Silva in Brazil). We are now talking mostly about political populism, associated with attempts to abandon what, until recently, belonged in the domain of 'political correctness' or 'rules of the game' accepted in the modern world (globalization, political equality, etc.). The influence of populist politicians is growing in Europe and America, and in a number of developing countries.

In the middle of the 2010s, there are two specific features of populism. First, both rightist and leftist populism is clearly rising. The former is mostly peculiar to developed countries in Europe and America, whereas the latter can be seen in poorer countries (including European countries such as Italy and Spain). The positions of rightist and leftist populism may coincide in some provisions of the economic programme (particularly with regards to globalization).[6] Second, macroeconomic (fiscal) populism remains quite a rare phenomenon, restricted mostly to the situation in Venezuela. This is important for the evaluation of the prospects of macroeconomic stability in the world's leading countries.

A populist reaction in the form of anti-globalism may manifest itself in various countries in the near future. Anti-globalism has become an altogether indispensable component of modern populism. In particular, the rise of the US dollar, which seemed logical in 2017, may lead to toughening protectionist measures in the USA, with retaliatory measures in certain countries. Various sanction regimes are also a form of populist response to political and, to a greater extent, economic problems.

The rise of populism seems to be based primarily on economic factors. Decelerating growth and protracted recessions are able to evoke a populist response to the problems. Sustainable growth is a natural, though insufficient, condition for overcoming populism. However, populism thrives under the favourable conditions of no clear present growth prospects. There are also social policy measures that may mitigate the risks of realizing populist slogans: they primarily include assistance for those who incur losses as a result of economic progress in adapting to new conditions, particularly support for education and other social spheres, which may be more important than directly handing out money.

In this political dynamic, a new political polarization is taking shape more and more clearly, replacing the confrontation between rightist and leftist forces (in other words, followers of the free market or socialism, liberalism or etatism). Currently, it is far more important to note the confrontation between populism on the one hand and traditional models of modernization on the other. Both rightist and leftist forces with a 'traditional focus' may concentrate on both sides. It seems unclear how stable or durable this new configuration is, or whether it is of a temporary nature, owing to the specific circumstances of the current global crisis.

Another consequence of the crisis could have been massive nationalization – actual (hidden) or explicit (open) – as well as the strengthening of dirigistic trends in economic policy. As the experience of the past four centuries has shown, it is the guarantees of private property rights that serve as the basis of temporary economic growth – that is, growth that provides a significant increase in per capita GDP. However, this thesis has undergone a revision: in rescuing debtors, filling the banks with capital and increasing guarantees for private deposits, the state began to assume risks generated by the actions of all the major economic players – bankers, depositors and borrowers (in practice, they are often the same people).

In the fight against the global crisis, the governments of most developed countries adopted measures actually undermining the institution of private property as a fundamental framework for a market economy, and a source of personal responsibility of an individual (and above all an entrepreneur) for their own decisions. The state (and society), ready to assume private risks through nationalization of losses, will, at the next stage, make the nationalization of risks inevitable.

Many big companies that found themselves in a difficult situation were practically nationalized through the provision of financial assistance. This took place via at least three channels: through the redemption of debts of individual firms, through recapitalization in exchange for corporate equity, and by inflation of the accrued liability. States tend to assume all liabilities of financial institutions, both through guarantees and direct capital injections. Such assistance to financial institutions naturally led to formal or actual dilution of privately owned stocks, which placed doubt on its very immunity.

Nationalization in the early twenty-first century is distinguished by one specific feature – its non-ideological character. Nationalizations of the twentieth century were ideologically motivated, and their authors – from the Russian Bolsheviks to the British Labourists – were convinced that public ownership was more effective than private. By the end of the twentieth century, the world had parted with this illusion, and massive nationalizations were replaced by deregulation and privatization. Today, nobody (or almost nobody) considers state ownership as an institution that provides economic efficiency. But, it is the public sector that turned out to be the main beneficiary of the anti-crisis policy.

In addition to direct nationalization, there has been an increase in dirigisme – that is, an increase in the number of individual decisions of state institutions, their choosing (rather than the market choosing) who is right and who is wrong, as well as the willingness of the state to dictate to the companies what services they should provide and what goods they should produce. The bankruptcy of Lehman Brothers in 2008, on the one hand, and support to Bear Stearns, AIG and Citibank, on the other hand, which were poorly explained by market interpretation, were the results of individual decisions: they matched the logic of the centrally managed economy.

The next natural step was the adoption of governmental decisions regarding the character of the activity of actually nationalized institutions. In autumn 2008, British Prime Minister Gordon Brown declared that he would encourage the banks under his control to invest more in small business. The same was required from the Russian state banks, with no regard as to how it would affect the quality of their portfolios. Supporting small business is, of course, 'a holy crusade' favoured by all modern governments. However, the consequences of such decisions are easy to predict: if the authorities give instructions about where to invest money, then they will need to support their banks when these politically defined investments prove to be ineffective – that is, the state support and the ineffectiveness of investments form a vicious circle.

Finally, systemic risks are associated with the emergence of 'the most favoured' (or more equal than others) market players – those that are said to be too big to fail. In modern Russian economic language, this phenomenon is called 'systemically important enterprises'. Of course, at all times, there were businesses the collapse of which led to greater social and political costs to society. However, the phenomenon of modern economic growth implies, not only the emergence of new businesses (and companies), but also their exit as a result of competition. Competition and the absence of the 'untouchables' form the basis of modern economic and social progress.

Meanwhile, politics in the contemporary world is to a large extent aimed at preserving many of those giants that are actually relics of the economy of the past. There are at least two arguments in favour of their support: first, because of the importance of their goods or services; and second, because of the social (and political) consequences that can result from their closure. Both these arguments are important, but the authorities should not seek to support potential business failures as a way of solving these problems.

Currently, most governments think that the problem of systemically important enterprises could be solved through better management and a more careful attitude towards them on the part of the authorities. Most often, such proposals occur in relation to the banking sector, although they are quite applicable to other industries (especially infrastructure). The efficiency of such regulation raises doubts: if previous attempts to build a similar system failed, why will it prove to be effective now? Overcoming the rigid linking of a given company with the service it provides, as required from a national point of view, is a far more efficient (albeit more complicated) method. The state should ensure the availability of assets and technology for the economic agent who can replace the management and owners of the "systemically important" bankrupts, and this is the real skill and arts of politics.[7]

The sociopolitical risks of bankruptcy should also be the subject of particular attention from the state, with regard to assistance in social restructuring and adaptation to new areas for employment of those working at the bankrupt enterprises. The successful experience of such actions is very well known, including in Russia in the 1990s: the restructuring of the coal industry enabled a large number of ineffective mines to be closed, with retraining and reorientation of the released workers, who found employment in other sectors.

Finally, one should emphasize the complexity and ambiguity of the mechanisms of the emergence and development of systemic crisis risks. In the wake of criticism of the liberal model of the past 30 years, a thesis became very popular about the need for greater state intervention in the economy, as a means of overcoming the risks of spontaneous development. However, a sound analysis of the situation reveals that this solution is not obvious, as state regulation itself bears systemic risks. "Top officials are calling for the creation of a systemic risk regulator. But the American government is the most serious source of the risk", rightly argued John Taylor, a professor at Stanford University.[8] These words should be applied not only to the US government.

## Notes

1. Thornhill 2008: 6.
2. See: Ferguson 2008; Rodrik 2008; Rogoff 2008.
3. See: Acemoglu *et al.* 2013
4. See: Mudde and Kaltwasser 2011.
5. A classic analysis of twentieth-century economic populism is contained in a book edited by R. Dornbusch and S. Edwards, *The Macroeconomics of Populism in Latin America*. In the book, it is defined as an "approach to the economy which focuses on growth and the distribution of income while neglecting inflation risks, budget deficits, external limitations, and the response of economic agents to aggressive non-market policies" (Dornbusch and Edwards 1991: 9; see also: Sachs 1989b; Dornbusch and Edwards 1990b). They provide a description of the populist political and economic cycle: Phase 1: The launching of populist policies in response to depression or stagnation results in a noticeable growth of the economy and, respectively, real income provided at the expense of both domestic production and imports. Phase 2: The appearance of 'bottlenecks' in the economy is caused by commodity shortages or the payment balance deficit, with a simultaneous gradual reduction of international reserves used to maintain the currency exchange rate. Phase 3: Rapid escalation of inflation and (or) commodity shortages, budget deficits, capital outflows and demonetization of the economy inevitably lead to devaluation, a substantial drop in incomes and, almost always, the loss of political control by the government. Phase 4 marks the transition to orthodox stabilization implemented by a new (often military) government (Dornbusch and Edwards 1991: 11–12).
6. The results of the referendum in the UK and the US election in 2016 are of interest in terms of the correlation between rightist and leftist populism in developed countries. Bernie Sanders, a leftist critic of the establishment, lost the Democratic Party primaries to Hillary Clinton, who represents the traditional elites. However, the presidential election was won by Donald Trump, who actively utilized rightist populist slogans and had much in common with Bernie Sanders in his anti-globalist agenda (Di Tella and Rotemberg 2016: 10). Similarly, in the UK, rightist populism is associated with leaving the EU and confidently dominates the leftist populism of the current Labour Party leadership.
7. "Too big to fail – whether it is a bank or a car manufacturer – is not a status we can put up with. Both politically and economically correct would be to help the collapse to come than to subsidize it" (Kay 2009: 9).
8. See: Taylor 2009: 9.

## References

Acemoglu, D., Yegorov, G., and Sonin, K. (2013). "A political theory of populism", *Quarterly Journal of Economics*, vol. 128, no. 2, pp. 771–805.

Di Tella, R. and Rotemberg, J.J. (2016). "Populism and the return of the 'paranoid style': Some evidence and a simple model of demand for incompetence as insurance against elite betrayal." Harvard Business School Working Paper 17–056. Cambridge, MA: Harvard Business School.

Dornbusch, R. and Edwards, S. (1990). *Macroeconomic Populism*. Amsterdam: Elsevier Science.

Dornbusch, R. and Edwards, S. (eds) (1991). *The Macroeconomics of Populism in Latin America*. Chicago, IL: University of Chicago Press.

Ferguson, N. (2008). "Geopolitical consequences of the credit crunch", *The Washington Post*, 21 September.

Kay, J. (2009). "Why 'too big to fail' is too much for us to take", *The Financial Times*, 27 May.
Mudde, C., and Kaltwasser, C.R. (2011). "Voices of the peoples: Populism in Europe and Latin America compared", *Kellog Institute Working Paper*, Issue 378.
Rodrik, D. (2008). "The death of the globalization consensus." Project Syndicate, 11 July. Available at: www.project-syndicate.org/commentary/rodrik21 (accessed 1 August 2017).
Rogoff, K. (2008). "America goes from teacher to student." Project Syndicate, 4 February. Available at: www.project-syndicate.org/commentary/rogoff39 (accessed 1 August 2017).
Sachs, J.D. (1989). *Developing Country Debt and the World Economy*. Chicago, IL: University of Chicago Press.
Taylor, J. (2009). "Exploding debt threatens America", *The Financial Times*, 27 May.
Thornhill, J.A. (2008). "A year of chocolate box politics", *The Financial Times*, 24 December.

# 10 In quest of a new economic model

Year 2010 marked the end of the first phase of the global crisis that had begun in 2008, a phase focused on preventing economic collapse. By this time, it was clear that the key challenge of the crisis was the elaboration of a new model of social and economic development. The world had been left weak after the first phase (Figure 10.1). However, the leading countries learned to take coordinated anti-crisis measures.

An important outcome of the first stage of the global crisis was the de facto refutation, by most leading countries, of the illusion that the crisis could be overcome just by government intervention. The shock of the first phase led to an increase in the popularity of accusations of a liberal economic model and calls to go back to the ideology and practice of the 'big government. The vulgar understanding of economic liberalism (neo-liberalism or supply-side economics) as the cause of the crisis was opposed by the revival of the vulgar understanding of Keynesianism (demand-side economics). However, soon came the understanding that the crisis could be explained both by the *lack* of government regulation and

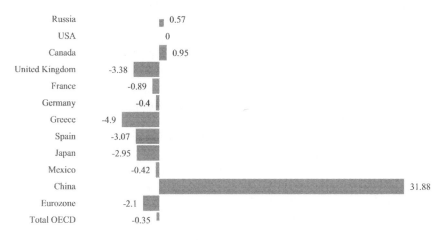

*Figure 10.1* Gross domestic product, 2010, percentage change from 2007
*Source*: IMF 2016

the *inability* of the government to ensure adequate economic regulation. It was understood that the response to the crisis should not be increased intervention in the economy, but the development of new tools for public regulation, and, particularly, regulation of the financial markets and regulation of the global market.

The resolution of complex economic problems requires deep structural reforms, the overcoming of imbalances accumulated in the world and the emergence of a new growth model. It was in 2010 that the debate about this new model began and gained traction throughout the world.

These discussions were all the more necessary because the world was facing a long period of instability. Systemic risks, as well as challenges, faced by the economic policies of the leading countries form the basis of a new phase of economic development. The world had entered a 'turbulent decade'.[1]

'Turbulent decade' does not mean constant recession and the emotionally charged atmosphere that the world experienced in the autumn of 2008. There are variations in the pace of growth, a period of unsustainable growth with local ups and downs, with spurts of inflation and attempts to control it.

In fact, 2013 and, especially, 2014 demonstrated some important changes on the world economic map. The year 2014 saw divergence in the economic development of key countries and regions of the world. The assumption made in 2008–9 about the new role of *emerging markets* as a possible powerhouse to overcome the crisis did not prove true.

The US has become the key factor in the formation of a new, post-crisis economic and technological structure. In this country, economic growth resumed quite early, new industrial sectors appeared, and the gap between consumption and savings began to shrink. The budget deficit declined from 8.4 per cent of GDP in 2011 to 2.9 per cent of GDP in 2014, and unemployment during the same period decreased from 8.6 per cent to 5.8 per cent and was declining further. Once again, the phenomenon of the 'flight to quality' manifested itself: the improvement in the American economy has led to increased demand for its currency, despite numerous warnings that the dollar is a "particularly risky security that is not secured by any tangible assets". A major structural shift is evidenced by the fact that high-tech companies (primarily IT and biotechnological firms) have become leaders in capitalization, outpacing the traditional corporations, including in the energy sector. Some 15 years ago, they saw the signs of a 'bubble' (*dotcom crisis*) here, but now it is a steady trend.

Despite maintaining high growth rates, China has not become a significant factor in the overcoming of the global crisis. An important transformation is taking place here: the role of internal growth factors is increasing. The huge Chinese market is becoming more important for the national economy, which demonstrates the fact that the Chinese political elite are aware of the importance of forming a new model of economic growth.

The Eurozone continued to show signs of poor health. The key problem remained the complexity of the model, based on a single currency without a single financial system. It can be assumed that a solution will be found over time, and a euro crisis will be avoided.[2] The situation partly resembles the overcoming of the crisis at the turn of the 1970s–1980s, when Western European countries began to increase their pace of growth, following the United States.

The prospects of energy prices were an important element of the global trend. Almost a twofold fall in oil prices over the last few months of 2014 led to the key question (or even puzzle): can this shift be sustained (similar to the mid 1980s), or will it be temporary (similar to 2008–9), followed by a rebound? A strict answer to this question is hardly possible: there are arguments in favour of both variants. There is no doubt that this factor will become important in the formation of the structure of the post-crisis global economy. For Europe, a steady decline in oil prices seems preferable; for the United States, it is neutral, because it is most likely to benefit (albeit differently) under both options. For importing developing countries, cheap energy is an obvious benefit. Finally, for oil producers, this is a period of difficult tests, which should encourage institutional reforms. However, the question of what kind of institutional response will be made remains open. Two options for institutional transformation were possible – mobilization (administrative), and liberalization (economic). As the global crisis expanded, a number of problems with national and global economic policies arose, which researchers and practitioners should focus on.

## *The problem of economic growth rates*

In the pre-crisis decade, the world economy grew at unprecedentedly high rates, which seemed to be the result of acquired economic and political innovations, which will always be in effect from now on. This concern was the main reason why the monetary authorities (particularly in the United States) were reluctant to restrain loan growth and thereby slow down the overheating of the economy. High rates were demonstrated both by developed and developing countries, which was a major achievement on the part of the economic policies, although it still resulted in overheating and crisis. But, in the midst of a slowdown, a number of questions have arisen.

For example: will the slow growth rates become a part of the 'new normality' that was discussed in the media at the beginning of the crisis? At that time, the term was associated mainly with the characteristics of the monetary policy (quantitative easing and lower interest rates). Later the main concern was that it might result in a stable period of low growth rates (*secular stagnation hypothesis*).[3] In other words, do the current growth rates reflect short-term problems, or is it an important characteristic of the future post-crisis model of economic development?[4] What are the perspectives of developing countries, particularly those from which an economic miracle was expected?

## *An alternative macroeconomic policy*

The macroeconomic situation in developed countries has led to a substantial revision of the understanding of the key macroeconomic threats. After the stagflation of the 1970s, the main macroeconomic task was considered to be controlling inflation: it dominated in developed countries and was put forward as the primary macroeconomic recommendation for developing countries. Now, after several decades of stability and as a result of deflationary problems in recent global crisis, inflation is no longer perceived as the main macroeconomic problem, at least in the developed world. Greater support is being given to proposals to raise inflation targets in the framework of inflation targeting.

Economic and political recommendations recently considered old-fashioned and actually taboo in economic and political discussions are gradually receiving careful recognition. In particular, talks about the possibility of introducing elements of currency control have become more frequent. The events of recent years show that capital market liberalization sometimes creates significant risks that cannot be ignored. The experience of the use of currency control by a number of Asian countries (e.g. Malaysia) also played a role in overcoming the crisis of 1997–8. It is stipulated that measures limiting the movement of capital may be justified under two conditions: first, if they are aimed, not at structural containment of capital flows, but at maintaining macroeconomic stability and the resilience of the financial sector, to mitigate fluctuations; second, if they are in effect for a short period during which institutional reforms enhancing the efficiency of the financial market and creating favourable conditions for investors are carried out. Without compliance with these conditions, restrictions on the movement of capital will not give permanent results and will only lead to corruption and an inefficient economy.[5] As shown by historical experience, it is very difficult to ensure the implementation of these conditions in practice, and most of the previous attempts were ineffective.

The situation becomes better defined with possibilities to stimulate economic growth by fiscal instruments. And governments of some developed countries began to conduct counter-cyclical measures as a traditional policy of escalating budget costs. But, most probably, such a policy can only be afforded by the country issuing the reserve currency – the United States. The European experience shows that countries that carry out strict fiscal policy against the backdrop of a soft money policy (primarily the United Kingdom and Germany, as well as Portugal) are more successful politically and economically. The attempts to conduct a soft fiscal policy in France can hardly be recognized as successful, either for economic growth or for the popularity of the Socialist government.[6]

## Perspectives of globalization and global imbalances

Over the years since the beginning of the crisis, global imbalances have somewhat softened, owing to the evolution of new technologies in the West and the rise of labour costs in Asia (including China). But there is another, more complicated issue of the perspectives of globalization as the most important phenomenon of the last quarter of the twentieth century. The growth of prosperity in developing countries resulted in a new market reality: they became less competitive in terms of labour costs. Now, they must compete primarily for institutional improvements, for the quality of the business climate. The role of commodity exchange between countries (and, consequently, separation of consumption and savings) was decreasing.

Increased costs in developing countries, on the one hand, and their growing domestic demand, on the other, might lead to a slowdown in the growth of world trade. In other words, there is a possibility of deglobalization. There is nothing unprecedented in this. It has happened before. It appears that periods of globalization and deglobalization replace each other from time to time. One of the factors of deglobalization may be another trend of recent times – the *reindustrialization of developed countries*. It is not a return of traditional industries to developed countries, but the emergence of new industries that are characterized by a decrease in the share of labour in costs and an increase in the significance of factors such as the proximity of the research base and basic consumer demand. The rise in the cost of labour in leading developing countries makes only a small additional contribution to this process.

An important factor in reindustrialization is the above-mentioned transformation of the energy market. Cheaper energy is associated with the newest technologies for the extraction of unconventional types of oil and natural gas, as well as the significant expansion of opportunities for their transportation. One consequence of this is the 'revolution in energy prices'.

All that is mentioned above does not mean the curtailment of production in the 'new industrial countries'. They are also important markets for the sale of products, including high-technology products. However, several conclusions for the post-crisis development can be drawn from the above.

First, the strengthening of competition for investment and for the deployment of production is inevitable, not only among developing countries but now also between developed countries. The decision to locate production in a particular country becomes the result of a greater number of factors than just the alternative between a higher profitably with worse institutions or a lower profitability with higher institutional credibility.

Second, developing countries should not only create conditions favourable for production (cheap labour and acceptable institutions, i.e. ensuring a proper investment and business climate), but also stimulate domestic demand. Internal (or regional) demand will become an increasingly significant factor in investment decisions, especially for global corporations. This will be a significant change to the model of successful economic policy accepted over the past 30 years (from Germany to China).

Third, the idea of the new industrialization of developed countries looks convincing. This was noted in the United States at the beginning of the crisis, and this is what is periodically discussed by Russia's leadership. It is not about the reconstruction of traditional industrial sectors, but about the emergence of radically new sectors, in which intellectual activities and production itself are closely intertwined, and the location of which throughout the world (depending on the cost of resources) is ineffective. Moreover, the idea of the 'new industrialism' is incompatible with the opposition of the industrial and financial sectors, although it is very popular among left-wing politicians in developed countries. (During his election campaign im 2012, François Hollande announced a "war against the world of finance").

Fourth, the division of industries into advanced and backward ones is finally becoming a thing of the past. In the contemporary world, any industry can be high-tech and old-fashioned. The sectoral structure of the economy by itself is not an indicator of the backwardness or advancement of a country's technological base.[7] The same applies to the ratio of production of goods and services, as the latter are increasingly becoming a continuation of the former, and the distinction between them is becoming blurred. (For example, Rolls Royce now actually sells, not the engine, but the time during which the engine delivers flight).

Fifth, governments should encourage economic growth and high-tech jobs, rather than increase production and maintain employment at any cost. This requires a major shift in the paradigm of economic policy. Governments of all countries, whether developed or developing, prefer to support existing enterprises rather than risky beginners. Moreover, even with a desire to focus on technological priorities, governments are always looking back at existing technological trends, dramatically increasing the probability of error when they are establishing budgetary priorities. The usual practice is financial aid for large firms and a negative perception of their leaders' attempts to dismiss employees in the process of modernization.

### *Modernization of the welfare state*

Another major problem of the current crisis is the need for a profound transformation of human capital sectors (primarily education, health care, R&D, pensioning, social support). In other words, the formation of a new model of the *welfare state* is on the agenda.

The crisis of the welfare state of industrial society is one of the fundamental causes of the current global crisis. Imbalances in developed countries were the result of steady growth of budgets aimed at redistributing resources in favour of certain categories of the population. At the beginning of its history (at the turn of the twentieth century), the magnitude of redistribution was small and covered small groups of the population, but the situation changed fundamentally by the beginning of the twenty-first century. The majority of the population is now covered by systems of education, health care and pension protection, and, to a large extent, their operation is based on the redistribution of resources through state budgets. The features of the demographic behaviour of many developed countries today are such that the share of those who provide resources for redistribution is declining, whereas the share of recipients is growing.

If we analyse the geography of redistribution, it is easy to see that the situation is most difficult in those countries where the burden of the welfare state is especially high (in Eurozone), and, among them, the most affected are the countries with high social obligations and low labour productivity (southern Europe). The crisis is relatively weaker in the United States and the former Soviet Union, where the welfare state collaped in 1990s and thus is less developed. And finally, the crisis has had less of an effect on the newly industrialized countries (here, we are not talking about a recession, but about some slowdown in growth): they have not managed to create social sectors conforming to the standards of an industrial society.

The global crisis not only called into question the redistributive model of the welfare state. The volatility of the financial market poses serious short- and medium-term challenges for private savings based on investments in securities: it is now difficult to find financial instruments that ensure reliability and, at the same time, liquidity and profitability of savings. The decrease in the profitability of securities raises a question about the unreliability of existing forms of social insurance, and about the need to substantially revise the insurance model of the welfare state and find new tools for its functioning.

Thus, the formation of a modern welfare state is a topical problem for the majority of the world's developed countries today. Incidentally, the resolution of this issue can minimally take into account the world experience: there are simply no effective systems that correspond to today's challenges. Moreover, a country that is able to form a modern, effective model of human capital will gain a powerful advantage in the post-industrial world.

A post-industrial welfare state will differ substantially from traditional industrial ones, and it is today that we are seeking to find its basic principles. We can already select a number of characteristics of a welfare state, which include:

- continuous, lifelong provision, enabling people to study and receive treatment throughout their life;
- individualization – that is, the ability to define your own educational goals, as well as the trajectory and mechanisms of health care and the selection of educational and medical services; in the case of the pension system, this means a substantial diversification of the forms of support for seniors;
- globalization of services and international competition for clients, where educational and medical institutions compete, not just with neighbouring universities (schools) and hospitals and relevant institutions in their own countries, but throughout the world;
- privatization of social services while the role of private expenditure on human capital is increased: private payments or co-payments are not only natural but the inevitable effect of the technological modernization of sectors and the increase in the well-being of the population;
- arrival of new technologies radically changing the nature of the services provided by these sectors.

Of particular interest from this point of view are the prospects for the development of fast-growing countries in Asia. It is only now that they are approaching the level of economic development from which the welfare state, based on redistribution, in Western countries and in Russia began to rapidly grow in the twentieth century. The key question here is: will they also go this way or, relying on accumulated experience, will they try to form a new model based on new principles? An interesting experience is offered by Singapore, which has not repeated the Western model. However, its model is a limited one, functioning in a country with a population of 5 million people.

## *Inequality*

This problem, including inequality in the developed world, is now being examined in a different light. This problem has two aspects: the dynamics of inequality in the course of economic growth and the impact of inequality on it. It is evident that the problems of inequality intersect with the long-term slowdown in growth and with the issue of contemporary forms of the welfare state corresponding to the demographic and political realities of the twenty-first century mentioned above.

Particular attention was drawn to this topic following the publication of Thomas Piketty's book.[8] He noted that, in addition to inter-country inequality, the modern world is facing a trend towards greater inequality in the distribution of incomes and, particularly, savings. The latter is typical both of developed countries and of the 'top' group of developing economies.

The inequality in the distribution of savings, according to Piketty, plays an important role in the observed slowdown of the economy. The concentration of large volumes of savings (formed, inter alia, by revenues from worldwide operations) belonging to a small percentage of the population creates conditions in the domestic market for the offer of resources to exceed the demand for investment. This pushes interest rates down; however, when economic growth decelerates and inflation becomes very low, this also deprives the monetary authorities of the possibility to pursue a policy of stimulation through low interest rates (the nominal interest rate cannot be less than zero – the so-called *zero lower bound*).

To address the issues raised, we need to rethink the theoretical basis of modern economic policy and the generally accepted practical recommendations (including the so-called "Washington consensus"). Although it is still important to ensure economic stability, economists and politicians are now facing the challenge of finding additional instruments of economic development regulation that would enable them to avoid lengthy stagnation with low inflation (or deflation).

## Notes

1. Alan Greenspan called his book of memoirs *The Age of Turbulence* (2007). It was written before the crisis and focuses on 1987–2002 – the period of rapid economic growth. Now it is clear that only today, after the publication of the book, has the real 'age of turbulence' begun.
2. The truth is that, as a dreadful joke in *The Economist* says, "the euro needs French reform, German extravagance and Italian political maturity" (see: *The Economist* 2012).
3. See: Summers 2014.
4. See: Teulings and Baldwin 2014.
5. Similar conclusions can be found in the IMF study (Saborowski *et al.* 2014). It shows that imposing restrictions on capital movement can be effective if at least one of three

conditions is met: strong macroeconomic fundamentals, well-developed institutional environment, and the existence of a fully-fledged monitoring system for a long time.
6 Supporting the position of the Socialist leadership in France, which does not wish to reduce the budget deficit down to the Maastricht criterion of 3 per cent of GDP in the foreseeable future, the left-wing Italian prime minister, M. Renzi, said that the higher deficit is better than the electoral victory of the right-wing forces led by Marine Le Pen (Politi 2014). This is one example of the dominance of politics over economics that is becoming a characteristic feature of the contemporary global crisis.
7 The situation in a sense goes back to the pre-industrial phase, when individual industries were not clearly advanced or backward. In those times, the most powerful, economically and militarily, were agricultural monarchies, but not the states with well-developed city industry and trade. Incidentally, this feature of the technological base was at the foundation of classical liberalism, laissez-faire, which encouraged countries to benefit from the freedoms of trade, rather than strive for artificial development of individual industries. In the logic of industrialism of the nineteenth and twentieth centuries, the supporters of this approach were accused of conservation of backwardness, not taking into account the fact that Adam Smith thought that a synonym of progress was the division of labour, but not the industry itself, in opposition to agriculture (see: Mau 2002).
8 See: Piketty 2015.

## References

*Economist, The.* (2012). "Europe's Achilles heel", *The Economist*, 12 May.
Greenspan, A. (2007). *The Age of Turbulence: Adventures in a new world*. London: Penguin.
IMF. (2016). "Gross domestic product." Available at: http://data.imf.org/regular.aspx?key= 60998124 (accessed November 2016).
Mau, V. (2002). "Post-communist Russia in post-industrial world: Elements of catching-up policy", *Voprosy Ekonomiki*, no. 7.
Piketty, T. (2015). *Capital in the Twenty-First Century*. Moscow: Ad Marginem Press.
Politi, J. (2014). "Berlin has no right to lecture, says Renzi", *The Financial Times*, 3 October.
Saborowski, C., Sanya, S., Weisfeld, H, and Yepez, J. (2014). "Effectiveness of capital outflow restrictions." Washington, DC: International Monetery Fund.
Summers, L. (2014). "Reflections on the new 'Secular Stagnation hypothesis'." Vox, CERP's Policy Portal, 30 October. Available at: http://voxeu.org/article/larry-summers-secular-stagnation (accessed 2 August 2017).
Teulings, C. and Baldwin, R. (eds) (2014). "Secular stagnation: Facts, causes and cures." London: Centre for Economic Policy Research Press. Available at: http://voxeu.org/content/secular-stagnation-facts-causes-and-cures (accessed 2 August 2017).

# Part IV
# Global crisis in Russia

# 11 The drama of 2008

## From an economic miracle to an economic crisis

The main feature of the year 2008 that guarantees it a special place in global and Russian economic history is the speed at which the economic crisis developed. In a matter of months, in Russia and in many other developed and developing countries, faith in the economic miracle was replaced by fear of collapse.

It cannot be said that the crisis came as a surprise. At the beginning of 2008, there were already signs of instability in the two main factors of Russia's economic growth – high prices for energy resources and cheap money on the global financial markets. However, the institutional environment, which serves as a stable platform for economic growth, was very poorly developed in Russia, and institutions (both economic and political) were barely able to mitigate and rectify the effects of a worsening economic and political situation.

The most significant sources of the crisis in Russia were the global recession, the decline in prices for oil and other commodities exported by Russia, a deficit in the balance of payments and the increase in the country's dependence on foreign investments, the rapid growth of Russian enterprises' external debt and the high risk of non-payment if the government abandoned anti-crisis support measures, and also the dubious effectiveness of many investment projects that had been launched during the boom period, but could not be continued under crisis conditions. It is also important to note that, in Russia, during the 8 prosperous years, a new generation of politicians had emerged who had become accustomed to 'managing the increase in prosperity', with no experience of crisis management, and ordinary people had become accustomed to rising incomes.[1]

The pessimistic forecasts turned out to be true, and events developed according to the very-worst-case scenario: the two main sources of growth in the Russian economy were depleted at the same time – prices fell on Russia's main export commodities, and cheap financial resources on the global market disappeared. The crisis had taken effect. Was Russia prepared for this, and to what extent?

## Characteristics of the crisis in Russia

For eight years preceding the crisis (2000–7), the Russian political and economic elite meticulously prepared for a default similar to that of 1998, seeking to avoid the mistakes of the past. This was successful to a certain extent; however, the new crisis turned out to be different. The default of 1998 in Russia was caused by internal factors – the weakness of the Russian authorities, which were incapable of conducting responsible macroeconomic (primarily budgetary) policies. Now, for the first time in 100 years, Russia was encountering a world crisis as part of the global economic and financial system. This can be seen as a sign of its conclusive transformation to a normal market country.

From the outside, it all seemed like a paradox: the crisis was spreading steadily through a country with an exceptionally favourable macroeconomic situation.

The situation was characterized by a double surplus (fiscal and the balance of payments), which attracted capital that was actively flowing into Russia, expanding leverage. Naturally, the emergence of the crisis led to the opposite effect: leverage decreased, which immediately resulted in a drop on the stock market.

The Russian stock market, despite rapid growth in 2004–7, demonstrated its infancy. It was capable of quickly shrinking to minimal values, although there was a certain internal logic to this. As can be seen from Figure 11.1, following the market decrease, the stock indexes ended up in approximately the same place as they would have been without the jump in 2005. The triangle shape on the graph clearly reflects the formation of a 'bubble' on the financial market, which was a result of the boom that caused the increase in disparities.

The inefficiency of the economics and export structure also played a role in this respect. With raw materials and investment goods dominating the export market, the country's balance of payments experienced a more severe dependency on cyclical fluctuations than it would in a diversified economy. The slowdown in growth and the decline of investment activity in importing countries was capable, owing to a multiplicative effect, of causing a dramatic halt in the raw materials economy, leading to a hard-landing scenario.

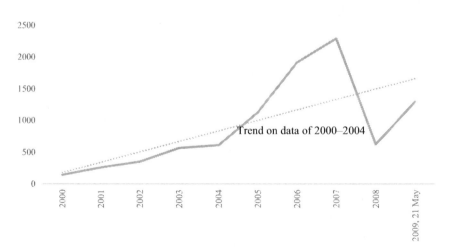

*Figure 11.1* Dynamics of the RTS index
*Source*: RTS Stock Exchange

This was the mirror effect of the situation experienced by Russia after the crisis of 1998. The increase in the growth rate of the global economy created demand for commodities from Russia, which caused a boom when energy prices were starting to rise. Much had been said in prior years of the need for structural diversification, but, during the boom period, nobody thought to take this matter seriously.

The rapid growth of corporate debt in foreign currencies became a greater problem. This was made even worse by the fact that most of them were in fact quasi state loans. Many lending enterprises were connected to the government and acted according to the principle of 'privatization of profits and nationalization of losses'. This is also how they were perceived on the financial market, whose agents understood that, if crisis happened, the largest Russian private borrowers would be able to rely on the support of the federal budget. This is how the moral hazard occurs, which has been known since the Asian crisis of 1997, when some could irresponsibly borrow money, and others could lend it without proper justification. When crises strike, it is the government that has to save debtors. One could note an increase in the trend for 'chaebolization' of a number of leading Russian companies, if we use the example of South Korean *chaebols* – firms that are actually under state control.

In 2007, an important change occurred in the dynamics of the external debt: prior to this, the total debt burden (state and corporate) had decreased, but now it was starting to increase.

This significantly increased Russia's dependence on the global financial situation (Figure 11.2). There was yet another error of Russian borrowers: they were quick to agree on security schemes, although the successes of the Russian economy in past years meant that, in many cases, it was possible to get by without securities. As a result, when the crisis started, they were faced with a rapid decline in the value of securities (margin calls came into effect – demands that further cash be deposited to cover a security deposit) and a real threat of losing their assets.

This situation had a serious impact on fiscal and exchange rate policies. On the one hand, large debts among politically influential economic agents (including those close to the budget), often in possession of strategically important assets, limited the opportunities to devalue the rouble, which would lead to a sharp rise in the cost of servicing their external debt. On the other hand, state resources had to be used to provide borrowers with financial assistance to cover or repay debts.

## Battling the crisis in Russia

The anti-crisis measures of the Russian authorities in 2008–9 partly repeated the steps taken by the most developed countries, but differed in certain key areas.

Measures were taken to prevent the collapse of the credit system. Banks received large financial resources to overcome the liquidity crisis. This was aimed at supporting economic activity. In Russia, the availability of banking loans and enterprises' deposits in the banks are the main sources of growth for the real sector, not the stock market. Maintaining the stability of the banking system is important

124  *The Russian version of the global crisis*

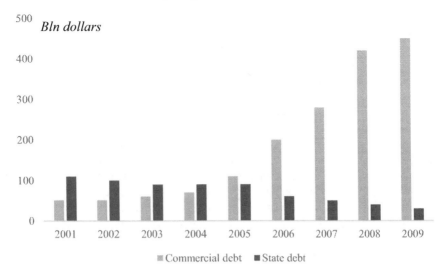

*Figure 11.2* Dynamics of external debt, 2001–8 (external debt of the Russian Federation at the start of the period)
*Source*: Federal State Statistics Service

for social and political stability. Losing money in banks would have been far more painful and politically dangerous in Russia than losses from falling stock markets.

There were, of course, some dubious schemes. Banks that received liquidity from the government preferred to convert it into foreign currency to hedge against currency risks and inflation or use it to reduce their own debts towards foreign creditors. That was entirely justified from a business prospective, but did not reflect the intentions of the authorities providing the funds. In addition, allocation of state money was sometimes accompanied by bribes, which was no surprise owing to the limited access to scarce resources at a reduced price. (It was assumed by financial authorities that money from primary beneficiaries would be provided to second-tier borrowers, not at market rate, but at a reduced rate slightly higher than the percentage for their primary distribution.)

At the beginning of the global crisis, the government also tried to maintain stock indexes, but abandoned this quite soon. In practice, such attempts could only help investors to earn large sums of money by selling their securities. Of course, the drop in share value is not pleasant for shareholders and creates problems with collateral (margin calls), but the solution to the latter problem lies in a different area.

Discussions began on the problem of preventing an output contraction. The rapid economic growth of preceding years was largely due to cheap financial resources on the global market that were borrowed by domestic companies. However, cheap money does not necessarily result in effective investment, especially where government-connected companies are concerned. They are more readily given money, as it is understood that, if anything goes the wrong, the state will provide support to these companies. This raises a problem of moral hazard.

Then, the situation changed. There were no more affordable loans, and securities used as collateral for loans rapidly decreased in price. Before the end of 2008, around US$43 billion had to be paid on these debts. The state expressed its willingness to provide US$50 billion through VEB (the Russian Development Bank) to resolve this issue.

Monetary policy was also ambiguous. In 2008–9, for political reasons, the authorities did not decide to completely abandon support for the rouble exchange rate and opted instead for a phased, long-term devaluation. The reasons for caution were clear: authorities were afraid that the third sharp depreciation of rouble savings in 20 years (after 1992 and 1998) would completely destroy confidence in the national currency.

This policy had one positive aspect and a number of serious negative effects. The positive thing was that the public was given the opportunity to hedge against the depreciation of the rouble. Almost everybody who wanted to was able to exchange roubles for dollars or euros (Figure 11.3).

However, the gradual devaluation increased the sense of panic on the market and led to a significant reduction in foreign exchange reserves. Uncertainty about the exchange rate paralysed credit institutions. The banks, anticipating the fall in the national currency, often refused to provide loans in roubles, and loans in foreign currency did not attract borrowers for the same reason. The sharp reduction in the rouble exchange rate became an important factor in maintaining internal production, protecting the domestic market from import goods, aiding exporters and also providing additional stimulus for the future inflow of foreign direct investment.

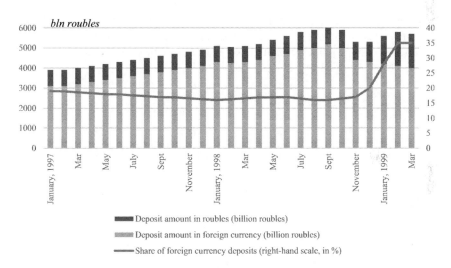

*Figure 11.3* Structure of private bank deposits (data on deposits of private individuals attracted by credit institutions)

*Source*: Central Bank of Russia, author's calculations

Finally, the government offered a large stimulus package, primarily tax incentives, including tax reductions, small business support measures and a list of core enterprises that could apply to receive special support from the state. These measures caused a mixed reaction. Support for small businesses is undoubtedly important for both economic and social reasons – this sector can have a significant impact on reducing unemployment. However, the problems of small businesses are not economic or legal: they are to do with law enforcement and politics. In Russia, there has always been a sceptical view of small businesses, as they are powerless against bureaucratic arbitrariness and extortion. The development of small businesses requires a profound change in Russian society's values system, and that of the national elite in particular.

There are serious doubts about the effectiveness of measures of direct assistance to large enterprises. The main problems were not so much about lack of money, but rather the disruption in the functioning of economic mechanisms, and ultimately the inefficiency of some enterprises. Major financial injections are not enough to increase industrial competitiveness and renovate the economic structure. In addition, existing social complexities may weaken these measures.

Russia's anti-crisis policy was supposed to focus primarily on preventing macroeconomic imbalances. Even with allowances for the budget deficit in 2009, healthy sources needed to be engaged to cover the shortfall, and internal loans had to be used, without resort to printing more money. The danger was in the belief that artificially stimulating demand (crass Keynesianism) would be able to solve the key problems of Russian social or economic development.

When a national currency does not have a long 'credit history', and it is not a reserve currency, weaker fiscal and monetary policies are highly likely to lead to a hasty retreat from the national currency, a greater velocity of money circulation, and inflation. And, against the backdrop of global recession, this option will inevitably lead to stagflation.[2] That was one of the most serious problems for Russia after 2008. And, this phenomenon makes the situation in Russia different compared with other developed and emerging economies.

## Notes

1 See: Mau 2008.
2 "There are alarming similarities between emerging economies today and the rich world in the 1970s when the Great Inflation lifted off" (*The Economist* 2008).

## References

Economist, The. (2008). "Inflation's back", *The Economist*, 22 May, p. 17. Available at: www.economist.com/node/11409414 (accessed 2 August 2017).

Mau, V. (2008). "Russia's economic policy in 2007: Successes and risks", *Voprosy Ekonomiki*, no. 2, pp. 4–25.

# 12 Economic policy of 2009

## Between crisis and modernization

The key feature of economic development in 2009 was uncertainty. The year began with expectations of a catastrophic, unprecedentedly deep economic crisis, including financial collapse, oil prices falling below US$30 per barrel, uncontrollable depreciation of the rouble, a deep slump in production, mass unemployment and social instability. None of this happened. Moreover, besides the anti-crisis measures of 2009, some new, positive trends appeared, including a reduction in inflation.

### The main outcome of the year of crisis: institutional stability

The results of 2008 demonstrated the stability of Russia's economic, social and political institutions. It was the second major crisis faced by Russia's post-communist political system based on the 1993 Constitution. In both cases, the system demonstrated stability and resilience, the ability to take on the challenges of the crisis and respond to them, preventing political disruption. There was even some progress. In 1998, the political institutions were not able to prevent the dramatic escalation of the crisis in time, and the government only began to conduct a vigorous anti-crisis policy when the country was on the verge of (or even beyond) financial disaster. In 2009, on the other hand, the political system proved to be capable of adapting to drastic changes from the very first days of the crisis and immediately launched an anti-crisis management regime.

There were many shortcomings and problems with Russia's anti-crisis policy in 2009, and there were many alternative options that could have been taken. All this is interesting from the standpoint of theoretical discussions and especially from the standpoint of economic historians of the future. However, it cannot be denied that the elite was able to consolidate and not lose control of the situation, although at first it seemed to many that the weakness of the Russian institutions and the immaturity of the political class would entail severe economic, social and political losses.

The global crisis once again underlined the need for the implementation of comprehensive modernization – in technological, economic and social terms. Russia turned out to be the country with the most fragile economy, both in terms of production (the decline in GDP and slowdown in industry were among the most severe among G20 countries) and stock market indicators. The depth of the recession was partly offset by strong growth before the crisis and the expectation of high rates of recovery (which was especially demonstrated by the stock market). However, serious threats to long-term development meant that tools had to be found to provide long-term stability for economic development. Such stability could be provided by modernization and diversification.

The year 2009 also demonstrated that Russian society had no demand for modernization. Political statements about the need for comprehensive modernization were not objected to, of course, but they clashed with the elite's expectations of 'business as usual' – the recovery of the old growth model based on the rents from oil and gas exports. Everybody agreed verbally on the importance of diversification, but the 2009 growth in oil prices, which contrasted sharply with the pessimistic expectations of the end of 2008, did not stimulate the real policies of modernization at all.

## Elements of the anti-crisis policy

The specific nature of Russia's anti-crisis policy was based on the following circumstances:

First, Russia was the only country in the G20 with two-digit inflation. With the rapid decline in GDP, the country was falling into the trap of stagflation; in other words, from the macroeconomic point of view, the nature of the crisis was significantly different from that in most other countries of the world, for which the main threat was deflation. Consequently, the Central Bank had to raise the interest rate to a real positive value, and then only lower it as inflation reduced.

Second, the high level of monopolization in the Russian economy reduced the effectiveness of budgetary incentives. The experience of the pre-crisis years convincingly showed that the increased budgetary demand used to result in the growth of prices, not supply. Accordingly, the role of fiscal incentives (primarily, investments in infrastructure and construction) could not be substantial. Tax cuts, which were implemented at the end of 2008, would be more likely to play a stimulating role.

Third, the weakness of the political and legal institutions further weakened the effectiveness of the budget support measures.[1]

Fourth, the crisis demonstrated the structural vulnerability of the Russian economy, its one-sidedness and inefficiency. For Russia, the problem of modernization was presented more acutely by the crisis, and this required a combination of anti-crisis and modernization measures.

### *The role of social policy*

In Russia, the most prominent anti-crisis measures were support for the population (increase in pensions, creation of the concept of welfare activities organized at the main place of employment) and support for individual enterprises. Even in the case of support for individual enterprises, the causes of such assistance generally had social undertones (Table 12.1).

*Table 12.1* Anti-crisis measures of 2009

|  | Plan (RUB billions) | Fact (RUB billions) |
|---|---|---|
| Sectoral measures | 1,625.80 | 1,734.90 |
| Support of households | 593.70 | 652.60 |
| Contribution to the EurAsEC anti-crisis fund | 24.50 | 24.50 |
| Total | 2,244.00 | 2,412.00 |

*Source*: The Ministry of Economic Development of Russian Federation

Russia's anti-crisis budget was one of the most socially focused compared with other countries.

This has, not only a political explanation, but also an economic one. The demand generated by social assistance comes primarily from the poor and therefore concentrates mainly on domestic goods (relatively cheap as a result of devaluation). It can be assumed that the increased demand here has a greater incentive effect than the budget's demand for infrastructural facilities or residential construction.

Single-industry towns ('monotowns") required special attention. The government considered them to be particularly dangerous, especially from a sociopolitical point of view, but also saw the opportunity to use their restructuring in order to begin to implement a real (and selective) modernization policy. There cannot be any universal solution to this; that is why proposals were made to prepare individual programmes to develop and transform them – from diversification to total elimination (in exceptional cases).

## *Support of the real sector*

The government began to provide support for a number of enterprises, having made a list of those that were 'critically important'. The main tools of support were state guarantees for loans that came into effect from mid 2009. On the one hand, this stabilized the social situation, but, on the other, it became an obstacle to business restructuring. This meant that the actual protection of interests and the support of owners and managers of companies that had got into difficult situations were some of the effects of the anti-crisis measures in Russia. Owners and managers of the companies rescued by the state were not replaced and suffered minimally. The government indeed put a lot of effort into supporting critically important enterprises, but this also had a negative effect: it demonstrated that they could blackmail the government (the 'too big to fail' effect). The government had to minimize this effect.

The Russian authorities had not applied fiscal stimulation, as was considered in other countries. The anti-crisis budget was only adopted at the end of April 2009, and injections of liquidity into the economy through the budget system were sterilized through the monetary channel. Liquidity remained in shortage, which led to a decline in inventories to 7.5 per cent of GDP, and inflation decreased in the second half of 2009.

## The banking sector

The anti-crisis policy included support for the banks, which enabled the Russian banking system to stay afloat without major upheaval. Emphasis was placed, as in other sectors, on preserving the current institutions and current owners. The main focus was to provide liquidity. The Central Bank had, for the first time, fully acted as the lender of last resort, preventing the destabilization of the banking sector. The banking panic was suppressed, and this is what distinguishes the situation from 1998.

However, this policy had adverse effects in the medium term, as there was no purification of the banking environment: almost all the institutions that existed before the crisis were preserved. It can be assumed that the Central Bank simply decided not to address structural challenges at the peak of the crisis.

It was all the more important that there were no significant improvements regarding bad debts (non-performing loans). The weakening of the standards of capital regulation helped to disguise the situation and maintain a semblance of the stability of the banking sector amid the decline in the quality of assets.

## Monetary policy

Russia followed a path of smooth currency devaluation, which ended in January 2009, and rejection of exchange rate targeting. It was an important and difficult decision. Throughout the entire history of post-communist Russia, the monetary authorities had been more focused on economic growth than was required by the Constitution. Beginning with low policy rates and "technical loans" in 1992, and ending with restraining the exchange rate in 2000, the Central Bank of Russia always sacrificed the task of reducing inflation for the sake of supporting the real sector. In fact, the negative effects of this policy were sterilized by the Ministry of Finance.[2] Now, attempts were made to create an anti-inflation policy, while fluctuations in the currency exchange rate were smoothed out. However, 2009 revealed that devaluation was not a universal cure for low competitiveness. Many expected a repeat of the miracle from 10 years ago – the beginning of rapid import-substitution growth due to the decline of the rouble exchange rate. This did not happen.

Although the anti-crisis policy did help to stabilize the situation and prevent non-managed developments, there were some serious flaws and limitations. The main one was the lack of real steps towards anti-crisis modernization. At the turn of 2008–9, many spoke of the need to take advantage of the crisis to speed up modernization, to highlight the modernization aspect of the anti-crisis measures. But, in practice, most attention was focused on preventing destabilization, which essentially meant maintaining the status quo. This was the aim of support for employment in enterprises, with virtually no bankruptcies, and conserving the banking sector, with no comprehensive solutions for bad debts.

Combining anti-crisis and modernization policies is a very complicated task that is virtually impossible to resolve within one calendar year. Anti-crisis measures must be started quickly; there should not be a carefully checked strategy of long-term development. Modernization, on the other hand, requires serious long-term efforts.

## Barriers and risks

The barriers to modernization and the risks that arise in its absence became more apparent by the end of 2009. Politics in the contemporary world are, to a large extent, aimed at preserving many of those giants that are actually relics of the economy of the past. This is well illustrated by the experience of guarantees provided by the Russian government in 2009. Virtually none of those who received this support or money were able to offer any coherent programme of modernization in response.

Another serious problem associated with the too-big-to-fail paradigm is the rebirth of the ideology of the 'big state'. The causes of the global crisis were explained by the lack of state regulation, which is why there were calls to expand state interference in economic life.

So far, the experts have mostly talked about the need for stricter regulation of the financial markets and institutions, including on an international scale. This is likely to entail a return to regulation of production and trade. The 2009 law "On trade" and the state's desire to actively intervene in pricing created a dangerous precedent, especially given the domestic traditions of dirigisme.

Following criticism of the economic liberalism of the past 30 years, an argument became popular (not only in Russia) of the need for greater state intervention in the economy as an instrument to overcome the risks of spontaneous development.

Finally, Russian society lacked demand for serious renewal and modernization. The desire to preserve the status quo meant waiting for the recovery of prices for Russia's commodity exports (fuel, energy resources and metals) and a return to the pre-crisis growth model. According to the prevailing view, the sources of the economic rise in 1999–2007, as well as the causes of the current crisis, were connected to the dynamics of oil prices (and also gas and metal prices). And the way out of the crisis associated with rising energy prices. The hope that "things will sort themselves out" (or business as usual) remained dominant.

## Notes

1 To read more about the quality of Russian political and legal institutions, see: Freinkman and Dashkeev 2008.
2 For further reading on the paradoxes of Russian economic policy, where the Central Bank is concerned with economic growth, while the Ministry of Finance focuses on the stability of the currency rate, see: Yudaeva and Godunova 2009: 39–40.

## References

Freinkman, L. and Dashkeev, V. (2008). "Rossiya v 2007 g.: riski zamedleniya ekonomicheskogo rosta na fone sohranyauscheisya institutsionalnoy stagnatsii" [Russia in 2007: Risks of slowing economic growth against the background of institutional stagnation]. *Voprosy Ekonomiki*, no. 4, pp. 75–93.

Smith, A. (1977). *An Inquiry into the Nature and Causes of the Wealth of Nations*. Chicago, IL: University of Chicago Press.

Yudaeva, K. and Godunova, M. (2009). "Lessons of crisis for Russia: Macroeconomic policy", *Economicheskaya Politika*, no. 6, pp. 30–41.

# 13 Economic policy of 2010

## In search of innovations

In 2010 the emphasis of Russia's economic policy was no longer on rescuing individual economic agents (companies, banks), but on maintaining conditions to ensure economic and social stability. Banks and companies started to repay debts to the state. Large business again started to increase external borrowings, but, in contrast to previous years, credits were now mostly taken by the non-financial sector. Economic growth in Russia had resumed (Figure 13.1), but the growth rate was significantly lower than in 2000–7: as in previous years, the growth was higher than in developed countries, but lower than in China, India and Brazil. However, owing to the significant decline in the midst of the crisis, economic recovery became much more acute problem. The task for Russia to be among five largest countries in terms of GDP by 2020 had become significantly more difficult.

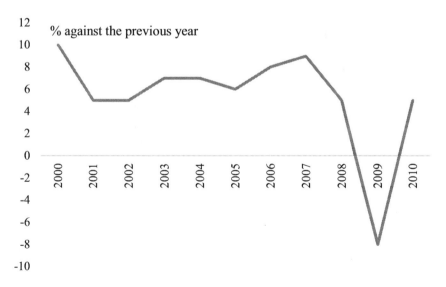

*Figure 13.1* Gross domestic product
*Source*: IMF

## At the heart of economic policy

The following issues were most important in Russia's economic development in 2010.

*First*, the significant worsening of the financial (fiscal) situation: Russia had again encountered a fiscal deficit, which had not been faced by the country for almost a decade (Figure 13.2). After the financial crisis of 1989–98, which hit its peak with the 1998 default, the government started to be particularly sensitive to budgetary problems and sought to balance the budget.

It was supported by rising oil prices. A balanced budget became a symbol of post-communist Russia and the subject of consensus of the new elite. Thanks to intense repayment of external debt, by the onset of the crisis, Russia had become one of the countries with the lowest debts in the world.

Of course, there were forces that pushed for an increase in budget expenditures, but they had limited political influence.

However, the situation changed, at least psychologically. The country tried to live with the deficit in 2009, and there was no disaster. The elite realized that they could gain access to far larger money resources than could be obtained through an increase in labour productivity and a favourable external economic environment, especially because all the most developed countries were doing the same. This resulted in a paradoxical situation: a fiscal deficit occurred at the oil price of US$80 per barrel, whereas several years ago even US$30 enabled a surplus federal budget (Figure 13.3).

Formally, the situation did not present much cause for concern. The sovereign debt remained low, and the country had ample opportunities for borrowing, both

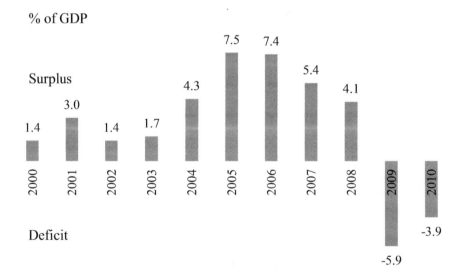

*Figure 13.2* Surplus (deficit) of the federal budget
Source: The Ministry of Finance of Russian Federation

Economic policy of 2010  135

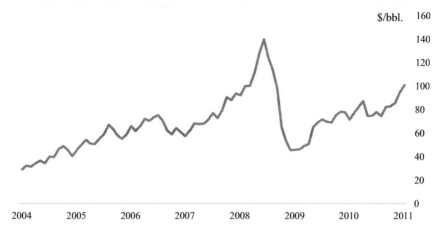

*Figure 13.3* Urals oil price
*Source*: IMF

in roubles and foreign currency (Figures 13.4 and 13.5). The budget deficit was not very large compared with that of many countries – 3.5–4 per cent of GDP. However, without the rental revenue, the budget deficit was higher than 13 per cent of GDP: in other words, the country turned out to be extremely dependent on the fluctuations of world energy prices – that is, on factors not controlled by Russia.

*Second*, after inflation fell in 2009–10, the consumer price index once again rose to 8.7 per cent at the end of the year. Inflation remained one of the highest

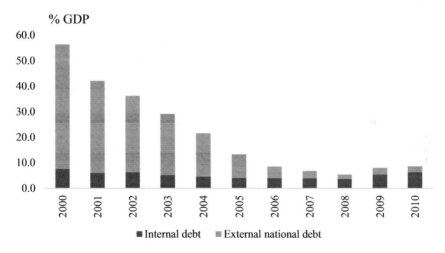

*Figure 13.4* National debt
*Source*: The Ministry of Finance of Russian Federation

136  *The Russian version of the global crisis*

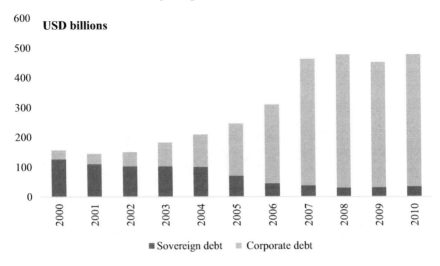

*Figure 13.5* External debt (year end)
Source: The Ministry of Finance of Russian Federation

among the G20 countries and was comparable only with inflation in India and Turkey (see Table 13.1 and Figure 13.6).

There were two important sources of inflation escalation. On the one hand, drought and extremely low crop yields affected the total price index of agricultural production (Figure 13.7). On the other hand, there was the fiscal policy, as far as the increase in budget expenditures inevitably influenced prices. Budget deficit

*Table 13.1* Inflation, consumer prices growth against the previous year

|  | 2007 | 2008 | 2009 | 2010 |
|---|---|---|---|---|
| Russia: |  |  |  |  |
| – According to OECD | 9.0 | 14.1 | 11.6 | 6.8 |
| – According to Federal State Statistics Service | 11.9 | 13.3 | 8.8 | 8.8 |
| G7 | 2.2 | 3.0 | –0.1 | 1.4 |
| Turkey | 8.8 | 10.4 | 6.3 | 8.6 |
| India | 6.4 | 8.3 | 10.9 | 12.0 |
| China | 4.8 | 5.9 | –0.7 | 3.2 |
| Brazil | 3.6 | 5.7 | 4.9 | 5.0 |
| Spain | 2.8 | 4.1 | –0.3 | 1.8 |
| Greece | 2.9 | 4.2 | 1.2 | 4.7 |
| USA | 2.9 | 3.8 | –0.4 | 1.6 |
| United Kingdom | 2.3 | 3.6 | 2.2 | 3.3 |
| Canada | 2.1 | 2.4 | 0.3 | 1.8 |
| France | 1.5 | 2.8 | 0.1 | 1.5 |

*Sources*: OECD, IMF, RBC, Federal State Statistics Service

covered from the reserve fund and foreign currency interventions also contributed to inflation.

Inflation in Russia was a much more problematic factor than in developed countries where the main risk was deflation. Inflation in Russia led to higher interest rates and to their being kept at a two-digit level, which was an obstacle to economic growth.

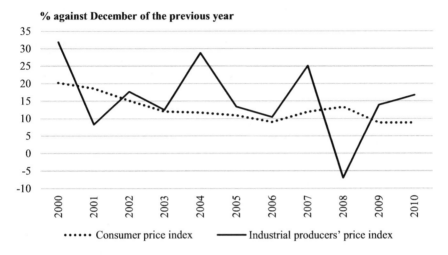

*Figure 13.6* Inflation
*Source*: Central Bank of Russian Federation

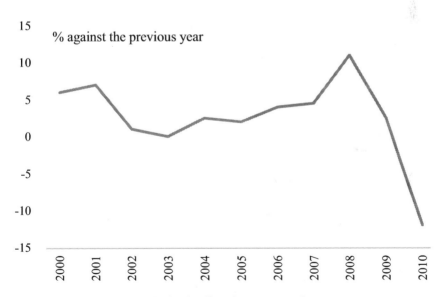

*Figure 13.7* Agricultural production in all producers' categories
*Source*: Federal State Statistics Service

138  *The Russian version of the global crisis*

In this situation, one could expect the enlargement of borrowings by Russian firms on foreign markets offering cheaper financial resources. The borrowings did grow in 2010, and the non-financial institutions were especially active (unlike in the pre-crisis time).

*Third*, Russia faced a significant outflow of capital, which, in 2010, amounted to US$32.8 billion. The idea of limiting the free movement of capital, introducing control of capital was rather popular, (Brazil, in fact, introduced the so-called "Tobin tax") for avoiding the dangerous outflow of capital (Figure 13.8). Capital outflows continued, despite the fact that the Russian stock market was one of the fastest growing. Its small scale (portfolio investment inflow was a small fraction in the dynamics of capital), small depth and volatility (massive fluctuations, much higher than a few per cent) led to the loss of interest from major international investors. The level of direct investment in 2010 was low (Figure 13.9).

There were evidently a number of reasons for capital outflow: the overall uncertainty of the crisis's development, and the uncertainty associated with the upcoming national elections in Russia and the high level of corruption, when a part of the funds spent by budgets of all levels remained in the hands of officials who preferred to hide the accumulated funds in 'safe harbours' (this is evidenced by the comparatively small amounts of one-time transfers of funds abroad, which was typical in 2010). Corruption grew from a microeconomic phenomenon into a macroeconomic factor.

The balance of payments on current operations decreased owing to considerable growth in imports, which in turn was a reaction to the increase in the budget's social expenditure (Figure 13.10). The situation of 1999, when the growth of

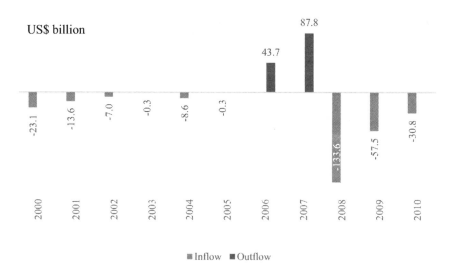

*Figure 13.8* Net inflow–outflow of capital in the private sector according to the balance sheets

*Source*: Central Bank of Russian Federation

*Economic policy of 2010* 139

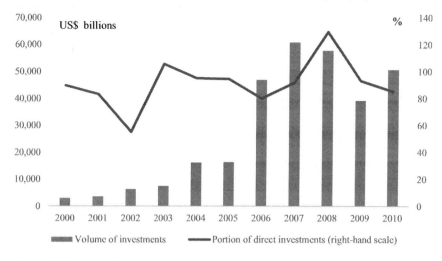

*Figure 13.9* Foreign investments
Source: Federal State Statistics Service

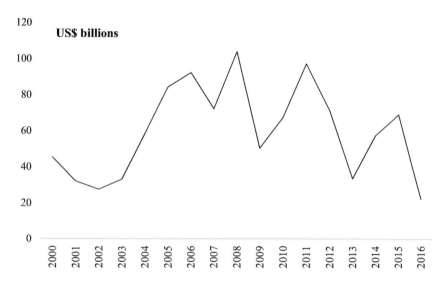

*Figure 13.10* Balance of payments, current account
Source: Central Bank of Russia

nominal payments to households increased the demand for domestic goods (import substitution), was possible only in the case of a huge devaluation of the national currency (as in 1998), not just a few percentage points as in 2010.

All the above suggests the following conclusion: 2010 demonstrated that Russia had ceased to be a cheap country, as it was in the 1990s and early 2000s. It concerns the value of assets, goods and services. In crisis times, with a relatively stable exchange rate, the ratio of return on market operations and country risks (risk/return) significantly changed because of the persistence of high risks and reduced profitability; other developing markets were more reliable, at comparable levels of return. Domestic consumer goods cannot generally compete with imports in terms of price/quality ratio either. These circumstances led to capital outflow and a decrease in the current account. The fears of a current account turned to negative values were justified. But, this scenario was not inevitable, as the growth of demand for import goods led to a weakening of the rouble, which in turn was a limiting factor. It depends on the actions of the monetary authorities and the fiscal policy. The Central Bank is able to control the exchange rate, gradually weakening the rouble in order to limit the influx of imports. However, it will contradict the tasks for inflation targeting and emphasize once again that the problems of domestic production are more important for the Central Bank than stability of prices and currency.

The prospects of the balance of payments depend on the character of the budget policy. Effusive budget expansion (particularly in the area of social benefits) can become a factor for sustained growth of demand for them – that is, the appearance of a double deficit (the budget and current account).

*Fourth*, by the end of 2010, the labour market was significantly better than expected at the beginning of the year. By December, the number of unemployed persons had decreased by 0.7 million people to 5.7 million, and the number of registered unemployed persons decreased by 183,100 people – down to 1.9 million. The phenomenon of jobless recovery (restoring production with a lag in restoring employment) was not observed in Russia. This situation can only be welcomed from the point of view of sociopolitical stability. But, there are two possible explanations that do not allow the strong labour market recovery to be evaluated as an entirely positive development (Figure 13.11).

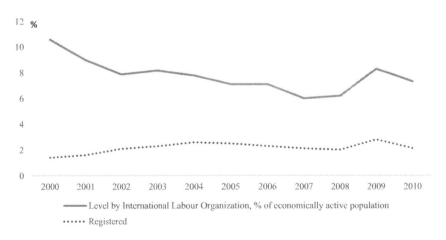

*Figure 13.11* Unemployment

*Source*: Federal State Statistics Service

On the one hand, the phenomenon of a jobless recovery is the reverse side of the coin and an indicator of structural transformation of the economy. It means increased structural unemployment – that is, the emergence of new jobs and a lack of people with relevant skills. The jobless recovery is an indispensable factor of the modernization that is needed to overcome a crisis. The absence of this phenomenon requires a special discussion on the existence or absence of modernization at the stage of recovery from crisis. Political pressure on businesses and regions with the requirement to ensure high employment affects the economy similarly.

On the other hand, in the specific demographic situations in Russia, the fact that employment is not lagging behind economic recovery can be an indicator of a higher level of retirement – that is, unemployment is reduced, not only owing to a rise in employment, but also because of a reduction in the workforce of working age.

These explanations do not contradict each other, and, most probably, they influenced the situation in 2010. Of course, in terms of social stability, these developments were useful. However, in terms of solving the problems of modernization, the labour market situation could not be interpreted unambiguously.

*Fifth*, in Russia, important steps were made in the area of international integration – both in terms of cooperation within the common economic space of the Customs Union and in accession to the WTO. There were significant advancements in both fields. Now, they are linked to purely political, rather than economic or technical, solutions, including the membership of the WTO. For Russia, both processes are important ways to stimulate competition and producers, as well as jurisdictions.[1]

In an effort to combine the anti-crisis measures with modernization, the Russian government used some new elements in its economic policy that were substantially different to those used in 2000–8.

First and foremost, this included the new macroeconomic reality – a persistent budget deficit and increased budgetary borrowing.

Another important innovation of economic policy in 2010 was increased taxes. Throughout the entire history of the post-communist transformation of Russia, after the establishment of the fundamentally new tax system in 1992, taxes had mostly gradually declined (with the exception of hydrocarbons, tobacco and alcohol). Decisive action to reduce taxes was taken in 2000–1. There was one important (yet undeclared) reason for tax cuts in the early 2000s: to set the tax rate at a level close to the effective rate.

In 2010, the trend changed. Social security payments were raised significantly (particularly payments to the pension fund); taxation of hydrocarbon production was increased. The fiscal logic of these measures was understandable – with a rise in budget expenditure, an increase in taxes was almost inevitable. However, it was obvious that increased taxation of labour discourages structural modernization, as it most painfully affects the industries with a high proportion of labour costs, in contrast to mineral mining sectors.

In an effort to mitigate the negative impact of the tax increase, the authorities became more active in using discrete (selective) economic policy measures. The most striking example was the Skolkovo Innovation Centre, the residents of which received an unprecedented set of fiscal and administrative privileges – from low rates of social payments to the creation of their own bodies for law enforcement, tax and customs. In fact, it was an attempt to create a point of innovative growth, managed, as it should be, in a modern, developed, post-industrial society.

The model of special economic zones (SEZs) began its transformation according to this logic. Initially, SEZs were seen as the areas for accelerated growth, defined as a result of competition between different regions that tried to offer the best conditions for stimulating business and innovation activities. Thereafter, the SEZs were 'appointed' – that is, created in a place appropriate from the point of view of the formation of a certain technological cluster.

In an effort to compensate for the rise in social taxes for small businesses (and realizing that a portion of the business would withdraw into the shadows), the government decided to reduce payments to the pension fund from 26 per cent to 18 per cent for small enterprises and individual entrepreneurs engaged in providing social services, for a period of 2 years.

Finally, in 2010, privatization once again became a hot topic. The government had adopted an ambitious programme of privatization: not only were stakes in enterprises in which the state was a minority shareholder put on sale, but also the minority shareholdings of state-owned companies or companies with dominance of state ownership, such as Rosneft, Russian Railways, RusHydro, Sberbank, VTB, and others. Presumably, the aims of privatization will be to attract strategic investors (and, respectively, obtain investment resources and improve corporate management), as well as increase budget revenues. However, with 2010 challenges, the first task should have been the most important.[2]

## New growth model

One of the illusions at the beginning of any structural crisis is expectation of the return of 'good old times', or business as usual. This strategy is wrong. A structural crisis delivers a new model of economic development, and only after it appears can this crisis be overcome. Only those countries that are able to form this model and implement it most consistently and resolutely may benefit from the crisis. The challenge of a new growth model is the stimulating element of a crisis, which gives a chance for individual countries to make an economic breakthrough.

Russia had two options for socio-economic policies, and it is the political elite that would have to make the choice.

*The first option* involved developing the pre-crisis model and adapting it to emerging challenges. The state is the main growth stimulator, as a source of financial resources, a neutralizing agent of free-market instability and a holder of the key institutions needed for economic growth. It identifies priorities, focuses political and financial resources on them, builds a financial system based on the state-owned banks and stock exchanges, and directly manages the key manufacturing companies (controls the 'commanding heights'). Government demand, not only for goods and services, but also for institutions is crucially important here. Households' demand also largely depends on the state.

*The second option* involves strengthening the role of private sources of growth (private firms and households) that will gradually replace the state and force it out of the business zone. The state must create the most favourable conditions for private economic operators to function and encourage their interest in development – that is, stimulate the supply of goods and services on the market.

This dichotomy is well known in economic theory and economic history. It appeared long before the current global crisis. The choice between supply-side economics and demand-side economics lies at the heart of the debate, which is characteristic of the most of the twentieth century.

This theme is even more relevant for countries with developing economies (or countries where modernization is catching up). However, excessive state intervention would come at a high political and economic price to society. The 'big government' stiffens and, at a certain point, becomes an impediment to modern economic growth, and overcoming this obstacle requires huge resources, and sometimes victims.

The Russian growth model that emerged from the 2000s was based on demand-side economics. The key elements of this model are ensuring a high level of social and political stability in society as the main objective of the government; high and increasing prices for hydrocarbons; expanding budget costs as the most important source of demand; the gradual increase of taxes; continuing high inflation potential; and strengthening the role of individual (selective) solutions, as opposed to the establishment of common rules of the game.

The model of economic growth that had formed by the 2000s was based on the availability of significant, cheap and 'unearned' financial resources, which comes, not from an increase in productivity, but from the favourable external economic environment. This model, with slight modifications, actually existed in Russia from the 1970s and, until recently, it was almost as popular as at the beginning of its existence. Fast-growing expenditure from the state budget either requires even more rapid growth of prices for energy resources, or results in a budget deficit.

The state is the most important source of demand in the economy. This demand is primarily from the middle and poor classes dependent on the state budget – pensioners, civil servants and military personnel, as well as workers in state corporations. An important role is played by the finances directed to the defence and law enforcement agencies in the form of military pay and arms purchases.

Another area of strong government demand is investment in infrastructure. But, being aware of the high level of corruption in this sector, the government was very cautious with its infrastructural investments, in contrast to social spending.

Choosing between the priority of infrastructural and social issues is difficult. Social costs go to a more competitive market, and they may indeed lead to an increase in consumption. Infrastructural sectors are more monopolized, and investing in them leads rather to higher prices (tariffs), than to an increase in the supply of relevant goods and services.

At the same time, social spending significantly affects inflation and increases the demand for cheap import goods. The practice of recent years showed that growth of demand for cheap goods was satisfied, not by domestic producers, but by supplies from countries with cheap labour (mainly from Asia).[3] This limits the incentive potential of budget expenditure.

To some extent, this demand could be compensated for by the exchange rate policy – that is, by controlling the strengthening of the rouble; however, the possibilities of monetary authorities in this area are very limited, especially with such high prices for hydrocarbons.

Another problem of social spending is its irreversible character. It is only possible to refuse officially assumed obligations in major political or (and) economic crisis. It is impossible to resort to the argument of a lack of budget revenues.

The priority of social stability in this model encourages a conservative labour market policy – policies that prevent the release of the workforce, which in turn prevents structural upgrades. The release will become acceptable, but very careful and controlled by the state. This will give serious positive results, as was demonstrated by Avtovaz in 2010. However, replicating such experiences on a massive scale is almost impossible.

Finally, an economy based on state demand is fundamentally more prone to preservation and supporting monopolies, as well as to inflation. The monopolies will ensure the stability of the economic and political situation, albeit at the cost of lower quality of goods and services, with higher inflation.

The dominance of government demand will soften economic agents' need for reduced inflation, as public investment will become more important than private, and, for a private investor, low inflation is more important, as it is a prerequisite for lower interest rates.

It seems that the state will reinforce the individual (selective) nature of its solutions by providing stimulating benefits for certain types of investor and manufacturer – the benefits compensating for increased taxes and interest rates, and administrative barriers.

*Growth with structural modernization needs supply-side economics.* During modernization, one must primarily focus, not only (and even not so much) on the pace of growth, but also on its quality. This requires the adoption of a new growth model, based on stimulating the supply of goods and services – that is, creating conditions for the successful operation and development of economic agents.

The following are the main elements of this model:

First is the decline rather than increase of the budget burden relative to GDP – that is, the reduction of budget expenditure and taxes. Almost all successful examples of catching-up development in the post-industrial world were observed in countries with a budget rate to GDP lower than in most advanced countries. (This is the fundamental difference between modern catch-up development and the catch-up development in the industrial era of the nineteenth and twentieth centuries.)

Second is restoring macroeconomic balance – that is, the reduction of the budget deficit along with streamlining and improving the effectiveness of budget expenditures.

Third is a monetary policy favourable for private investment. This means a gradual movement towards the rouble as a regional reserve currency. Owing to the fact that the effectiveness of stimulating domestic production curbing appreciation of the national currency decreased, it was necessary to start carrying out inflation targeting, which would maintain the interest rates at a level acceptable for investors.

Fourth is ensuring the openness of the economy as the most important condition for stimulating internal competition, including the development of the Eurasian Economic Union, joining the WTO and the prospects of OECD, and the future perspective of moving towards a common economic space with the EU, which could be seen as a strategic objective

Fifth is the neutralization of rent revenues – the return to the ideology and practice of forming the stabilization fund out of the funds derived from the sale of hydrocarbons at a price above a certain level (fixed for several years).

Sixth is reform of human capital sectors, particularly education, pension and health care systems, keeping them in line with the demographic and financial realities of a post-industrial society, and strengthening the private and individual principles of functioning of these sectors, as well as linking their development to the formation of sources of long-term investment.

And, finally, there is the consistent implementation of privatization with a prime focus, not on fiscal, but on social and political, objectives – the formation of a wide layer of non-oligarchical owners of companies, the middle class and the attraction of strategic investors. This kind of privatization will create the demand for modernization, macroeconomic improvement and structural reforms described above. (That is what happened in the 1990s, when the beginning of privatization opened up the path to both macroeconomic and political stabilization.)

As demonstrated by 2010, restoring economic growth did not mean recovering from the crisis. The economic situation remained volatile and greatly dependent on government demand.

Overcoming of the crisis was not reflected in the growth indicators – in the same way that the beginning of the crisis did not coincide with the start of the recession. The question was about a new quality of growth, a new growth model, and a new model of managing socio-economic processes – now, evidently, on a global scale.

## Notes

1   For further reading on the competition of law jurisdictions, see: Shuvalov 2010.
2   Privatization may have three objectives – political, economic and fiscal. The first is to strengthen the political regime by systematically expanding its social base. The second is to attract effective owners, to accelerate economic growth and increase its quality. The third is to increase budget revenues. In the 1990s, as in the case of any large-scale revolution of the past, the first objective was dominant. In an environment of political stability, the economic objective takes precedence, although the two others also play a role – they are quite compatible (for further details, see: Mau 2001).
3   According to Alexei Vedev, 75 per cent of the growth in domestic demand resulted in inflation and rising imports, and only 25 per cent stimulated domestic production (see: Centre for Strategic Studies of the Bank of Moscow 2010).

## References

Centre for Strategic Studies of the Bank of Moscow. (2010) "Development of the banking system of Russia in 2010–2011. On the way to 'cheap money'."

Gerschenkron, A. (1962). *Economic Backwardness in Historical Perspective: A book of essays*. Cambridge, MA: Belknap Press.

Mau, V. (2001). *Ekonomika i revolyutsia: uroki istorii* [Economy and Revolution: Lessons of history]. *Voprosy Ekonomiki*. No. 1.

Shuvalov, I. (2010). "Rossiya na puti modernizatsii" [Russia on the path of modernization], *Ekonomicheskaya Politika*, no. 1.

# 14 Economic policy of 2011

The global crisis and the search for a new growth model

### Economic dynamics

The social and economic development of Russia in 2011 was determined by two main factors: the upcoming elections for the Duma (December 2011) and the president of the Russian Federation (March 2012), on the one hand, and the global crisis, on the other. These were substantially different groups of factors, both in terms of strength and direction of impact. However, they shaped the behaviour of all participants in economic and political life.

There are three main mechanisms of influence of the global economy on today's Russia: through demand for export goods, through the availability of investment resources (direct investments and loans) and through demand for Russian securities on the stock market. The slow growth of the world economy led to a decrease in the demand for Russian exports, but the prices for its main export commodities remained high, although they did not increase at the rate that had been usual for several years before the crisis. The Russian stock market is extremely vulnerable to external shocks, but it did not yet play a significant role in ensuring the country's economic growth. External borrowings by the corporate sector continued to grow, surpassing the pre-crisis level (see Figure A.4).

Standard mechanisms of electoral influence on the economic life of a society include growing uncertainty about future economic policies, as well as the rise of populism if an incumbent seeks re-election. Both mechanisms proved to be relevant to Russia in 2011, despite the fact that the probability of power being retained in the hands of the ruling party and its leaders seemed exceptionally high to all, and the maintenance of stability did not require additional financial resources. However, it did not prevent the country's leaders from announcing their intention to implement large-scale financial infusions over the next few years, mainly in the social sphere and in defence and law enforcement agencies.

In 2011, Russia demonstrated sufficient stability of economic development. Economic growth remained moderate and, in general, quite natural for a country of an average level of economic development: Russia's growth was higher than Germany's, but lower than China's.

Macroeconomic parameters remained formally favourable: the budget at year-end had a surplus of almost 1 per cent of GDP, and inflation reached its historic minimum of all 20 years of Russia's post-communist existence.

However, macroeconomic situation remained extremely vulnerable. It was based on budget revenues from high oil prices, which were at a historic maximum compared with the level at the turn of the 1970s–1980s (see Figure A.5).

Basing budget commitments on oil revenue was an extremely dangerous construction, as was demonstrated by the experience of the Soviet Union in the 1980s. Meanwhile, the non-oil deficit of the federal budget in 2011 totalled approximately 10 per cent of GDP, and the budget deficit reached 4.5 per cent of GDP at the average 10-year oil price.

In 2011, capital outflows increased and reached US$80 billion. There were various reasons for that: a poor investment climate, the demand for foreign assets from major Russian investors, increased competition for capital from the emerging markets of Asia and Latin America, the global crisis leading to growing demand for US dollars, and also the political risks of the pre-election period.

The economic crisis is always considered as the starting point of modernization. As the accumulated reserves were able to prevent bankruptcies and forced structural modernization, the Russian authorities developed a modernization agenda from the top. During 2011, there was an active discussion about principles for stimulating modernization and selective innovations.

Modernization cannot be realized by directives, even from a very high level. Modernization requires competition between both economic agents and institutions. In this regard, modernization factors could include two major economic and political steps in 2011: WTO accession and the breakthrough in integration of the post-Soviet space (the start of the Customs Union and the agreements on the Common Economic Space of Russia, Belarus and Kazakhstan). The WTO had to ensure expansion of competition between producers; the Customs Union and the Common Economic Space had to add competition of institutions to the competition of products.

A characteristic feature of the economic life of this period was the high level of politicization, which was very well traced both in Russia and worldwide. This included the above developments, anti-government protests in Arab countries, as well as the "Occupy Wall Street" movement in the developed world and the increased public political activity of 2011–12 in Russia. Of course, the causes and mechanisms of politicization in various regions were different, but it was impossible to ignore the fact they were juxtaposed.

## Continued debate on the growth model

Before 2011, the global crisis had a limited impact on the situation in Russia. But it also did not contribute to structural changes, to modernization of the Russian economy and policy. And, at the turn of 2010–11, Vladimir Putin requested the expert community to work out Russia's development strategy until 2020, which in fact had to be a programme of institutional and structural modernization.

There were two groups of reasons why this new strategy was demanded.

First, of course, was the global crisis itself, which is an intellectual challenge, as noted above, and which requires a rethinking of socio-economic policy. "You never want a serious crisis to go to waste" – these words from Rahm Emanuel, the US president's chief of staff (2008–10), very accurately reflect the tasks faced by the governments of all developed countries.

There were also specific Russian reasons for updating the economic policy. The model of economic policy of the beginning of the 2000s was formed under the powerful intellectual, political and even psychological impact of the post-communist transformation of 1991–9, in general, and the financial crisis of 1998, in particular.

The economic policy of 1999–2009 (demand-side economics) had the following characteristics and features:

- It was to ensure political and social stability as a *sine qua non* condition.
- The role of the state was gradually increased as the source of this stability. This was manifested in at least three ways: increased state ownership (formal and actual); increased budgetary revenues and expenditures (in total and in proportion to GDP); compensation for distrust of financial institutions through the development of government financial structures (which was typical for the countries of catch-up industrialization).
- It was to achieve a positive fiscal balance. However, the fiscal balance was unstable amid strong fiscal expansion. Stoppage (or even a significant slowdown) of revenue growth brought about a budget deficit.
- It was to restrain the increasing exchange rate while maintaining high inflation and high interest rates. This was seen as a source of incentives for domestic producers.
- It offered state corporations and quasi-private and private firms wide access to the international capital market. The high cost of internal credits was compensated by the possibility of borrowing on the international market.
- The government became the most important source of demand in the economy. Demand from the middle and poor classes – pensioners, unemployed persons, public servants and military personnel, as well as the workers of the state corporations – was dependent on the state budget. An important role was played by the finances directed to the defence and law enforcement agencies in the form of military pay and arms purchases. It was especially strong during the global financial crisis of 2008–10.
- There was limited public investment in infrastructure. Being aware of the high level of corruption in this sector, the government was rather cautious in its infrastructural investments, in contrast to social spending.
- There was support for large, inefficient enterprises as a means of overcoming social destabilization – hence, the political and administrative constraints on the release of employees in inefficient industrial enterprises.
- Administrative reform was reduced to constant clarification of the range of functions carried out by various public authorities, while there was a refusal to fundamentally revise the system of public administration.
- Taxes were raised to ensure macroeconomic and social stability.

It is easy to see some inevitable consequences of this economic policy.

There were *budget problems*. Escalating budget expenditures with oil prices led to a budget deficit. Russia's economy became dramatically vulnerable to external shocks associated with the unpredictability of oil prices.

The duality of the Stabilization Fund (the government's reserves associated with superprofits from oil exports) was revealed as the strategic social and economic goals were ensured. On the one hand, these reserves helped to avoid budget populism, sterilize the monetary mass and create a security cushion for a possible crisis. On the other hand, the availability of significant reserves in crisis was a strong factor inhibiting modernization, as it helped to douse social tension at the cost of slowing down the pace of the restructuring of enterprises in default. The situation in the banking sector was similar.

*The monetary policy* was based on restraining appreciation of the rouble, which had a side effect – inflation. Nevertheless the rouble was strengthening, and in real terms (by purchasing power parity) it exceeded the level of 1997, having reached 65 per cent of the nominal level (25 per cent in 1999) by 2008. The competitiveness of Russian firms naturally decreased owing to exchange rate dynamics. But, high inflation resulted in twoe-digit interest rates on loans, which made it impossible to get the funds needed for domestic business and hindered mortgage lending.

"Scissors of competitiveness" created the most severe structural trap in Russia. In the early 2000s, Russia was a country with institutions of average quality and cheap, skilled labour, but now the situation was considerably different. From 1999 to 2010, there was a steady increase in labour costs, with the quality of institutions stagnant or even declining (Figure 14.1).[1]

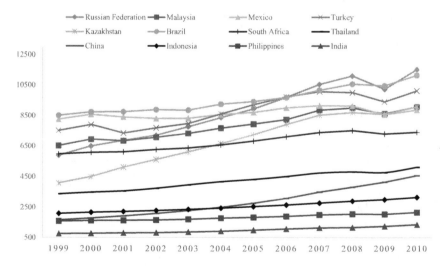

*Figure 14.1a* Structural constraints of economic growth: 'scissors of competitiveness' in terms of GDP per capita. In these terms, Russia was first among the most dynamic countries with emerging markets

Source: The World Bank 2016

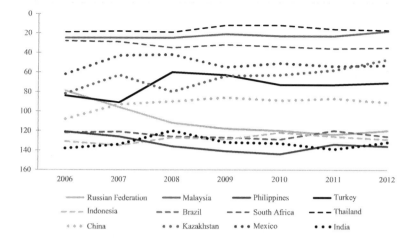

*Figure 14.1b* Structural constraints of economic growth: 'scissors of competitiveness' in terms of business environment. Russia's position became worse and it was by now in the group of lagging countries, along with Brazil, India and Indonesia, while their per capita GDP was below the Russian level

*Source*: Doing Business index, the World Bank

Of course, any indicator is important, not on its own, but in comparison with countries with a comparable level of economic development that compete with Russia in raising capital and developing production capacity.

Thus, Russia became less attractive for investment, and this concerns both foreign and domestic capital. This is evidently part of the explanation for capital outflows observed at this time.

Russia found itself in a structural trap, with (relatively) expensive labour and (relatively) bad institutions. It is clear that, in such a situation, only the services and raw material sectors (natural resource management) may be competitive.

The high cost of labour, weak institutions and low productivity were limiting opportunities both for increasing industrial exports and for covering the increase in internal demand by domestic production.

There were two ways out of this trap: either institutions should improve substantially, or wages could come down in accordance with the quality of the institutions.

The demographic crisis is another impediment to economic growth. There is a the reduction in the working-age population, which started in the mid 2000s (Figure 14.2). It is thought that the demographic problem can be offset by external migration. But, modern migration can only solve quantitative problems with a decrease in the quality of the labour force. Migrants flow to Russia from less developed countries, and they have a lower demand for political institutions and institutions of human development. The problem of improving the quality of institutions and human capital has reached an impasse.

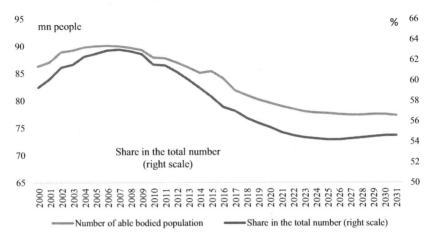

*Figure 14.2* Structural constraints to economic growth (decline of Russia's able-bodied population)
*Source*: Federal State Statistics Service

Another problem is the active adoption by members of the creative class of the idea of changing their country of residence – in other words, an exit strategy. This is a fairly new phenomenon that requires serious consideration. It is, perhaps, the first time that the concept of leaving the country is associated, not with a deterioration in welfare, but with a substantial improvement. Globalization, coupled with the rapid growth of standards of living in the country, resulted in the rapid growth of an educated, mobile class of people who feel competitive in the global market. They are in demand in most developed countries and can easily move around the globe. As a result, Russia has to compete for its own creative class, as if it were international.

This situation creates fundamentally new institutional challenges. To a large extent, the creative class is no longer demanding improvements in the quality of institutions in its native country because it can get what it desires (political system, education, medicine) in any other country. The lack of demand for modern institutions in Russia will result in a lack of their supply. This is what is becoming the most important structural obstacle for modernization.

The business climate is another important challenge. In Russia the quality of institutions was at a lower level than that in countries with comparable levels of per capita GDP (Table 14.1).

In terms of the level of development, Russia was in fiftieth place among almost 200 countries, and, in terms of the quality of institutions, it was below 200th place.

Fast-rising oil prices and the increased economic activity of the government compensated, at a certain stage, for the negative impact of the business climate on economic growth. The Doing Business index in 2011 reflected very poor performance on many indicators of international competitiveness. Russia was at

*Table 14.1* The level of economic development and quality of institutions

| GDP per capita | 50 |
|---|---|
| Economic competitiveness (VEF) | 65 |
| Competitiveness of higher education | 50 |
| Competitiveness of health care | 63 |
| Life expectancy | 150 |
| Medical expenses per capita | 70 |
| Quality of institutions | 118 |
| Level of corruption | 154 |
| Human development index | 65 |

*Source*: Doing Business index, the World Bank

the bottom of the list – below 120th position in this rating. This applied to customs regulation, opening and closing a business, management of a construction business and investor protection (see Figure 14.3 and Table 14.2).

The condition of the basic (law enforcement) and financial institutions was a major limiting factor.

Russia's spatial development was another structural limiter of competitiveness. Weak responsibility of regional and municipal authorities resulted in an excessive burden on the federal budget, which further discouraged the regions from identifying their own resources. The appointment of regional authorities from above (by the president) also motivated them to lobby primarily for the redistribution of federal funds.

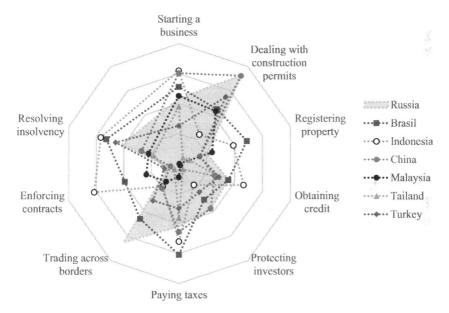

*Figure 14.3* The most significant institutional constraints to economic growth
*Source:* Doing Business index, the World Bank

*Table 14.2* Doing Business rating

| Doing Business, 2011 (183 countries) | |
|---|---|
| Ease of doing business | 123 |
| Starting a business | 108 |
| Registering property | 51 |
| Obtaining credit | 89 |
| Trading across borders | 162 |
| Resolving insolvency | 103 |
| Protecting investors | 93 |
| Paying taxes | 105 |
| Dealing with construction permits | 182 |
| Enforcing contracts | 18 |

*Source*: Doing Business index, the World Bank

The lack of incentives for the regional consolidation of human and financial resources, as well as the mechanisms of such consolidation, would constantly place financial pressure on the federal government and cause a deliberate irrationality of budgetary expenditure.

## Note

1 The issue of the quality of institutions was examined, inter alia, in the paper by Freinkman and Dashkeev (2008).

## Reference

Freinkman, L., and Dashkeev, V. (2008). "Rossiya v 2007 g.: riski zamedleniya ekonomicheskogo rosta na fone sohranyauscheisya institutsionalnoy stagnatsii" [Russia in 2007: Risks of slowing economic growth against the background of institutional stagnation], *Voprosy Ekonomiki*, no. 4.

# 15 Economic policy of 2012

Between modernization and stagnation

### Restoring growth in times of crisis

Amid global problems, and particularly in comparison with developed countries, the Russian economy in 2012 seemed to be doing rather well (see Table A.1).

The economy continued to grow, albeit at a slow rate – about 4 per cent of GDP and about 3 per cent in the industrial sector. One important, positive result was that economic growth was mainly caused by domestic demand (investment grew by approximately 7 per cent and consumption by approximately 6 per cent).

Inflation was rather high but remained under control and with a tendency to fall. Sovereign debt was low, and the budget was balanced. The current account was also positive. Direct foreign investment increased, but with a substantial outflow of capital.

There were some new trends: positive interest rates, as well as an excess of lending over deposits, which reflected a change in household saving behaviour and the transition to the credit model of consumption.

Most of the macroeconomic parameters did not change significantly, compared with 2011. Russia was a country with sustainable growth focused on domestic demand, a balanced budget, low debt, significant monetary reserves.

Despite favourable economic indicators – both in absolute terms and in comparison with other countries – the strategic situation did not give grounds for exclusively optimistic forecasts. The most visible was the slowdown of economic growth at the end of 2012. It was a matter of concern because many politicians and economists thought that a growth rate below 5 per cent would not ensure social and even political stability. In fact, the problem of growth rates was not so critical. On the one hand, it would be strange to expect high growth rates, when the main foreign trade partner, which accounts for almost 60 per cent of turnover (the EU), slowed down and seemed on the brink of a recession. On the other hand, it is not only the rates that are important, but also the quality of growth, its structure and its ability to ensure modernization. A nervous reaction from the government to the slowdown of growth, which could lead to an artificial increase in public demand, accompanied by the destruction of the macroeconomic balance, would have been more dangerous.

It was far more important to focus on four long-term socio-economic problems, which ultimately result in low, ever-decreasing growth rates.

*First* was the lack of positive structural changes for modernization. The recovery to the pre-crisis level came with deterioration in the sectoral structure: mining exceeded the pre-crisis level by 5 per cent, manufacturing by approximately 1 per cent (see Table 15.1 and Figure 15.1).

The output of traditional Russian exports (coke and oil products, chemical production, manufacture of rubber and plastic products) was restored, but the rate of metallurgical recovery was low, owing to low demand for metals and a decrease in world prices due to the slow global economic recovery.

There was active growth in vehicle production (mainly at the expense of the automotive industry), which had been close to exhaustion.

The recession in the production of investment goods (building materials, machines, electrical equipment, electronic and optical equipment) was not overcome: in 2012, it was approximately 14 per cent below pre-crisis levels, and the volume of construction works was 10 per cent lower.

*Second*, the significant outflow of capital exceeded its inflow. One can say that, with high prices for Russian export products, the country generated more capital than it could 'digest', given the limited material and human resources. But, in the

*Table 15.1* Results of growth adjustment: growth of industrial production (January–September 2012/January–September 2008, per cent)

| | |
|---|---|
| Total industrial production | 2.7 |
| Mining | 5.0 |
| Manufacturing | 1.2 |
| Consumption goods (food and other consumer goods) | 6.6 |
| Food | 9.3 |
| Textiles and textile products | −9.3 |
| Leather, leather goods, footwear | 9.9 |
| Other goods | −0.3 |
| Goods of intermediate demand | 3.2 |
| Coke and petroleum products | 9.2 |
| Chemical products | 7.9 |
| Rubber and plastic products | 23.3 |
| Metal and fabricated metal products | −3.5 |
| Manufacture of transport means and equipment | 17.0 |
| Forestry, woodworking and pulp and paper industries (FWPP) | −7.1 |
| Manufacture of wood and wood products | −8.2 |
| Pulp and paper production; publishing and printing | −6.6 |
| Production of investment goods | −14.1 |
| Building materials | −10.4 |
| Machines and equipment | −19.1 |
| Electrical, electronic and optical equipment | −13.0 |
| Electricity, gas and hot water generation and distribution | −15.4 |
| Additionally | 0.7 |
| Fixed capital investment | −6.9 |
| Commercial transport turnover | −0.6 |
| Construction | −10.7 |

*Sources*: Federal State Statistics Service, Centre of Strategic Research

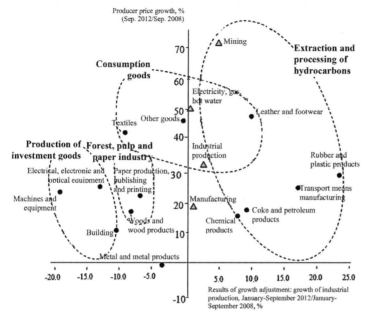

*Figure 15.1* Recovery of production and price competitiveness
Source: Federal State Statistics Service

open economy, the restricted possibility of the productive use of capital is also an indicator of a bad investment climate.

*Third*, unemployment was low. This factor contributed to social and political stability, although it also pointed to a lack of real structural changes. Modernization implies that employment would lag behind economic growth, and therefore recovery might appear to be jobless; meanwhile, governments are reluctant to accept the role of unemployment in modernization.

*Fourth*, a significant number of highly educated Russians (the creative class) want to leave the country, and it is not about a formal change of residence. An increasing number of wealthy Russians seek to receive health care and study abroad, to acquire real estate, to provide education for their children and then get permanent residency for them. According to the polls ("Valdaysky Club", October 2012), about 70 per cent of Russians with incomes above the average would like their children to study and work abroad, and more than a third of them want their children to leave Russia. This is politically dangerous, because it means that high-quality, effective demand for education and health care will leave Russia, and good universities and clinics usually only appear in places with a demand for them. The elite's exit strategy is further facilitated by the fact that the transactional costs of leaving the country are declining, because of globalization and the increase in welfare. As a result, over the past 25 years, radical changes have occurred in the formation of the sociopolitical position of active citizens: in the past, the creative class sought to improve living conditions in their country, but today it is easier and cheaper to change the country of residence, especially as, in today's global society, one can earn money in one country, while taking advantage of home comforts (and creating an effective demand for these comforts) in another.

There is no quick fix for the above-mentioned circumstances: they reflect the problems of the quality of Russian society and its limited capacity for modernization, not to mention its ability to make an innovative breakthrough. It is not only time that is required to remedy this situation, but also the political will to implement institutional reforms.

## Scenarios and traps

The forecast of social and economic performance until 2030, prepared in 2012 by the Ministry of Economic Development, offered three scenarios: conservative, innovative and forced (targeted).

The conservative scenario implied inertial growth at a slowing pace of 2.7–3.1 per cent. The growth was based on the competitive advantages in the commodity sector, while the high-technology and medium–high-technology industries still lagged behind. It was anticipated that macroeconomic stability would be ensured through conservative fiscal policies. Modernization had to rely on imports of technology. Accordingly, innovation activity should mainly focus on the energy and raw materials industries.

The innovative scenario complemented the conservative one with increased diversification of production and exports, based on institutional and industrial modernization. The emphasis here was put on improving the investment climate, fostering entrepreneurship and significantly improving the quality of public services and the efficiency of public administration. It also stressed the development of transport infrastructure and a number of Russia's traditional technological industries (the aviation and space industry, nuclear technology, space-related services, etc.). The state had to implement modernization of the social infrastructure to ensure the dynamic development of human capital. Budget policy would apparently remain conservative, and GDP growth was about 4 per cent.

The third, forced scenario was based primarily on a structural manoeuvre, where the rate of gross accumulation of equity capital would be raised up to 30–33 per cent of GDP (from about 20 per cent). It meant the increased use of national savings and increased inflow of foreign capital – up to 6 per cent of GDP. Public expenditure on production and transport infrastructure would be significantly raised. It was assumed that exports would be diversified, with a tenfold increase in exports of machinery and equipment by 2030, but the share of exports in GDP would decline from 27 per cent to 19 per cent. Consumer imports would decrease significantly. In addition, this scenario assumed a breakthrough in the demographic trend and an increase in the population, including people of working age. Of course, this scenario was fraught with macroeconomic risks, as it was based on a steady budget deficit, the growth of public debt and a current account deficit. As noted by the forecast's authors, this would increase the vulnerability of the country to external shocks (and these shocks would come soon – in 2014).

The fact that there were three scenarios for economic policy that were designed to implement major structural reforms and achieve a modernization breakthrough was not simply logical, but also had deep roots in the Russian economic history of the twentieth century. We mean the economic and political battles and practical experience of the 1920s and 1980s, and, in both cases, the Soviet leadership faced serious structural challenges, not only at the national level, but also on a global scale, and had to respond to them.

It was in the 1920s that the prospects of industrialization and the ways to achieve it, while preserving market institutions in the USSR, became a topical issue. Three different approaches to meet this challenge were developed, and the future demonstrated that they were fundamentally incompatible.[1]

*First*, industrialization through the development of the agricultural sector would deliver resources that would gradually be transformed into industrial investments. It was a model of organic growth based on the so-called genetic methodology of planning (reliance on the extrapolation of existing trends in the growth of peasant households). The supporters of this theory included Nikolai Kondratiev, Nikolai Makarov, Leonid Shanin, Albert Weinstein and other economists, who were mainly grouped around the Ministry of Finance (Narkomfin) and the Institute of Conjuncture. Grigory Sokolnikov, who headed the Ministry of Finance, supported this group. He was concerned about maintaining the fiscal and monetary balance. The essence of the model was to use revenue from agriculture (including exports) as a source of demand for industrial output – to accumulate the necessary resources for investments in industrial growth.

The *second* model assumed a more active industrial policy, which, however, did not imply any serious macroeconomic imbalances, but included more active institutional transformations – that is, greater shifts in the socio-economic structure of society. The main idea of the model was a combination of genetic and teleological approaches to planning; it assumed a more active financial policy to speed up the growth of industrial production. One can include Vladimir Bazarov, Abram Ginzburg and the prominent politician Nikolai Bukharin among the supporters of this model. This course can be defined as balanced industrialization.

And *third*, there was a policy of forced industrialization, the supporters of which stated that a balanced budget was now not needed and blamed controversy over the budget as being a 'numbers game'. Radical structural changes here were based on a sharp, forced reallocation of funds from consumption to accumulation, from agriculture to industry. This involved a fundamental institutional change in all sectors of the economy, as well as radical macroeconomic destabilization. Evgeny Preobrazhensky developed the theory of this model, Valerian Kuibyshev put it into practice, and Joseph Stalin was the political leader who included it in his economic programme. It is well known that it was this 'forced' model that eventually prevailed and was implemented by exceptionally stringent methods. It was at that time that the famous words, which explain the political essence of this model, were uttered: "It is better to stand for high rates of growth than to sit (in jail) for low ones".

These three approaches are also well known from the experience with the economic policy of the 1980s. In fact, they repeat the models known as 'stagnation', 'reconstruction' ('perestroika') and 'acceleration'. Stagnation meant continued economic development based on favourable external economic factors, with expanding imports of consumer goods and production means. Reconstruction put the emphasis on institutional reforms, activation of human capital (through an anti-alcohol campaign, publicity, increased self-management of enterprises and workforces, and the development of cooperative and individual entrepreneurship). Acceleration implied a structural manoeuvre aimed at enhancing the rate of GDP accumulation, while reducing the share of consumption, as a basis for the growth of investment and technological modernization. The last two approaches were accompanied by massive forign and domestic borrowings, initially for investment in technology imports, and then increasingly for purchasing food.

The macroeconomic risks of this policy were obvious, as the very beginning of structural and institutional manoeuvres coincided with a sharp decline in energy prices, which at that time were the foundation of the stability of the Soviet economy. The Soviet system soon collapsed.

The year 2012 was not a turning point in the development of the Russian and global economy, but nobody expected this. It was a time for the accumulation of resources (technologies and institutions) to shape the post-crisis world – the new geopolitical and geo-economic balances.

But, it became clear again that global instability and macroeconomic risks do not mitigate the importance of modernization – the central point of any economic policy debate. And, the key challenge of this policy is how to provide consistency and integrity in modernization. In fact, fivefold modernization should be implemented, including in technological, economic, social, military and political areas.

## Note

1   See: Erlich 1960.

## References

Erlich, A. (1960). *The Soviet Industrialization Debate, 1924–1928*. Cambridge, MT: Harvard University Press.

# 16 Economic policy of 2013

Reconstruction or acceleration?

In 2013, Russia entered a new phase of socio-economic development. This year marked the end of the period of explosive growth, which had lasted for almost 12 years (1999–2012) and which was based on recovery trends and patterns. The 2009 recession did not cancel this growth model, but, on the contrary, extended it for the period necessary to return to the pre-crisis level. Now, the issue of a new model has come into play, as the pace of economic growth has fallen to an unprecedented low, and this inhibition can no longer be explained solely or even predominantly by external factors.

The problem faced by the country in 2013 was clear and challenging: at the time when major world economies witnessed a turning point in overcoming the crisis, Russia was clearly just starting to enter it. Things were not so simple of course. The crisis in the West remained severe, the effects of the anti-crisis fight were still evident, and the macroeconomic situation had not become any easier. One must also note the slowdown in China, with all that it implies for the global economy. Nevertheless, the change in trend was obvious, which was mostly evident in the increase in economic growth (see Table A.2).

The developed world once again demonstrated its resilience and strategic effectiveness. The US was again the driving force behind the overcoming of the global crisis, and the economic power of Germany laid *the foundation for overcoming the crisis in Europe.*

## Outlines of Russia's socio-economic development

Amid the situation in the developed world, Russia looked stable in 2013, from a formal, macroeconomic perspective (see Table A.1). The economy was growing, albeit at a decelerating pace, the budget balance was maintained, debt was low, employment was high, inflation was under control. However, a development trend such as this cannot help but raise concerns.

There are two circumstances that mark a fundamental change in the situation, compared with the development of Russia over the previous 12 years (after 2000).

The first is the rapid deceleration in economic growth, which, in 2013, was below the average world level (1.5 per cent of GDP in Russia against almost 3 per cent as the world average). It was a situation unprecedented in the previous 12 years, with the exception of 2009. But, that year, deep recession was the result of an external shock, it was short and it was quickly neutralized by the government.

In 2013, the situation looked different. The global economy had emerged from the crisis, and its growth rates were increasing, whereas the situation in Russia turned out to be opposite to the global trend. Of course, one can give examples of other BRICS countries in which economic growth also slowed down, but it does not look convincing from either an economic or political point of view. In 2013, the issue of economic growth became the top priority in the discussion about economic policy, and below we will look at this more closely.

The second major problem was the increase in budgetary tension. Since 1999, the excess of revenues actually received over those planned in the budget had been a tradition in the Russian budget process. This was the result of rapidly rising oil prices and higher inflation compared with the parameters included in the budget. The opposition was constantly accusing the government of poor budget planning, but everyone understood that this approach created an additional reserve of stability, which meant that the superprofits could be used to resolve, not only economic, but also sociopolitical, problems.

That year, this reserve was over. Oil prices, which remained at an exceptionally high level in 2013, stopped growing and even began to decline in real terms. Although inflation was slightly higher than forecast, it was increasingly approaching the budgetary target, and, with a fully-fledged introduction of inflation targeting, this source of additional national revenue faded away. Finally, lower economic growth automatically meant lower tax revenue, which could be partly compensated by an increase in revenues from income tax (primarily associated with the growth of salaries in the public sector).

Against this backdrop, the Russian economy demonstrated a number of trends that are important in terms of the country's medium-term development.

## *The problem of modernization*

Productivity grew slowly, which was evidenced by the high level of employment. However, a structural crisis is a time when modernization shifts must be significantly intensified.

A comparison with the sectoral structure of the first half of *pre-crisis* 2008 illustrates these problems (see Table A.3). In comparison with the pre-crisis period of 2008, the volume of industrial production in 2013 reached 104.5 per cent (data for the 12 months against the same period in 2008). This excess was achieved owing to the growth in mining, chemical production and production of transport means and food. The majority of processing sectors had not reached the level of 2008. Moreover, according to the 2013 results, production of investment goods was even further from reaching the pre-crisis volumes than it was in 2012.

The determinant of such a vector of industrial development is the dynamics of domestic demand for industrial products. Producers of investment goods were actively recovering during the period between Q1 2010 and Q2 2012, showing two-digit growth rates. This growth took place amid the increasing recovery of investment activities: investment in fixed capital during this period grew at moderate rates – nearly 10 per cent in annual terms. But, after Q3 2012, investment activities began to slow down, which was accompanied by a fall in the production of investment goods. It is important to note that the majority of these producers started to reduce production prior to their achieving pre-crisis volumes. According to the results of 10 months of 2013, production of machines and equipment was 25 per cent lower than the pre-crisis level, electrical equipment dropped by 16 per cent, and construction materials dropped by 8 per cent.

## *Employment*

Employment was kept at a high level. Unemployment remained low, and, after a certain increase in Q1 2013 (5.8 per cent), amounted to 5.4 per cent at the end of the year. It is an extremely low level for post-communist Russia (the absolute minimum of 5.1 per cent was registered in October 2012), as well as compared with other leading countries in the world. Among other important parameters, one should take into account the following: wages growth in the public sector and continued growth of income in relation to productivity; a parallel increase in the number of advertised vacancies; increased revenues from individual income tax and lower revenues from corporate income tax and value-added tax (VAT); and growth of contributions to the Pension Fund and other social off-budgetary funds.

Low unemployment is, of course, an important factor in social stability, especially in a political system based on democratic elections. However, a high level of employment in the absence of significant natural population growth is poorly compatible with another key task – creating 25 million new, high-skilled jobs.

Labour-market behaviour has been standard for the past 20 years. Employers did not want to reduce employment in times of crisis. But, there was also a new phenomenon: maintaining high employment and a slowdown in growth rates were accompanied by an increase in wages. This can be explained by high wage payments in social sectors in accordance with the Decree of the President of Russia, "On the measures to implement the state social policy" (dated 7 May 2012), as well as the ongoing reduction in working-age employees, which increased pressure on the labour market and made it grow (in terms of the level of employment and wages).

## *Social focus and financial strain*

One important characteristic of the present Russian economy is the increase in the share of wages, with a reduction in the share of profit, in GDP. In Marxist political economics, this is a classic problem of the correlation between labour and surplus value ($m/v$). In other words, in socialist terminology, the balance between labour and capital shifts towards labour. The system becomes more socially oriented, but also less investment-attractive. This is reflected in the structure of taxes, characterized by growth of revenues from individual income tax, with a reduction in the collection of corporate income tax and VAT.

During 2013, the growth of the Russian economy was still largely determined by the factors of consumer demand supported by an increase in wages and consumer lending. Wage growth steadily exceeded GDP growth and labour productivity (Figure 16.1). With the increase of GDP in 2013 of only 1.5 per cent, the growth in real disposable income amounted to about 4 per cent; the growth of wages was more than 5 per cent, and the volume of loans to individuals increased by 28 per cent. As a result, the volume of retail trade grew by almost 4 per cent, and the volume of paid services increased by 2.5 per cent.

However, the growth of retail turnover slowed down, although it was still higher than GDP growth, which in turn was owing to slower growth in real disposable income and retail lending. Figure 16.2 shows the periods when consumption was noticeably stimulated by bank lending or an increase in wages.

Wages exceeded 50 per cent of GDP, which not only strengthens the consumer character of the economy, but could also indicate an approaching crisis. In 1997–8 and 2007–8, when the share of wages exceeded 50 per cent, Russia entered into a crisis: either the currency was devalued, or production volumes declined, or both happened together.

Alongside the rise in personal income, the enterprises' financial situation deteriorated: the balanced profit of major activities decreased almost by 20 per cent. Profit is one of the main sources of investment for an average Russian

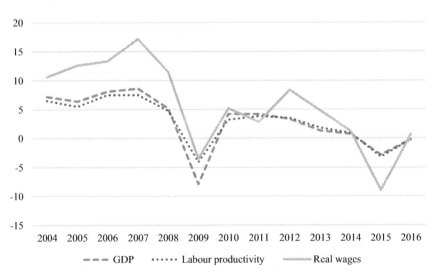

*Figure 16.1* Growth rates of GDP, labour productivity and real wages
*Source*: Federal State Statistics Service

*Economic policy of 2013* 165

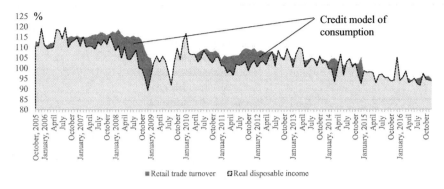

*Figure 16.2* Growth rates of real disposable income and retail turnover (year on year)
Source: Federal State Statistics Service

enterprise, and profits in the production and investment demand sectors declined significantly more than in the consumer demand and trade sectors (see Table A.4). The share of profit in GDP is qute low (Figures 16.3 and 16.4). Moreover, since the beginning of the global crisis, there has been a trend towards increasing the share of one's own funds in investments, while reducing borrowings and budget funds (the latter is true for regional budget investments). In fact, it resembled the situation in the early 2000s.

As 50–75 per cent of investments in today's Russia were financed from profits of enterprises, and about 60 per cent of profit was generated in the oil and trade sectors, the decline in the share of profit meant fewer investment opportunities, mostly in non-primary industries.

*Figure 16.3* Gross profit and mixed income, wages of employees
Source: Federal State Statistics Service

166 *The Russian version of the global crisis*

*Figure 16.4* Gross operating surplus and mixed income (per cent GDP, 2015)
Sources: Eurostat, Federal State Statistics Service

## The growth of wages in the public sector

The growth of wages in the public sector became an important factor of the social and economic policy of 2012. There was a substantial increase in payments to military employees, law enforcement agencies and federal civil employees, and, in 2013, the Decree of the President of Russia on raising the wages of employees in the education and health care systems came into effect. Thus, the authorities sought to increase the attractiveness of human capital sectors, implementing their priority role in the country's socio-economic policy. However, it was assumed that wage growth would be accompanied by a profound institutional transformation of the relevant sectors, with highly qualified specialists being attracted to them.

## The budgetary situation

The budgetary situation in 2013 looked quite favourable, especially against the backdrop of a fiscal crisis in most developed countries. The federal budget was balanced, the debt, although somewhat raised, remained exceptionally low (10 per cent of GDP, of which external debt accounted for less than 2.5 per cent of GDP). The partial change of the budgetary rule concerned only the fall-out budget revenues and, in this sense, it did not yet create additional risks in terms of non-controlled escalating budget commitments. However, abandoning the principle of income balancing, with a focus on a multi-year average oil price, eased the fiscal policy and later led to a further increase in the non-oil deficit of the budget. The non-oil budget deficit, after rising from 6.7 per cent of GDP in 2008 to 13.8 per cent in 2009, remained precariously high.

Therefore, one cannot ignore the problem of the high dependence of welfare and stability on oil prices (a parameter that is outside the national government's control), as well as the habit of living in conditions of growing revenues, which have occurred over the past decade. The stagnation of oil prices and their reduction aggravated the struggle for the resource, which 'suddenly' became rare.

## Regional finances

Regional finances were in a more difficult position. In 2013, there was a significant reduction in income, and it was impossible to quickly and adequately reduce expenditure, and these factors explain the increase in subnational borrowing.

According to the Federal Treasury, the decline in the total income of consolidated budgets of regions in 2013 was more than 5 per cent in real terms, compared with 2012. Tax revenues shrank by 3.8 per cent, and transfers from the federal budget decreased by 11.5 per cent.

The general reduction in tax revenues was due to the dynamics of the income tax revenues, which declined by 19.8 per cent during this period. The reduction in total taxes received by regional budgets could have been larger, had it not been for the growth of revenues from other taxes, notably from personal income tax, which grew by 4.2 per cent. However, the expenditures of consolidated regional budgets over a period of 10 months in 2013 declined by only 0.8 per cent in real terms. As a result of lower revenues, and with the need to keep expenditure at a certain level, the subnational authorities were forced to increase the volume of borrowing: the regional debt (excluding municipal budgets) for 2013 rose by more than 10 per cent in nominal terms. At the end of 2013, the total regional debt reached about 2.5 per cent of GDP, or 22.8 per cent of the tax and non-tax revenues of subfederal budgets. However, there was a trend towards stable growth of the debt.

Over the previous 5 years there had been an increase in regional social spending, with a decrease in investment expenditure. The share of social spending in the total expenditure of the consolidated budgets of the constituent entities had increased by 10 per cent since 2009, reaching more than 62 per cent in 2013. Spending on housing and transport (they are more associated with investment than other items) declined to approximately 21 per cent (see Table A.5).

## *Monetary policy*

Monetary policy in 2013 remained conservative and focused on a transition to inflation targeting. Disinflation occupied the foreground, and lower interest rates were only possible on this basis and as long as this issue was resolved. Contrary to common criticism of the conservative approach adopted by the Central Bank, the approach was quite justified. The poor credit history of the national currency and the continuing risks of high inflation meant that the monetary authorities had to be extremely cautious in increasing the money supply – all the more so as stagflation might have been a significant problem in the face of a slowing economy.

Inflation at 6.5 per cent exceeded the Central Bank's targets and remained a major problem of monetary policy. According to this parameter, Russia radically differs from most of the leading countries of the world (primarily the G20 states), for which deflation is a more dangerous problem. The continued high level of inflation is associated with both macroeconomic and institutional factors: the former includes stimulating household demand, and the latter concerns the growth of tariffs of natural monopolies.

Finally, an important feature of 2013 was the 10 per cent rouble devaluation that is explained by both internal and external factors. The internal ones include the slowdown of the Russian economy and the business climate, which led to the withdrawal of capital from the country. However, it would be incorrect to limit the explanation to this factor alone; the global process is no less important: the increasing recovery of the United States and the easing crisis in Europe led to the 'flight-to-quality' (outflow of hard currency from developing to developed markets), which is a characteristic feature of such situations. The money flows into the dollar and the euro. It is an absolutely inevitable process, very well known to the markets of the past 50 years.

It would be a mistake to consider devaluation only as one factor in reviving the national economy and stimulating import substitution, as was the case after the 1998 crisis. In 2013, the positive effects of the weakened rouble became very limited: there was an increase in exporters' revenues, as well as a certain increase in the competitiveness of commodity producers, but it had no impact on the structure of exports (i.e. it did not reduce the share of raw materials and energy) and did not stimulate technological exports. To radically improve import substitution, devaluation must have been much deeper – not in percentages but in times (as in 1998). Moreover, devaluation in the present situation will punish those who are involved in technological chains of cooperation and who depend on supplies of imported components or equipment. In 2013, 65 per cent of imports were components and investment goods – that is, the devaluation of the rouble negatively influenced the pace of economic growth and led to a decline in GDP (at least in the first stage).

## *Regulation of the financial markets*

In 2013, significant changes occurred in the regulation of the financial markets. The Central Bank became a single regulator. This decision looked natural, because it relied on the general trend to strengthen financial regulation.

A new development at the time was that the Bank of Russia increased its activities to clean up the banking system. Not only did insolvent banks lose their licences, but also those involved in illegal financial transactions. However, these actions posed a certain risk associated with provoking banking panic, which could have led to the outflow of deposits from private banks into state-owned banks. In terms of the strategic objectives of development of the national bank system, this would not have been a good result. It would have been reasonable, in addition to clearing up the banking system, to conduct measures to stimulate the consolidation of banks, encouraging mergers between healthy banks.

## Problems of economic growth

The main development of Russian socio-economic life in 2013 was a significant slowdown in growth. The country faced a decline in investment activities, virtually zero growth in industrial production, and a slowing consumer demand.

The slowdown was a result of several factors. The external economic environment played a certain role. Recession in the EU – the main external trading partner of Russia – could not help but have a negative impact on the dynamics of the Russian economy. Another factor was the particular features of the investment cycle within the country. Major state-run companies play an important role in investment processes in Russia, and, in 2012–13, it was these companies that completed major investment projects, which affected growth rates accordingly.

However, it was factors not related to the economic environment that were most important. The *braking mechanism* was activated in Russia. This mechanism was associated with the exhaustion of the growth model that had existed since 1999, and it was of a purely institutional nature.

As we mentioned above, the 1999–2011 growth model relied on the rapid increase in demand (internal and external), which was satisfied by significant unused production capacities. In fact, it was highly fortunate that the possibilities to strengthen internal demand (owing to the extremely low starting level that was formed after the post-communist transformation) coincided with the dynamic development of the world economy, which formed the external demand. Recovery growth, and certainly in a favourable external environment, is almost insensitive to the investment climate – the main task was to ensure social and political stability. However, recovery growth has two important and unpleasant features: it diminishes over time and it is finite. The exhaustion of reserves leads to a slowdown, which can only be compensated for by favourable conditions for investment activities and the emergence of conditions for new growth.[1]

The exhaustion of the post-transformation (recovery) growth model had been exhausted, but it had some internal reserves, including retained high oil prices and accumulated financial reserves. In addition, a certain role was played by the 7 per cent fall in GDP in 2009, which resulted in some recovery of production reserves, which had been exhausted again. The slowdown started in the second half of 2012, when Russian GDP surpassed the pre-crisis level (i.e. the recovery reserves were exhausted), and export growth virtually stopped.

As existing experience shows, a recovery period may last longer than predicted by economists'. Therefore, at some stage, when a forecast is made that the rate should start to fall, but it does not decrease significantly, politicians begin to believe that high growth in the recovery period is an inevitable result of their ruling and will continue indefinitely. But, it is quite possible that an economic crisis will begin amid this confidence.

Let us denote the following basic elements of the braking mechanism in Russian economy of the 2010s.

The first element is domination of consumer demand (wages) to the detriment of investments (profits). This is demonstrated by the rising share of wages and declining share of profits, as well as by the advanced growth of wages compared with the growth of GDP and productivity. The level of savings remains low – 21.8 per cent over the past 5 years. However, for the past half a century, a steady dynamic growth has been demonstrated by countries with share investments of no less than 25 per cent of GDP, with investments in education and health reaching about 7–8 per cent of GDP. Bridging the gap in labour productivity requires a higher level of investment, and the consumer growth model operates at the cost of a certain decline in the share of investment.

Second, low efficiency of markets impedes the inflow of labour and capital to the most developed sectors and brings the risk of the preservation of the existing economic structure. The low level of competition in domestic markets is associated with adverse conditions of doing business, the existence of an excessive non-market or monopoly sector of the economy, as well as an excessive public sector; low efficiency of the labour market is against a background of high and ever rising labour costs.

Third is low efficiency of state regulation, including the lack of an institutional and macroeconomic environment for long-term investments, as well as the lack of efficiency in the use of public spending against the background of a high level of this spending – all this also brings macroeconomic risks.

Fourth, a low level of engagement in world trade (excluding raw materials) is an obstacle to the expansion of non-commodity exports and the integration of Russian firms into international value chains, which also means a high level of tariffs.

All this suggested that Russia fell into the 'middle income trap'. This problem may occur when a country, having reached a high level of well-being, faces limitations in terms of both the cost of the workforce (already high) and institutions (they are not good yet). That is, a country is not able to compete, either with developed economies that have highly skilled workforces and export technological innovations, or with economies with low incomes, low wages and cheap industrial goods. The key problems of the Russian economy now concern the inefficient use of labour and capital – the absence of conditions for increasing the share of products and services with high added value, which turns out to be a critical factor of the background of relatively high costs.

This situation requires a fundamental reshaping of institutions – those formal and informal rules under which economic development is taking place. There have been many discussions about institutional reforms in recent years. However, they remained only wishes, until economic dynamics showed definitely that the existing institutional environment was exhausted. Of course, one can try to accelerate without changing the institutional environment; however, such a policy is unlikely to give a stable result.

The last conclusion brings us to the question of the risks that may get in the way of the development of the Russian economy and society in the coming period.

## Short- and medium-term socio-economic risks

First of all, it is necessary to emphasize the risks associated with the formation of the economic growth model, or, more precisely, the risks of an inadequate response to braking. In our view, there are two types of risk, both of an opposing nature: passive acceptance of the current pace of development as historically inevitable, on the one hand, and acceptance of artificial (in fact, inadequate) measures to turn the tide, on the other hand.

In 2013, there were significant changes in the official assessments of the prospects for socio-economic development. Previous economic forecasts by the government were more like a menu approach and included the desired (sometimes even fantastic) development scenarios, but, from 2013, the official forecast had been made mostly on the basis of extrapolation of existing trends, that is, it almost completely excluded institutional reforms. The forecast included 3 per cent economic growth until 2030, which is much less than the 5 per cent growth rate that is desirable, according to official statements made over the past several years. This is partly true, because a forecast, by definition, cannot include any changes in economic policy that have not yet occurred. Thus, there is a great danger such a forecast will be fulfilled, low growth rates will be accepted at the political level and institutional reforms will be abandoned.

The opposite (and potentially more dangerous) risk is of choosing a course for a formal acceleration – increasing economic growth without ensuring quality growth. An acceleration policy comes against the backdrop of a weakening fiscal and monetary policy, particularly in the case of a rejection of the 'fiscal rule'. A conservative macroeconomic course is always subject to sharp criticism, and its supporters are in the minority and were opposed by the united forces of representatives of all sectors and industries. Arguments in favour of increasing budget spending, lowering interest rates and monetary manipulation are always very spectacular and attractive, because their authors believe (quite sincerely) that they will be able to ensure high rates of economic growth. Alexey Kudrin was not the first who was harshly criticized for his reluctance to understand the needs of producers, narrow 'book-keeping' opinions and a desire to senselessly save money. Before him, similar accusations were made against Sergei Witte, Vladimir Kokovtsov and Gregory Sokolnikov, who, at various times, headed Russia's Finance Ministry and who provided shining results – a stable currency and economic growth. Their resignation entailed heavy turbulence (not only financial and economic, but also political). It is clear that a conservative policy would be difficult in a country with many pressing socio-economic problems. Such a policy is particularly difficult to carry out when the government has accumulated large monetary reserves. But, this policy has always provided steady growth, whereas the policy of rampant fiscal expansion has always resulted in severe crises – whether it be the 'big leap' of the 1930s or the 'acceleration' of 1985–8.

The economic policies of the last Soviet decade are very instructive in hindsight. Today's macroeconomic realities surprisingly resemble the period of the 1970s–1980s: the oil price in those times was at about the same level; the USSR grew at a moderate rate of about 3 per cent per year; the Soviet budget was balanced, but all proceeds from the export of hydrocarbons were used to cover budget expenditures; the country was actively building gas pipelines; prices were stable, although the trade deficit was increasingly making itself felt (this is an indicator of inflation hidden under fixed prices); external debt was small; employment was guaranteed, albeit with low labour productivity; and the political system of the USSR was exceptionally rigid, unable to respond flexibly to the emergence of new global challenges (technological, economic or political).

All this was in sharp contrast to the situation in Western countries, which faced a deep structural crisis of the 1970s, named the "third phasis of the general crisis of capitalism" in official documents of the Communist Party of the Soviet Union.

At that time, it seemed that the Soviet economy was growing steadily, amid the crisis of the West. In fact, the market democracies were going through structural and technological modernization and they were forming the basis for a leap forward, whereas the Soviet Union was preserving its economic structure, becoming a hostage to fluctuations in commodity prices uncontrolled by the national government. As was revealed later, by the end of the 1970s, the crisis was already coming to an end, a new paradigm of economic policy was being formed, based on reducing the regulatory role of the state (deregulation), and, most

Economic policy of 2013  173

consistently and successfully, this policy was implemented by the governments of Margaret Thatcher (from 1979) and Ronald Reagan (from 1981).

By 1985, the Western economic growth rates exceeded those in the Soviet Union, and the lag of the system based on central planning was clear to all. The new dynamic Soviet leadership, which came to power in 1985, tried to turn the tide through aggressive fiscal stimulation. It started to inject investments at the cost of increasing soverign debt (which doubled between 1985 and 1990) and the budget deficit (which appeared in 1985 and started to grow rapidly). The growth rate really grew and almost caught up with the US debt (though remained lower than in the UK), but it lasted only for 2 years – 1987 and 1988. The system collapsed under the weight of financial problems – the economic downturn began in 1989 and lasted for almost a decade (see Figures 16.5 and 16.6).

Of course, the economic system of post-communist Russia is substantially different and much more resilient. Currency reserves are stable and high. Public debt is much lower than that of the USSR. Russia does not depend on the supply of food to the extent the Soviet Union did.

The existence of private property fundamentally changes the situation. The political system is undoubtedly much more flexible than in Soviet times.

However, the analogy to the situation of 30 years ago is also obvious. The structural crisis in the developed countries is gradually being overcome. The United States is showing rapid technological innovation, which will also extend to Europe. The recovery of growth in developed countries usually gives rise to a popular Russian idea "to catch up and overtake", and, usually, at any cost. The problem is how to avoid populism and macroeconomic destabilisation while fighting for high growth rates.

Budget and cash incentives, in addition to the dangerous consequences described above, can drive the country into the trap of stagflation – low or negative growth,

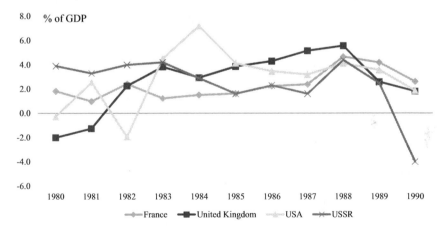

*Figure 16.5* GDP growth: USSR, USA, United Kingdom, France (1980–90; * produced national income)

Source: IMF, World Bank

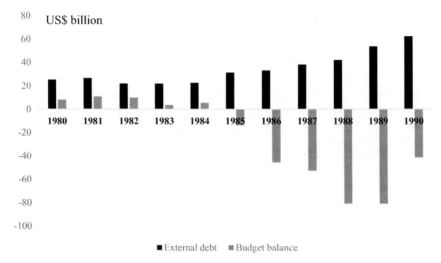

*Figure 16.6* National income, budget balance, external debt of the USSR (in actual prices, 1980–90)

*Source*: CIA Factbook

with persistently high inflation. The way out of stagflation is very difficult and painful. Retaining significant inflation is a feature that significantly distinguishes today's Russia from most other countries. And so, here one cannot apply the measures so popular in Western countries since 2008: low interest rates and heavy infusions of money. But thus policy is unacceptable from macroeconomic point of view.

*The stimulus spending policy appeared ineffective and risky.* As it was shown, growth of effective demand without raising productivity and competitiveness results in the demand going into inflation and imports.[2] In fact, we witnessed this when we could not achieve acceptable inflation of below 5 per cent, and imports grew faster than exports. In a country with high demand and low productivity, there was a distinct tendency of the rich to buy goods from rich countries and the poor from poor countries. As a result, it is mainly the sectors of raw materials and services that were internally competitive, while all other goods were imported.

The budgetary system was still exposed to *the risk of rising uncontrolled indebtedness of the regions*. It required special institutional solutions limiting (or even prohibiting) the deficit financing of regional budgets. The risks are even more exacerbated if the federal government has no superprofits that can be quickly used in case of social tensions.

Attention also should be drawn to *the risks associated with wages growth in the public sector*. The tasks of this growth are the fundamental upgrading of personnel, increasing the attractiveness of these sectors to highly skilled specialists. However, a serious problem in this field is the lack of synchronization between the institutional reforms and the growth of wages, and this results in the preservation of inefficiency, as existing personnel are not interested in giving up places to newcomers, and newcomers are not interested in coming owing to the dominance of old principles in organization of these sectors.

There are also macroeconomic risks in the rise in wages. In fact, the public sector begins to set the level and dynamics of wages in the economy, competing with the private sector. In an environment where overcoming the crisis requires greater efficiency, including in wages, the economy receives a signal about the feasibility of raising costs. Public sectors do not exist in isolation from the others, and their wage dynamics have an impact on other industries. By 2015, the public sector ceased to be non-competitive by its attractiveness for employees. Taking into account the employment guarantees, intensity of work and level of wages, budget organizations (along with state corporations and bodies of state administration) are quite attractive for a large part of the population. This results in problems of competition of the public sector with the private sector for labour, which adversely affects the competitiveness of the national economy.

The dramatic increase in the attractiveness of the public sector became one of the major obstacles to private business. This is one of the factors of the investment climate that is undervalued at present. The times when the public sector was uncompetitive for the highly skilled workforce are gone. Now the public sector (in a broad sense, i.e. including state-owned companies) has become extremely competitive in terms of attracting employees. To some extent, the situation resembles the situation on the financial market in the mid 1990s, when short-term state bonds (GKOs), thanks to their yield, had pulled investments from the private sector.

There were also *risks of rising unemployment*. Traditional Russian business reacted to the economic problems by preserving employment, lowering wages and a transition to part-time employment. Such measures had hampered modernization possibilities, but helped to maintain social and political stability. There was a possibility that the situation could change this time. Business tends to adopt the model of employment more accepted in market economies, and, in the autumn–winter of 2013, the government signalled that it was not going to impose political restrictions on lay-offs, with the purpose of promoting modernization.

Owing to possible market changes, another *risk factor in 2013 was a high and increasing level of consumer lending*. The accumulated debt of Russians is low compared with developed market economies – a little more than RUB10 trillion (13.5 per cent of GDP).

However, in view of the significantly higher interest rates (an average of 17.5 per cent per annum) and short terms of credit (the average term is less than 3 years), servicing bank debt (the cost of the entire loan portfolio) accounts for approximately 12 per cent of disposable income in Russia (in the United States, this indicator is about 11 per cent, with a debt of about 80 per cent of GDP). The debt burden was already higher than in the USA, with a much lower amount of debt (see Figure 16.7).

Among the *institutional risks*, one should also mention the often-changing 'rules of the game', even if they change for the better. When the law enforcement practice

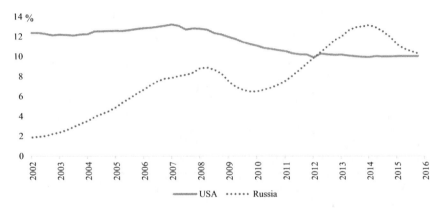

*Figure 16.7* Household debt servicing compared with disposable income
Source: IMF

changes (not the law itself), and a business practice that had previously been normal turns out to be illegal, it can seriously affect the willingness of entrepreneurs and members of the public to create new businesses and organizations, especially as, in Russia, private initiative and entrepreneurial spirit have always been perceived with suspicion and mistrust – both in the nineteenth and twenty-first centuries.

## Notes

1 The problems of recovery growth, its opportunities and limitations were well studied by the economists of the 1920s, and the practice of that time demonstrated the exceptional political vulnerability of this growth model. Its exhaustion results in a political crisis, with painful consequences both for economists and for society. See: Bazarov 2014, vol. 1: 356–83; vol. 2: 331–2.
2 See: Vedev and Kosarev, 2012: 50–65.

## References

Bazarov, V. (2014). *Izbrannye proizvedeniya* [Selected works], 2 vols. Moscow: Delo.
Vedev, A. and Kosarev, A. (2012). "Nekotorye kolichestvennye otsenki vozdejstviya institutsionalnyh ogranichenij na ekonomicheskij rost v Rossii" [Some quantitative estimates of the impact of institutional constraints on economic growth in Russia], *Ekonomicheskaya Politika*, no. 1.

# 17 Economic policy of 2014

## A new frontier and old challenges

The key characteristic of the economic, social and political development of Russia in 2014 was a combination and juxtaposition of several crises. In this case, we do not mean a crisis with one simple meaning (e.g. economic), but several trends and developments, each of which goes beyond a sustainable, inertial trend and significantly complicates decision-making.

**Juxtaposed crises**

One can observe the following crises and problems, which had emerged in Russia in by 2014:

- the continued global structural crisis resulting in profound changes in the economic and political life of leading countries and the emergence of new geo-economic and geopolitical balances; in Russia, this crisis is lagging behind;
- the crisis of the 2000s growth model of Russia, based on increasing demand (including consumption), which was caused by the availability of unused production capacities and the long rise in prices for Russian export products;
- a worsening geopolitical situation after deteriorating relations with Ukraine followed by sharp conflict with most developed countries;
- the external shock from sanctions imposed on Russia, particularly in the financial sphere;
- the external economic shock as a result of a fall in oil prices, which are the main source of income in the Russian budget;
- the currency crisis as a result of the dual external shock (most notably due to the fall in oil prices, and partly due to the financial sanctions);
- a cyclical crisis associated with the decrease in investment activity.

Each of these problems can be solved within the framework of a responsible economic policy. But, the fact that they are juxtaposed created additional difficulties, as it was necessary to take, not just diverse, but sometimes diametrically opposed, anti-crisis measures.

These crises affected the situation in Russia in different ways. The global crisis led to structural shifts in the world economy and politics and demanded the development of a new growth model for Russia. Starting in 2012, the fall in the growth rate once again demonstrated the need for structural and institutional reforms.[1] Geopolitical factors (including sanctions), no matter how important they are, play a secondary role, exacerbating the difficulties, but to some extent creating additional opportunities for anti-crisis manoeuvring and institutional renewal.

The internal and external circumstances led to a number of significant new challenges and strengthened the mutual influence of political and economic processes. Politics starts to dominate over economics, which is a characteristic feature of crisis periods and transformations.

## Economic situation in 2014

What were the main features of the economic situation in 2014, which influenced the medium-term development of the country (see Table A.1 and Figure A.1)? First and foremost was the slowdown in growth, which began as early as in 2012. The economic downturn itself is not such a big problem, if it is short. It is long-term recession and the related risks of an inadequate anti-crisis policy that could bring the real danger. An example of a type of wrong anti-crisis policy was the 'acceleration' of 1986–9, which was discussed in the previous chapter.

The year 2014 was a year of devaluation of the national currency. It would be wrong to say that the sharp devaluation of the rouble in December was the fault of the monetary authorities. The main reason for the devaluation was the structural problems of the Russian economy, which had been clear to all economists for the previous 10 years. Low diversification, the low competitiveness of many enterprises, a low level of trust in society and a background of high inflation that continued for 20 years made the Russian economy extremely sensitive towards the dynamics of oil prices and access to cheap external financing. Therefore, the isolation from external financial markets, coupled with falling oil prices, made devaluation inevitable.

The combination of said circumstances explains why the rouble turned out to be much more vulnerable than the currencies of other resource-based economies. This significantly contrasted with 2009, when rouble fluctuations were comparable with the dynamics of other currencies (Figures A.2 and A.3).

The political uncertainty became another factor that reduced business and investment activity. This led to a capital outflow comparable with that of 2009.

Influenced by the rouble devaluation, inflation accelerated to a two-digit number (11.4 per cent), and that exacerbated the economic (through interest rates) and social situation. Fighting inflation again became one of the most important tasks of the Russian economic policy.

A serious problem was caused by the de facto ban on Russian companies' access to international financial markets. This affected both the ability to raise loans (including for the refinancing of accumulated debts) and to allocate shares of Russian companies abroad. Compared with 2013, the volume of M&A (mergers and acquisitions) transactions decreased by a factor of three, and the amount of attracted syndicated loans decreased by more than a factor of four (from US$48.4 billion to

US$11.7 billion). Eurobonds attracted by companies fell from US$52.6 billion to about US$10 billion.

It is not just about the direct limitation of access to the capital markets of countries that officially declared sanctions (United States, EU, Canada, Japan). First, substitution of capital through the markets of other countries, including Asian, was problematic, because, in the globalized world, the financial institutions of third countries are very cautious about dealing with corporations affected by sanctions, being unwilling to spoil relations with the regulators of the countries that imposed them. Second, access to capital markets was getting more and more complicated, even for companies formally not affected by sanctions, as investors assessed country risks as high. Third, Russian business depended on the global environment – that is, quite unclear prospects of global growth and reduced demand for basic positions of Russian export (energy, metallurgy, etc.).

The devaluation of the rouble and limited access to financial markets, coupled with the declining investment ratings of the country and individual companies, made it difficult to pay the external debt of banks and corporations, which reached US$651 billion by early 2014 and fell to US$548 billion by 1 January 2015. Although it was a certain positive result for macroeconomic stability, in the short term, the reduction of the presence of Russian companies in global financial markets became an additional negative factor for economic growth.

Capital outflows increased significantly. It would be reasonable to compare the outflow dynamics, not only with the more stable level of 2013, but also with the crisis period of 2008–9, when capital outflows surged from Q3 2008 to Q2 2009 and amounted to US$182.6 billion, which was US$31 billion more than in 2014. However, during that period, Russian non-banking corporations could build up external assets, including direct investments. In 2008–9, these assets had grown to US$41 billion more than in 2014 – US$142 billion against US$101 billion. Capital outflow from the banking sector during the 2008–9 crisis period was US$32 billion more than for three-quarters of 2014, and, in addition to a significant redemption of external debt, banks actively built up foreign assets.

In 2014, the main cause of the increase in net capital outflow was the slowing inflow of foreign loans and investments, as well as investments in cash foreign exchange. If you take the indicators for 2013 net from the impact of Rosneft's transaction to purchase TNK-BP and from foreign loans for this purpose, the 2014 net outflow rose by US$98 billion and amounted to US$151.5 billion.

Almost all growth in foreign investments on the part of the non-banking sector was provided by the increase in investments in foreign currency cash. In 2013, according to estimates by the Bank of Russia, Russian residents' cash foreign exchange decreased by US$0.3 billion, but, in 2014, it rose to US$34.1 billion, almost the same as in 2008–9.

The growing problems in the Russian economy are demonstrated by the dynamics of wages and profit in GDP. We have already discussed the fact that, over the past 20 years, if the ratio of wages to GDP exceeded the 50 per cent level, it indicated an approaching crisis.[2] As seen in Figure A.6, the key role is played by the real exchange rate of the rouble.

Its strengthening leads to a lower share of exports in GDP (even in the face of rising oil prices) and growth in the share of labour. Under devaluation, the labour share falls, which becomes a factor in improving competitiveness and increasing the rate of exports to GDP.

At the same time, one could, in 2014, trace a number of positive features, mostly in macroeconomics, that might create grounds for sound anti-crisis measures. These include:

- a stable budget kept under control thanks to the 'budget rule';
- small public debt, especially denominated in foreign exchange;
- considerable foreign exchange reserves at the disposal of the Central Bank and the government;
- low unemployment providing social and political stability.

Russia substantially improved its position in the World Bank's Doing Business ranking. However, such an improvement would appear paradoxical, because an improvement of position in the ranking correlates with a falling growth rate, whereas, in the previous decade, the Russian economy grew rapidly amid consistent dropping of positions in the ranking. This does not mean this indicator is irrelevant, but it is also clear that economic growth is a result of the interaction of different and divergent factors.

Another positive result of 2014 was that the Central Bank demonstrated its ability to act independently, contrary to the opinion of the bulk of the economic and political elite. This concerned both the interest rates policy and the consistent work to clean up the banking sector. In 2014, the Central Bank withdrew eighty-five licences – seventy-two from banks and thirteen from non-bank credit institutions, which was a result of the disclosure of various schemes for misrepresenting balances of payment. And, this was only beginning of the purge of financial institutions, which will continue for several years.

With all the drawbacks of the decision to transfer to inflation targeting in a previously defined timeframe (by early 2015, and in fact, even a little earlier), it seemed appropriate and well timed. This helped to preserve foreign exchange reserves. The latter is especially important in comparison with the situation of 2008–9, when, in 5 months (from September 2008 to January 2009), the Bank of Russia sold about 40 per cent of its reserves (US$209 billion) to maintain the rouble exchange rate, in the face of uncertainty and a decline in oil prices. By that time, the Central Bank ensured currency stability and then accrued reserves, as long as oil prices started to rise (although not to the pre-crisis maximum). However, the flip side of this was the currency appreciation, which did not correspond to the new situation and, accordingly, inhibited structural modernization – after a rebound in 2009–10, the model of *business as usual* started to prevail once again.

## Discussions on economic policy: two models

Needless to say, economic growth continued to be a central point of economic debate. Increasing international tensions influenced this debate, which was reflected in two approaches to a growth model. Growth needs investments. In the face of limited access to external markets, special attention should be paid to internal sources of investment. There is a traditional crossroads: who should primarily support the investment – the state or private business?

The first scenario is administrative and mobilizational. A state that has given up hope concerning the willingness of businesses to invest should concentrate resources and direct them to priority sectors of the economy. This path is well known from the twentieth century. It can lead to higher growth, but, with this way, it is difficult to ensure the efficiency and global competitiveness of the national economy – at least based on the technologies of the twenty-first century. To meet the challenges of accelerated industrialization, the best thing was to rely on state budget and state banks. The sources include: taxes, accumulated reserves, government borrowing and the printing press (lending by government or by the lender of last resort). The two last sources are intertwined – state loans are ultimately financed by the Central Bank.

One of the most popular demands for the Bank of Russia was to issue loans for large investment projects (apparently approved by the state) at 'affordable' (significantly lower than inflation) interest rates. Obviously, mobilization implies intensive spending from centralized funds – if not through the budget, then through quasi-fiscal operations. It inevitably comes down to three steps: collect or print more money, give it to "properly selected" enterprises and impose foreign exchange controls in order to prevent the issued money from entering the foreign exchange market. At the next stage, this logic would inevitably lead to freezes on prices (price controls) and wages. These ideas are never voiced from the beginning, but they are inevitable component of the administrative (mobilization) scenario.

Another option is an economic policy (essentially based on liberalization) aimed at creating stimulus for the generation of private savings, their transformation into investment and, on this basis, the acceleration of economic growth. It is more difficult intellectually and organizationally, because many decisions require discussion and careful consideration. It does not give quick results, because time is needed for confidence to be generated among economic agents (businesses, employees and the state). The advantage of this approach is that it provides more consistent results and significantly reduces the amplitude of political and economic fluctuations.

The liberalization option was not popular in the context of classic catch-up industrialization in the first half of the twentieth century, but, in the 1990s and 2000s, it became widespread in different countries.

The most striking example is China after 1978, and especially after the suppression of the students' unrest in 1989, when economic sanctions were imposed by some Western countries. In spite of the fact that the Chinese Communist leadership was dominated by proponents of the mobilization, Deng Xiaoping insisted on taking steps towards consistent liberalization and expansion of private initiatives. As a result of this policy, the country has been showing rapid growth in investment and GDP since 1992.[3] There are other examples of accelerated growth through liberalization (Chile, Finland, Ireland, South Africa, Poland), but there are no similar examples within the frames of the mobilization model over the past half a century.

As each structural crisis leads to re-evaluation and revision of the regulation model, the question about the prospects of the liberal model and the possibility of returning to large-scale state interference arose in 2008, immediately after the collapse of Lehman Brothers. At first, it seemed that the crisis would result in the return of 'big government'. But soon there came warnings not to allow rough state intervention in economic life, and to avoid using the ideas of vulgar Keynesianism (crass Keynesianism). One of the first politicians to give such a warning, in early 2009, was Vladimir Putin in Davos:

> It is well known that in times of crisis the temptation to use simple and populist solutions is strong. A possible error is the excessive intervention in economic life on the part of the state, the blind faith in the omnipotence of the state. Yes, strengthening its role in the face of crisis is a natural reaction to failures in market regulation. But instead of improving market mechanisms, there occurred a temptation to maximize direct state involvement in the economy ... last century in the Soviet Union, the role of the state was absolute. That ultimately led to the total non-competitiveness of our economy, we have paid a heavy price for it. It came at a high cost. I am sure that nobody would like to repeat it.[4]

## *Mechanisms of growth*

The role of fiscal and monetary stimulus is one of the most popular topics in economic discussions. Developed countries actively use these methods afte 2008, with mixed results. Often, there are calls to use these tools in Russia. However, the macroeconomic situation in the country is radically different from that of Western states.

Unlike the developed countries, where the main challenges are high levels of debt and (or) a budget deficit with exceptionally low inflation (or even deflation), in Russia, economic deceleration is occurring under the conditions of a quite stable budget, low public debt and high inflation, which, in 2014, returned to two-digit rate. In other words, Russia faced stagflation, which could not be overcome by of quantitative easing. On the contrary, overcoming it required monetary policy to be tightened and inflation to be suppressed to levels acceptable for the renewal of economic growth, and only after that could interest rates be lowered.

Russia could not follow the path of monetary stimulation (quantitative easing), because it would result in further destabilization, high inflation and deepened recession.

The often recommended administrative lowering of policy interest rates could not solve the problem of stimulating growth either. High-interest credit resources in Russia are explained, not so much by the policy rate of the Central Bank, as by the low level of trust in economic policy, as well as in business partners. It is easy to note the gap between the Central Bank of Russia policy rate and the

*Table 17.1* Spread between credit rate and refinancing rate in some countries (2013)

| Country | Rate, % p.a. | | Spread, p.p. |
|---|---|---|---|
| | Refinancing | Credit | |
| USA | 0.75 | 3.25 | 2.50 |
| Canada | 1.25 | 3.00 | 1.75 |
| Japan | 0.30 | 1.30 | 1.00 |
| Brazil | 16.49 | 27.39 | 10.90 |
| China | 3.25 | 6.00 | 2.75 |
| India | 8.75 | 10.29 | 1.54 |
| RSA | 5.00 | 8.50 | 3.50 |
| Russia | 5.50 | 9.47 | 3.97 |

*Source*: IMF IFS Database

commercial rates used to issue loans to businesses. In Russia, it is large compared with that in other developed countries (Table 17.1).

An important factor of confidence is the stability of the national currency. In this respect, 2014 was extremely difficult for the rouble, which was under pressure from two powerful external factors: aggravation of the geopolitical situation and the dynamics of oil prices. In the midst of sanctions, combined with falling oil prices, the rouble proved to be one of the most volatile currencies, which sharply distinguishes the situation from 2008–9. In 2014, the Russian authorities repeatedly denied the possibility of imposing currency controls.

The monetary situation in Russia was significantly more complex than in the West, but the budget situation was, by contrast, more favourable, thanks to low public debt and a relatively small fiscal deficit. This seemed to create some space for fiscal stimulus. In reality, the possibility of fiscal stimulation was also very limited.

First, there were limited sources of financial resources. External debt markets were closed to Russia. An increase in national debt in the face of low or zero growth would pull resources from private investments or would result in the redemption of public debt by the Central Bank. In both cases, there was a risk that, instead of stimulating economic growth, the additional budget spending would only increase inflation.

Second, a question remained about the availability of internal reserves for an adequate response to higher demand. The assessments of production capacity discussed by economists were contradictory. On the one hand, a number of studies showed that the economy was practically at the limit of production capacity, and further growth would require increasing factor productivity.[5] On the other hand, according to Rosstat data, the load of productive capacities was about 60–65 per cent, and similar results can be found in market surveys of enterprises held by the Gaidar Institute for Economic Policy.[6]

However, low unemployment and the reduction in the working-age population diminished prospects of a positive reaction to increased demand anyway. External migration also ceased to be a source of additional labour, as the rouble devaluation reduced the attractiveness of working in Russia, and the migrant inflow started to decrease at the end of 2014.

Third, there was the imperfect structure of budgetary expenditure in terms of its impact on economic growth.[7] Over the previous few years, it had undergone significant negative changes. It had shifted from expenditure that provides growth (human capital and infrastructure) to 'non-productive' expenditure (public administration, military, police).[8] Fiscal stimulus by itself required appropriate institutional reforms and the effectiveness of budget expenditure to be improved.

The role of the budget rule was another matter. In 2014, the question of whether or not it would be appropriate to maintain the rule, which required that oil and gas superprofits be reserved, was at the centre of a fierce debate. While oil prices remained high, the Ministry of Finance was pressured to direct all revenues to the budget, in order to compensate for the reduction in business activity through government injections. When oil prices fell sharply, and, in accordance with the budgetary rule, the accumulated reserves should have been directed to compensate for the falling revenues, the Ministry of Finance proposed declaring the budget rule void and sequestrating expenditures in order to retain reserves for the future.

The debate on the budget rule was also important from the standpoint of economic policy principles in a country with significant influence over natural resource rent. One should use special mechanisms to mitigate the dependence of the budget (and the whole economy) on unpredictable market fluctuations. During the previous decade, this problem had been resolved by a portion of the superprofits being transferred to sovereign funds. It was better than spending all the rent in the current budget, as was done by the Soviet Union in the 1970s and 1980s. However, the experience of 2009–12 demonstrated a serious drawback of these savings: having an 'airbag' discourages modernization. A crisis is a time that encourages it, but the availability of resources helped to soften the impact of the crisis, following the principle of *business as usual*.

Russia needs to rethink the very ideology of using market superprofits and, respectively, the budget rule. Taking into account Russian political realities, it is advisable to define the cut-off price of market superprofits more tightly (to fix it at a fairly low level) and to balance the current budget (the budget of renewable obligations) at a level of income providing maximum protection from fluctuations in external factors. If additional revenues from the natural resource rents occur, they should be allocated to form a budget of development – that is, to finance expenditures with a finite timeframe which provide increase of total factor productivity (TFP) and without renewable commitments. This model would allow more investments in the case of a favourable market situation and would not create a temptation to 'pour' money into the problem (say, to bail out bankrupt firms) when a crisis breaks out.

## Notes

1   The thesis of the primacy of structural reforms in relation to crisis, in developed countries in general, and Russia in particular, is common to almost all researchers. "To emerge from the downturn with improved long-term prospects Russia will need a combination

of cyclical and structural policy measures. As the relative weight of the reasons for Russia's downturn is tilted toward structural factors, structural measures will need to lead the rebound. The lack of more comprehensive structural reforms in the past has led to a gradual erosion of investor confidence" (World Bank 2014: 5).
2   See Chapter 16 of this book.
3   See: Kissinger 2011; Kadochnikov and Ptashkina 2014.
4   See: Putin 2009.
5   See: Sinelnikov-Murylev et al. 2014; World Bank 2014.
6   "The average level of production capacity utilization, according to assessments of top managers interviewed in December 2014, amounted to 62 per cent. 91 per cent of respondents believe that their production capacities will satisfy the demand for production expected in the coming 6 months, and 11 per cent of them indicate the redundancy of available capacities" (Rosstat 2014).
7   See: IMF 1995; Moreno-Dodson 2013.
8   See: Knobel and Sokolov 2012; Idrisov and Sinelnikov-Murylev 2013, 2014. The problem of optimization of the budgetary expenditure structure in terms of the priorities of social and transport infrastructure in the economic policy is not new to Russia. The statement made by the minister of finance, A.A. Abaza, in the State Council on 31 December 1880 identified the following contours of the budgetary policy: "First and foremost, it is important to reduce military expenditures". Then, savings in other parts of the administration had to be made, except those on which the government could not save money, because they led to improvements in the people's welfare; such expenditures, according to Minister Abaza, included secondary and non-secondary schools, the court system and railroads. In strict compliance with the savings in public expenditure, it was necessary to encourage hard work and thrift of individuals – the main source of people's wealth (Peretz 1927).

## References

Idrisov, G. and Sinelnikov-Murylev, S. (2013). "Byudzhetnaya politika i ekonomicheskiy rost" [Budget Policy and Economic Growth], *Voprosy Ekonomiki*, no. 8, pp. 35–59.

Idrisov, G. and Sinelnikov-Murylev, S. (2014). "Formirovaniye predposylok dolgosrochnogo rosta: kak ih ponimat'?" [Forming sources for a long-run growth: How to understand?], *Voprosy Ekonomiki*, no. 3, pp. 4–20.

IMF. (1995). *Unproductive Public Expenditures: A pragmatic approach to policy analysis*. Prepared by K. Chu, S. Gupta, B. Clements, D. Hewitt, S. Lugaresi, J. Schiff, L. Schuknecht and G. Schwartz. IMF Pamphlet Series, no. 48.

Kadochnikov, P. and Ptashkina, M. (2014). "Liberalizatsiya vneshnej torgovli v Kitaye: otvet na vyzovy nachala 1990h godov" [Liberalization of foreign trade in China: Responding to challenges of the early 1990s], *Ekonomicheskaya Politika*, no. 6, pp. 103–13.

Kissinger, H. (2011). *On China*. New York: Penguin.

Knobel, A. and Sokolov, I. (2012). "Otsenka byudzhetnoj politiki RF na srednesrochnuyu perspektivu" [Evaluation of Russia's budget policy in medium-term perspective], *Ekonomicheskoye razvitie Rossii*, no. 12 (19), pp. 23–32.

Moreno-Dodson, B. (ed.) (2013). *Is Fiscal Policy the Answer? A developing country perspective*. Washington, DC: The World Bank.

Peretz, E. (1927). *Dnevnik (1880–1883)* [Diary (1880–1883)]. Moscow, Leningrad: Gosizdat.

Putin, V. (2009). Speech at Davos meeting, 29 January. Available at: www.vesti.ru/doc.html?id=246949 (accessed 4 August 2017).

Rosstat. (2014). *Delovaya aktivnost' organizatsij v Rossii* [Business activity of entities in Russia]. Available at: www.gks.ru/bgd/free/b04_03/isswww.exe/stg/d04/264.htm (accessed 4 August 2017).

Sinelnikov-Murylev, S., Drobyshevsky, S. and Kazakova, M. (2014). "Dekompozitsiya tempov rosta VVP Rossii v 1999–2014 godah" [Decomposition of GDP growth rates in Russia in 1999–2014], *Ekonomicheskaya Politika*, no. 5, pp. 7–37.

World Bank, The. (2014). *Confidence Crisis Exposes Economic Weakness*. Russian Economic Report, no. 31.

# 18 Economic policy of 2015
## Sanctions and anti-crisis agenda

### Delayed crisis in the rent economy

The economic situation in Russia in 2015 was defined by two groups of factors. On the one hand, there was the continuing effect of external shocks, including sanctions (especially in the financial sphere) and a simultaneous drop in prices of Russia's main export commodities. On the other hand, serious structural problems caused a decline in growth potential in the middle of the last decade and then a slowdown in the Russian economy.

Both groups of factors created a negative dynamic, already recorded in 2014 and manifested in lower GDP in 2015. Almost all experts recognized that, for all the importance of external shocks, structural crisis was the key factor. A weakening of investment activity has been observed since 2012, when growth rates slowed – these negative processes began before the introduction of sanctions and the decline in oil prices. The reason for this slowdown was the decrease in the potential economic growth, noted from the second half of the 2000s.[1]

As we wrote earlier in this book, the crisis in Russia is an element of the global structural crisis, which is pushing all developed countries to a reconsideration of the growth model. But, in great part, it has been created by Russia's domestic problems, primarily exhaustion of the model of extensive growth, based on the use of spare resources (capacity and work force) after the 40 per cent GDP decline in the 1990s, and quick-growing external and domestic demand. The issue of a new model for economic growth was raised back in "Strategy 2020" elaborated in 2011.[2]

Historical precedents can help us understand the nature of these problems, even though they do not offer simple remedies for an anti-crisis agenda – either positive (what should be done) or negative (what should not be done). One must pay attention first to the problems that the Russian economy faced in the second half of the 1980s. We can find many commonalities, from macroeconomic, institutional and geopolitical points of view:

- an analogous scale in the drop in oil prices;
- a double budget shock (the fall in income from exports and excise tax as a result of the anti-alcohol campaign of 1985);

- a deceleration of growth, especially in comparison with the developed West and rising China, and an active search by the elite for a new model for accelerating economic growth;
- the presence of geopolitical resistance, including external military actions and sanctions.

In both cases, we are talking about a postponed structural crisis that began a decade earlier in more developed countries and set new parameters for an economic model. The large-scale revenues from fuel exports in both cases helped Russia avoid a crisis (or mitigate its effects) at an earlier stage, when the more developed countries were going through a period of turbulence. But that just makes the struggle with its consequences all that much harder, when other countries complete their institutional and structural adaptation to new challenges.

For Russia to overcome this structural crisis it must leave the rent economy based on commodities' export. This does not mean a rejection of the role of commodities: they are not synonymous with rent. Unlike in the nineteenth and twentieth centuries, in the modern world the division of industries into leading and backward is blurred. Instead, there is a division into leading and backward technologies, and either one can occur in any industry.

Experience of the last 50 years proves that a country can be highly developed technologically, institutionally and economically, with a significant share of its economy in commodities, and hydrocarbons in particular (i.e. Norway, Canada, Australia). The problem lies not in the commodity per se, but in the inefficiency of technologies and institutions. The solution to this problem calls for a system of measures, primarily institutional, which cannot be reduced simply to removing rent revenues from the current budget (e.g. by a 'budget rule'). This raises the question of whether the national elite is able to provide an adequate business climate, the quality of human capital (including migration of qualified workers) and thereby the efficiency and competitiveness of the country and its institutions. As we have seen in the past half-century, managing the development of a commodities economy is very difficult: the presence of rents complicates rather than eases the tasks the government faces.[3]

An important political economy conclusion regarding Russian performance follows from this point. The interest groups that support alternative patterns of economic policy cannot be attributed to definite industries (sectors of the economy). Real watersheds are between technologically advanced and backward enterprises – not only in terms of production technologies, but also in terms of management technologies. One can also trace a split between the interests of rent-revenue firms, state-controlled enterprises (supported by public funds) and private firms. The departure from the sector approach to interest groups makes the analysis more complicated, but more accurate.

For all the similarities, the situation was quite different from the mid 1980s. The Russian economic and political systems are much more flexible and stable than the Soviet ones. 'Automatic stabilizers' (market prices, flexible exchange rate) are nowadays at work. There are significant gold reserves and a more flexible labour market, and there is no burden of being a global superpower. Russian authorities have a lot of experience of economic functioning, in both favourable and unfavourable conditions in the global economy.

But, there are also additional complications of a strategic character that cannot be ignored. At the moment, no one can be sure whether hydrocarbon prices will sometimes be comparable with their peak in 2008 or even in 2012. The cyclical character of the price fluctuations is only a hypothesis. Apparently, a 'new oil reality' is forming. So, it would be wrong to build Russian economic policy in expectation of high oil prices. A new 'budget rule' and a more responsible policy of expenditures, if there is added revenue from exporting oil, is only one of the possible areas for discussion.

Another important question: what is the mechanism for developing the country, with its rich stores of raw materials, in conditions where the accumulation of rent is not the issue? As noted earlier, the key problem is not limiting the role of commodities, but the substantial change in the technological base of these industries, primarily through stimulation of the development of higher redistribution and transition from the production and export of fuel to organic chemistry and concomitant production (fertilizer, polymers, plastics, and so on). Russia has the material and intellectual conditions for this, but it lacks the institutional capacity.

Which interest groups may support the path to structural modernization and overcoming rent dependence is still an open question. The experience of 2008–14 shows that the dominant sentiment among the elite continues to follow the lines of the logic of *business as usual* – that is, the expectation of a recovery of high oil prices. This is mostly important for those groups whose well-being depends on public budget spending. Their number in the last decade has substantially grown. In contrast, demand for modernization has notably fallen in the last decade, despite the active use in official political rhetoric of the terms 'innovation' and 'the creation of highly productive jobs' (the term 'modernization' is now used significantly less frequently). However, it is possible to stipulate that, with the continuation of low oil prices for a sufficiently long period, demand for modernization will rise.

In the elaboration of this policy, the government must not make fatal mistakes, with far-reaching consequences. In a crisis, there is always the temptation to find solutions that are as simple as they are dangerous. There are various exotic or populist economic and political decisions that lead to macroeconomic destabilization with the belief that "*this time is different*", as observed by Carmen Reinhart and Kenneth Rogoff.[4]

## The channels of sanctions' impact on the Russian economy

One can distinguish several channels of the sanctions' impact on the dynamics of Russian GDP. Among them are the strengthening of economic and political uncertainty, the rising cost of debt financing, and restrictions on technology transfer, as well as on imports.

The most important channel is a dramatic increase in uncertainty in economics and politics, which affects the decisions of economic agents, both internally and abroad. There are two mechanisms of the impact of uncertainty: through consumption and through investment.

## *Consumption*

The overall increase of uncertainty in economics and politics creates uncertainty regarding future incomes. As a result, an economic agent reduces consumption in the current period and increases savings, to mitigate possible variations in income and consumption in the future.[5] Taking into account the Russian specifics (low confidence in the national currency, the economic policy and the banking system, as well as high inflation and exchange rate risks), such savings are mainly made in the form of foreign currency cash. As a result, demand for real rouble cash balances declines (owing to the transaction component of demand and demand to store value), and demand for real cash balances in foreign currency increases (owing to demand to store value and for precautionary reasons).

Thus, total consumption in the economy declines, dollarization occurs, and inflation accelerates. These processes were clearly seen in Q1 and Q4 2014, when, in addition to increased capital outflows (in the form of dollarization of assets), the volume of bank deposits decreased, and households transferred their savings from banks to foreign currency cash and to bank safe deposit boxes (Table 18.1).

## *Investments*

Growing uncertainty about future incomes and output increases the current value of holdings of capital and reduces its desirable amount in the future. Thus, there occurs a decrease in investment needed to achieve it, and companies are willing to implement only those projects with a guaranteed profitability that exceeds the current increased cost of capital (interest). As, in this case, we refer to the increase in risk premium within an interest rate perceived by economic agents as an indicator of the relative profitability (cost) of the capital between the present and the future, the decrease in the nominal interest rate in the financial market cannot change the investment behaviour of companies. They will not start new investments in fixed capital and will prefer to save money in deposits or in the form of liquid assets.

*Table 18.1* Capital outflow and dollarization of the Russian economy in 2014

|  | *Q1* | *Q4* |
|---|---|---|
| Net capital outflow from the public sector, US$ billion | −47.6 | −76.2 |
| Dynamics of rouble accounts with banks, RUB billion | −798.4 | −289.1 |
| Dynamics of cash foreign currency, US$ billion | 10.2 | 15.1 |

*Source*: Central Bank of Russia

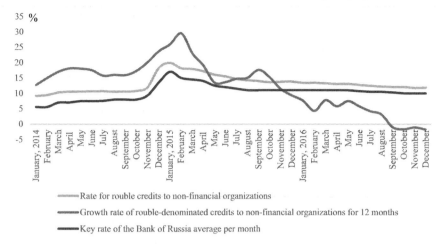

*Figure 18.1* Interest rate and growth rate of rouble-denominated credits to non-financial organizations

*Source*: Central Bank of Russia

Similarly, increasing the political interest rate of the Central Bank and the nominal rates in late 2014 had little impact on the non-financial sector: higher risks were integrated in advance.

The demand for rouble loans briefly increased as a result of the replacement of loans in foreign currency (Figure 18.1). But, as devaluation expectations ease and inflation decreases, which should reduce the risks of investment in real projects, the level of nominal rates again begin to play an important role in the credit market.

Note that the opposite monetary policy of several central banks in developed countries, after the crisis of 2008 (the Federal Reserve System, European Central Bank, Bank of Japan), gave similar results in terms of stimulating investment lending. Despite extremely low or even negative interest rates, companies are reluctant to take credit, because uncertainty is high in respect of the overall growth prospects of many developped countries and in respect of the specificity of the structural priorities of post-crisis development.

The second channel of the sanctions' impact on the Russian economy is a higher cost of borrowing, especially in the long term. As the majority of 'long-term' financing in previous years was obtained in the international market, apart from the increase in interest rates for Russian borrowers, an additional negative factor was the increased exchange rate for loans issued in foreign currencies. On the one hand, this channel reduces investment and negotiation opportunities for companies that, in spite of the mechanism of reduction of the desired amount of capital described above, intended to make investments at the present time. On the other hand, it limits the possibility of refinancing the current indebtedness of companies, which limits their current business capacity, as current financial flows are diverted to pay off existing debts.

The third channel of the sanctions' impact is the reduced total factor productivity due to the lack of access to technology transfer from abroad, the decline in foreign direct investment and the weakened competition with foreign producers (the latter is due to restrictions on foreign trade operations in both directions and the effect of the price advantage due to the decline in the rouble exchange rate). In the face of a declining population of working age and an incomplete process of renovation of fixed assets, it is the total factor productivity that turns out to be the only way to increase the structural (potential) growth rate from the current 1–1.5 per cent up to at least 3–3.5 per cent per year.

The possible channels of the sanctions' impact should also include the effects of restrictions on imports to Russia. The production of certain goods in a number of sectors of the Russian economy is critically dependent on imported components, the replacement of which is, at least in the short term, technically or technologically impossible. This effect will occur regardless of whether this restriction is the result of discrete solutions for specific categories of goods or the result of imported goods being more expensive owing to devaluation. In particular, a significant negative impact on the dynamics of output from a weaker rouble was expected in the pharmaceutical industry, automotive sector, textiles and apparel, plastics and products thereof, production of equipment, electrical equipment and electric machines, and furniture.[6]

Finally, one more channel of sanctions' impact is the restriction on Russian exports of certain types of goods, primarily energy and raw materials. As the production of such goods considerably exceeds the possible volumes of their consumption in the domestic markets, as well as technical limitations to the geographical destinations of exports in many cases, the reduction in export volumes of such goods would have clear negative effect on the output and financial status of companies in those sectors.

## Anti-crisis programme

The effect of external shocks on the Russian economy is distinguished by the fact that the crisis here is in form of stagflation. It is not classic stagflation, with the imposition of higher prices and unemployment. Russian stagflation has two characteristics. Employment was not very sensitive to the crisis – it fluctuated insignificantly in 2014–15. However, the cause of inflation was neither monetary or budgetary expansionism, nor an attempt to counteract the decline with Keynesian methods (as in the West in the early-1970s); it was brought on by a deep devaluation of the rouble. Thus, the ability of the authorities to curb inflation or prevent GDP contraction was limited.

The reaction to external shocks must be monetary and budget consolidation. Infusions of money in this situation lead to the growth of inflation and undermine, rather than stimulate, investments. Expanding budget financing on a healthy basis was also very difficult, because of the sharp fall in budget revenues with a simultaneous increase in the need for defence financing.

In December 2014, the situation seemed near catastrophic. The rouble was in free fall following the sanctions and the plummeting oil priced, and the financial authorities decided to protect the reserves and not spend them on supporting the national currency. The budget just passed by parliament became unrealistic in a few weeks.

In early 2015, the Russian government passed a package of anti-crisis measures, including revising the budget by cutting an average of 10 per cent in spending. The government examined concrete questions on the functioning of individual sectors tied to economic and social stability. The implementation of these measures stabilized the situation, but negative trends were not completely stopped. The government was criticized for not fully realizing the anti-crisis programme (actually, for not fully spending the amount allotted to it); however, this evinced the effectiveness of the measures taken.

The results of 2015 in Russia looked better than expected in late 2014. There was a risk of serious destabilization, and of the government and monetary authorities losing control of the macroeconomic situation. A timely switch to a floating currency exchange rate (called a switch to 'inflation targeting'), consolidation of budget expenses and the implementation of the government's anti-crisis plan prevented events from getting out of control and supported the level of international reserves.

Below, we examine the main elements of the anti-crisis economic and social policy in 2015–16.

## Economic dynamic

The GDP fell by 2.8 per cent in 2015, and this was the second episode of decline after 2009 (when the Russian economy shrank by 7.8 per cent on the wave of the global crisis; Table A.1). Although the decline of 2009 took place in the majority of developed countries, they are now experiencing a faster rate of growth. Throughout the year, politicians and analysts discussed wheter contraction 'reached the bottom' – that is, the point when the decline had to stop.

Two important factors determined the character and duration of the decline in 2015 and made it hard to predict: the industrial structure and the dynamics of the rouble. Changes in trade terms and devaluation[7] affected different industries in different ways, as shown by the varying dynamics in the previous year. Industries oriented on export demonstrated growth; those tied primarily to domestic consumption shrank. The ones that suffered the most were those that had benefited most in the past from the inflow of rent revenues – services, trade, construction. In fact, an analysis of problems related to the 'Dutch disease' showed that a powerful influx of rent revenues undermines the competitiveness of industries producing tradables, but promotes the development of sectors of non-tradables that do not compete with imports (mostly services – commercial trade, construction, financial and non-financial services), and, therefore, there can be no import substitution in them. Services benefited from growing demand in the growing economy and do not suffer from import competition. These sectors grew very actively in the past, but, for this very same reason, they are the most sensitive to the decline in demand as a result of devaluation. The dynamics of each sector were strongly affected by the share of imports and the debt load in foreign currency.[8]

The combination of these factors determined the GDP dynamics. When the devaluation processes ceased in mid 2015, many industries showed signs of reanimation. However, a new spiral in falling oil prices and the consequent further weakening of the rouble led to further GDP decline.

The situation with investments, which by early autumn had seemed stabilized, developed in the same way. The uncertainty in the rouble exchange rate, and consequently the business climate, led to a continued decrease in investments.

From a macroeconomic point of view, what was important for the restoration of growth in Russia was not whether oil prices were high or low, but that they were stable, which would be followed by consumer price index stabilization.

## *Structural policy and import substitution*

Devaluation of the rouble was widely considered as a source of import substitution and the diversification of the economy, particularly export. However it was also clear that the effect of 1999 (when economic growth automatically resumes after devaluation) would not be repeated, for a number of reasons: the gloomy global situation (political and economic); the lack of significant spare capacity and work force; a much deeper involvement of the Russian economy in the global value-added chains – that is, dependence of domestic production on deliveries of imported equipment or parts; and the fact that devaluation had become a widespread element in the policies of many other emerging countries competing with Russia.

In the past, and this does not apply only to Russia, the effect of devaluation was not immediately apparent, but the main result emerged in the first year after devaluation. But with current multifaceted devaluations and global shrinking demand, this effect would be unequal in different countries and at best would be postponed – if the devaluation can be supplemented by appropriate institutional reforms. This is demonstrated by the experience of a number of countries – most strikingly, Japan, which has not been able to start up the mechanism of growth for a quarter of a century.

Deavaluation may be important for import substitution, but it does not act directly or automatically. We can list the following causes that modify the influence of devaluation on economic growth in Russia in the mid-2010s:

- The structural consequences of a lengthy period of 'Dutch disease' damaged production (and the labour resources allocated to it) that could have been the source of import substitution – they simply cease to exist and cannot be resurrected automatically. That is why the export sectors, which have the ability to expand production without significant investment, revive first.

- In the absence of spare capacity, import substitution requires investment and, therefore, a good investment climate. Devaluation can compensate to a certain extent for a bad entrepreneurial climate, lowering the risk–profit ratio. However, in the context of making investments – that is, in long-term decisions – devaluation is not the most important argument.
- Devaluation makes the country attractive for foreign investment. However Russia's situation has been worsened by imposed sanctions.
- A country's involvement in international trade (in the global value-added chains) also limited the possibility of using devaluation, as some of the components were more expensive as a result. Therefore, the influence of devaluation on import substitution can be discussed only with a proper analysis of specific sectors and products.

By the beginning of 2015, a few sectors showed the ability to take advantage of devaluation, mostly those that related to export. At the same time, devaluation helped expose the weak points and showed an excessive dependence on imports in many manufacturing areas, as well as in the consumer market. A business model based on foreign currency loans and purchases of imported equipment began to collapse.

As a consequence of devaluation, Russian manufacturers received a few additional competitive advantages in domestic markets. Non-commodity export rose by about 6 per cent in physical terms over 2015. It is the new driver of import expansion, and the most stable positions in the Russian economy were held by companies that export non-commodities.

In 2015, the government commission for the support of import substitution was created, as was the Russian Export Centre, to support non-commodity export. The character and mechanisms of that support have been gradually developed. Prime Minister Dmitry Medvedev spoke out in favour of support for import substitution to the ability to produce goods and services that are competitive in foreign markets.[9] This meant that the government recognized the risk of ending up with protectionism, where the local market was closed to international competition and dominated by domestic, but more expensive and lower-quality, goods. This 'import substitution' is well known from the experience of many countries (especially in Latin America).

There were attempts throughout 2015 to limit the export of items the competitiveness of which benefitted from devaluation (grain, metals, chemicals). This was based on concern about shortages of these items for domestic consumption and expectation of a sharp rise in domestic prices to the world level. Essentially, these are the same argument, but in the former it is a 'phantom pain' of Soviet shortages and in the latter a part of the rhetoric of the market economy. However, no serious actions were taken, except for an extension of the ban on exporting hides and, in December 2015, the introduction of a ban on exporting waste paper for recycling.

The Russian government has repeatedly stated its firm intention to support import substitution. However, there are two interest groups presenting significantly different requirements to the authorities regarding this course. On the one hand, there are those who benefit from the devaluation effect of sustainable development and who are able to produce competitive goods, including for export. They usually require stability of national legislation and economic openness (not only for export, but also to import equipment and spare parts needed to produce export goods), in addition to devaluation.

On the other hand, there are less efficient manufacturers, for whom the devaluation is insufficient and who require protection from foreign competitors, as well as budgetary subsidies or loans on non-market conditions (with an artificial or subsidized interest rate). These groups are interested in the sanctions being retained as long as possible. Politically, they are supported by representatives of military and intelligence structures (*siloviki*).

## *Budget policy*

With external shocks, the government had to pursue a cautious budget policy, even though it cannot be called a fully restrictive (conservative) one. The federal budget deficit was 2.4 per cent GDP, compared with 0.4 per cent in 2014, keeping the state debt at the 14.3 per cent level – a very low number by international standards, especially as debt denominated in foreign currency even went down a bit (as a result of sanctions, and not because of conscious budget conservatism).

With the reduction in export income, the Russian government corrected the federal budget with a reduction in expenditures by March 2015. The instrument chosen was a sequestering of approximately 10 per cent. This is technically the simplest solution, and does not preclude using it again in the future. But, it will probably have negative medium-term consequences.

The problem is that, in the last 7–8 years, the expenditures structure of the budget has gotten worse: the share of 'productive expenditures' has been declining, whereas 'non-productive expenditures' have been growing larger.[10] The former includes the expenditure on human capital and transport infrastructure. The latter includes the expenditure on government, as well as defence and enforcement agencies (*siloviki*).

The country needs investment in human capital and transportation infrastructure in order to solve long-term socio-economic development issues – these state expenditures contribute to growth potential. Yet, it is these sectors that have less 'political weight' and lose the most as a result of sequestering.

A further sequestration of expenditures without structural reforms created risks for economic, social and political stability in the near term. Without structural reform, budget policy would lose its manoeuvrability, which might be needed in 2017–18 (as 2018 is a year of presidential election).

The structure of budget expenditures becomes no less important a problem than balancing the budget (low fiscal deficit). Balancing at the expense of productive sectors is fraught with the risk of a vicious circle: reducing expenditures on the productive sectors will undermine economic growth, thus leading to shrinkage of the revenue base of the budget. Therefore, the key task now is improvement of the expenditure structure – that is, finding more complex methods of economizing budget funds through structural and institutional reforms, rather than simple sequestration.

In 2017–18, the government has to increase the deficit in the federal budget in view of worsening prices for hydrocarbons. A complex search for compromise will likely ensue – how to maintain sociopolitical stability, while avoiding macroeconomic deterioration.

It is often noted that low debt creates additional macroeconomic problems, in particular, by depriving the monetary system of adequate instruments of collateral. There have even been proposals to limit state debt, not from above, but from below (not 'no more than', but 'no less than' a certain level).[11] This is hardly possible or advisable. On the one hand, there is no large volume of private savings in Russia that the government could borrow without damaging private investment. On the other hand, bearing in mind Russia's weak 'credit history', a substantial growth in borrowing would lead to a serious rise in its cost. Guaranteeing macroeconomic stability condemns Russia to a rather lengthy period of living with low sovereign debt.

The fiscal situation in subjects of the Russian Federation remains complicated. Despite the fact that tax income has fallen in real terms, the situation with debt has not worsened significantly. The nominal growth of revenues helps retain control over the development of events. The growth of expenditures in consolidated regional budgets slowed; it increased by only 1.4 per cent.

An important trend was the deceleration of debt growth in the consolidated regional budgets compared with 2013 and 2014 – growth was around 11 per cent (it was 29 per cent in 2013 and 20 per cent in 2014). In 2015, a part of regional commercial debt was replaced by debt to the Ministry of Finance, and, even as the budget debt grew, the commercial part was reduced. The share of commercial debt went down in 2015 from 64 to 60 per cent, whereas the share of budget credits, on the contrary, went up from 31 to 35 per cent. This improved the debt structure, reducing the cost of servicing it. However, the political elite periodically discusses the question of writing off part of the regional budget debt.

## *Monetary policy*

The transition to a floating rouble exchange rate made it possible to save the Central Bank's international reserves, which is important for long-term development. Raising the 'key interest rate' (or Central Bank policy rate) was another important and responsible decision, despite harsh criticism from a large part of the political and business elites. It was no less important that Vladimir Putin, president of Russia, frequently expressed his support of the Central Bank's policy. The monetary authorities continue to declare their goal of reducing inflation to 4 per cent by 2018, which would create completely new conditions for business.

Besides saving reserves, the policy of the Bank of Russia reduced capital outflow, and a significant part of the outflow was the result of paying foreign debt by Russian borrowers (Table A.1). Thus, in 2015, the pure outflow of capital was US$57 billion

(US$153 billion in 2014). The main channel of capital outflow was repayment of debts to non-residents, which went down by US$64 billion (US$37 billion in 2014). The geopolitical factor affected the dynamics of the outflow, as the fear of possible expansion of sanctions could have made investment abroad less attractive. This, in part, is confirmed by a decrease in direct foreign investment from US$18 billion in 2014 to US$7 billion in 2015.

The tendency to dollarize private savings decreased. Whereas, in 2014, Russian banks, companies and private individuals actively increased their investment in foreign assets, in 2015, the foreign assets of Russian residents went down slightly in the context of intensive payment of foreign debt. In 2014, the main channel of outflow was the growth of foreign assets (by US$116 billion, including US$30 billion in cash savings), whereas, in 2015, it was down by US$7 billion. This reduction is almost fully explained by the reduction in savings in foreign currency.

The harsh criticism of the policy of the Russian Central Bank, which is often blamed for all the problems of the Russian economy, is unjust. Paradoxically, it is those who most harshly criticize the 'monetarists' who are, in practice, real monetarists, exaggerating the ability of monetary authorities to neutralize the negative consequences of foreign policy and geopolitical crises. (See the next section of this chapter.)

*The banking sector* remains the object of continual attention from the authorities. The policy of cleaning it up continues. Ninety-three credit organizations lost their licences in 2015. The process of financial recovery (rehabilitation) was started with fifteen banks in 2015. The volume of assets in banks that lost the right to continue in 2015 was not great: they had approximately 1 per cent of the total assets of the banking sector.

A number of the biggest banks received major financial support from the state, as a crisis in the banking sector would have terrible consequences, not only economic but also sociopolitical. Most state support went to state banks. The capital of the biggest banks affiliated with state ministries or state companies (the VTB group, Gazprombank and Rosselkhozbank) grew from early 2015 by almost RUB900 billion, whereas the growth of all the other banks was less than RUB100 billion. The consequences of this accent in state support may be considered to be strengthened positions of state banks in the main segments of the bank services market, primarily in retail loans and attracting savings.

Lending to companies, although slowed down, still showed a positive dynamic – almost 7 per cent – whereas the debt of individuals went down by about the same amount – a much gentler reaction than in 2009. The quality of bank loans was worrying. Companies' arrears on rouble loans reached the maximum level of 2009, and individuals' arrears set new records. The quality of loans continues to deteriorate in all segments of the markets.

The main problem with the low financial results of the banking sector in 2015 was the unprofitability of a large number of banks. In 2015, almost 30 per cent of banks were losing money, whereas, in 2009, it was only 11 per cent. Unlike the situation 6 years ago, the decrease in the profitability of banks was caused, not only by a worsening of the quality of assets and the need to sharply increase expenditure on forming reserves, but also by the reduction in profitability of the main banking operations. The latter was the result of high interest rates. The cost of bank liabilities turned out to be more sensitive to higher policy rates than the profit of their credit portfolio, which led to a significant decrease in the banks' net interest income.

As in other developed countries, sharp criticism from different political forces and interest groups caused both actions by the authorities: support for the banking sector and closing down inefficient banks. In the first case, the arguments are standard and largely ideological: the need to support producers (companies), rather than financial intermediaries. In fact, the banking sector cleaning-up policy objectively contributes to strengthening the positions of two or three of the largest banks controlled by the government. Thus, the process of reforming the financial market turns out to be trapped: reforming the banks entails strengthening the state-owned banks and the monopolization of the financial sector.

## *Social stability and the labour market*

As in previous post-Soviet crises, in 2015, the population's income went down with a rather stable labour market. Unemployment fluctuated around 5.5 per cent, which was significantly lower than in Eurozone. In conditions of a tense demographic situation and a reduction in the working-age population, businesses are not willing to lower employment, but instead they cut working hours and, accordingly, wages.

The level of prosperity went down significantly during 2015 – real disposable income went down by 3.5 per cent, and real payments went down by more than 9 per cent. This fits the 'Russian model of the labour market' – reducing wages (and working time) instead of employment.

At the same time, savings in banks were growing, primarily in rouble form. This means a transition from a consumer model to a savings model, which in the short term becomes an additional braking factor on the economy: demand becomes even more limited, and the crisis uncertainty does not promote the transformation of savings into investments. Accordingly, retail trade went down by about 9 per cent.

The number of people in poverty was growing. The share of Russians considered poor has gone back to the level of the mid 2000s (20.3 per cent with income below the living wage). This phenomenon is new for recent years. In 2008–9, despite the fall in GDP by 7.8 per cent, this indicator was 19 per cent, and it then fell significantly. Back then, the state had large budget savings (the reserve fund) that were used to support the standard of living. Of course, it was paid for by a budget deficit of 6 per cent of the GDP in 2009, and the non-oil deficit reached a record 14 per cent. This time, there were no such resources in the budget.

Analysts have noted the erosion of the middle class in Russia,[12] even though we must distinguish between the problem of flows (lowered income flow) and assets (accumulated prosperity, formed stereotypes of behaviour). The crisis situation has led to a certain reduction in inequality – the Gini coefficient was down from 0.414 to 0.399, and the decile ratio is down from 15.8 to 14.2.[13] However, this could hardly be called a positive trend.

The results of 2015 showed that the situation was complex and had a tendency to worsen, but it did not threaten sociopolitical destabilization. Whereas, in the period of high economic dynamics, excess consumer demand worsened the structure of growth and raised the question of increasing stimulating factors in production, now the situation was changing. The dynamics of income and consumer behaviour indicate that the way to increase economic growth calls for elaborating special measures to stimulate demand. That said, we do not deny the need for activating factors on the supply side as well.

## Discussion on economic growth: the alternatives

The idea of a new model of economic growth was raised in Strategy-2020,[14] elaborated in 2011, and discussion on those issues has continued through all these years.

The policy of the government and monetary authorities was reflected in their programme documents, and it was more or less consistently implemented in 2014–16.[15] By this time, economic policy debates had intensified, and new economic policy ideas were put forward by various political and intellectual groups, which is quite natural when the economic situation becomes dire. A wide range of alternatives were suggested: from tough regulation of economic life by the state, with substantial easing of monetary and fiscal policies, on the one hand, to liberalization of political and economic life and tightened macroeconomic policy, on the other. A prominent place in the discussions was held by proposals in which dirigisme and populism were intertwined, which is typical for crisis stages in many countries.

Among the presentations and proposals of such a type, one can distinguish the presentations that were developed as part of two 'clubs': 'Izborsk' and 'Stolypin'. These proposals are basically similar, though, in their recommendations, they place different emphases: on politics and macroeconomics in the first case, and on the business climate in the second. Our analysis of these approaches is based on two materials. The views of the Izborsk Club find the most consistent presentation in the works of Sergei Glazyev, which we are considering here "The report on urgent measures to strengthen Russia's economic security and leading the Russian Economy on to the trajectory of advanced development".

Various versions of the Stolypin Club report were submitted in 2015–16, with reference to the following authors: Boris Titov, Andrei Klepach, and Anton Danilov-Danilyan. Given the obvious cross-over of authorship, the recommendations of both documents are comparable, although the first report is more consistent and theoretical.

The Glazyev report is based on two assumptions. First, Russia is the victim of aggression by the USA and NATO, and the "main goal in keeping with the old Western European geopolitical tradition is once again the destruction of Russia".[16] Second, the world is moving to the next wave of "technological structure" (in keeping with the logic of the "Kondratiev cycles"). The first assumption leads to the need to distance ourselves as much as possible from the aggressor countries, separating the Russian economy from them in trade and finance, as "a key position in the hybrid war against Russia is the financial and economic front".[17] The second sets the goal of taking special measures to 'ride' the new technological wave and become leaders of technological development.

This report sees the source of all of the difficulties of the Russian economy in the erroneous Central Bank policy on managing money supply and interest rates, as well as the excessive openness of the Russian economy. The paradox is that, although the author is one of the main critics of monetarism, he is monetarist himself, reducing all the problems to mistakes in monetary policy.[18] The way out of crisis calls for feeding the economy with money, while tightening administrative control on how it is spent, introducing banking and currency control, fixing the exchange of the rouble (at a low level), essentially protecting the economy from foreign competition, while increasing the role of state investments. The 'hard currency assets of the aggressor countries' should be replaced by investment of sovereign reserves into gold and securities of nations of the Euro-Asian Economic Union, the Shanghai Cooperation Organization, BRICS, and so on. Paradoxically, the report proposes not following the "recommendations of Washington", but recommends the "policy of Washington" on monetary stimulation (quantitative easing) for the Russian economy.

The concept of the Izborsk Club most consistently reflects the ideas of deeply conservative and isolationist circles. It is based on the interests of the part of the defence industry whose existence depends on the availability of powerful budgetary infusions and a lack of foreign competition. For this group, the backbone of economic and scientific activity is fulfillment of the state defence order. Foreign economic relations exist mainly in military and technical form and are implemented within intergovernmental agreements and at the public expense (or under state guarantees).

The proposals made by the Stolypin Club and those by the Izborsk Club share sharp criticism of the government and a willingness to implement a broad currency issue to support business. This approach reflects the interests of mid-size and relatively big business, mostly oriented to the domestic market. This group of businesses does not benefit from international trade and does not get money from the global financial market. They do benefit from cheap loans and budget subsidies, as well as restrictions on competition from foreign companies. Public-sector employees would support this policy too.

However, the main thrust of the Stolypin Club's report is to develop private business and reduce the government share in the Russian economy. It puts a premium on the formation of a nurturing business and investment environment and advocates institutional reforms required for this purpose.[19] This is the most important difference from the Izborsk Club.

The Stolypin Club elaborates similar theses, but they are less consistent.[20] Naturally, they leave out the thesis about the war being waged against Russia.

The main proposals of the Stolypin Club can be reduced to the following:

- High rates of economic growth must be guaranteed, and the proposed measures will bring rates of 10 per cent, according to the authors. This requires a beneficial investment climate, as well as special measures in monetary and budget policy to stimulate growth.
- The erroneous policy of the Central Bank is to blame for everything, because it focused on macroeconomic stability instead of economic growth. It proposes changing the Bank of Russia's mandate, with economic growth as the cornerstone. Suppression of inflation, therefore, is not a prerequisite for economic growth, but its outcome.
- Low monetization of the Russian economy (compared with leading developed and developing countries) requires and simultaneously allows for major monetary injections that will not lead to inflationary spirals. "The Russian variant of quantitative easing" looks like a harsh lowering of the key rate (below inflation level) and offers significant amounts of financing for special elaborated and approved industrial projects.
- Institutions of development, which will concentrate their activity on the priority sectors of the economy, must play a substantial role.
- There must be a return to targeting the hard currency exchange rate of the rouble. "Targeting the real effective course of the rouble" should be "maintained at the level depreciated by 10 per cent against market level".
- Raise the quality and improve the structure of budget expenditures, with the emphasis on the national economy and human capital.
- Use the mechanism of budget stimulation more. Increase the state debt substantially – it may reach no less than 60 per cent GDP – and the fiscal deficit – 5–6 per cent.
- Discourage the export of commodities and low-value-added products. In particular, levy payments into the budget when they are exported in foreign currency.
- If necessary, introduce capital control ('temporary', of course).
- Change the regulation of infrastructure companies (natural monopolies), which should be managed like service businesses, oriented towards performing quality services and not at making profits.
- There should be tax reform aimed at stimulating business.
- Reform and radically simplify the state's control and supervisory role.
- There should be rule of law, with effective court and law enforcement systems.
- There should be consistent expansion of the openness of the economy – 'limited protectionism' – bearing in mind the interests of domestic business.
- Improve the quality of state administration. Create a system for administrative reform, and particularly improving state administration of economic development.

This programme consists of obvious solutions, limited only by the political will to implement them. The list of institutions cooperating in economic growth is well known and has been proposed many times in various expert documents. However, in macroeconomic policy, the realization of many of these measures would lead to serious destabilization and shocks. Moreover, attempts to implement such measures were made often (in Russia and other countries) and always led to destabilization and, in some cases, to economic catastrophe.

First of all, one should be very cautious about the thesis that economic growth leads to a slowdown of inflation, and not the other way around. This is wrong at the core: economic growth as a rule is tied to a certain increase in inflation, and economic crisis is tied to its deceleration (deflation). Besides this, this thesis applies to a standard economic crisis, whereas Russia is dealing with stagflation, and monetary stimulation in a period of stagflation always leads to very negative results. There is no reason to assume that *it will be different this time* in Russia.

Finally, the illusion that low monetization of the economy is overcome by an injection of money into the economy is a very dangerous one. Even more dangerous is the idea that low monetization *provides an opportunity* for aggressive monetary stimulation of growth without serious inflationary consequences. Russia has its own experiences in this sphere. The most recent was in the 1990s, when the injection of money into the economy, despite very low monetization (in some periods, below 20 per cent), had a powerful inflationary effect. Even more interesting is the experience of 1925–6, when the leading economists of Gosplan (V. Bazarov, V. Groman and S. Strumilin) explained the need for inflationary pumping up of the economy by the gap between monetization and the level of recovery of the national economy. Their opponents (who included N. Kondratiev, L. Yurovsky and N. Makarov) pointed out that monetization was a very complex phenomenon that was not simply printing money. However, the inflationary model won and it led to a rapid increase in goods shortages, a crisis in agriculture and, in the final analysis, to the end of the market economy and the triumph of administrative socialism.[21]

The low level of monetization is not a consequence of restrictions on money, but the result of low money demand – that is, a low level of economic agents' trust in the national economic policy. In other words, low monetization is first and foremost an institutional problem, and only after that, a macroeconomic one. Its cure calls for measures that stimulate savings and improve the entrepreneurial climate, as well for lowering inflation as a condition of restoring trust in the national currency. That is why it is not economic growth that guarantees low inflation, but the lowering of inflation to acceptable levels that becomes a factor in economic growth.[22]

One must bear in mind the limited possibilities for fiscal stimulation in contemporary Russian conditions. On the one hand, Russia lacks significant capability for state borrowing – foreign markets are mostly closed because of sanctions, and the domestic financial market is narrow, and the growth of budget borrowing would compete with possible private investments. At the same time, the 'credit history' of the Russian budget policy over the last 25 years is not good, and growth of the fiscal deficit will lead to a significant increase in the cost of debt servicing.

In an analysis of the proposal to ease macroeconomic policy (monetary stimulation and growth of state debt) and the activation of budget and quasi-budget investments, it is appropriate to recall the experience of 1986–9, when, in the hope of accelerating economic growth, an analogous complex of measures was implemented. Its result is well known.

In addition to the two outlined concepts, which obviously opposed the government's course of economic policy in Russia in 2015–16, a new liberal view of the economic policy began to form (conventionally, it can be labelled as a 'liberal approach'). This approach is most consistently expressed by two former members of the Russian government, Herman Gref and Alexei Kudrin; in any case, it is shared by the Russian leaders, who are usually combined under the term 'government economic block', as well as Elvira Nabiullina, governor of the Central Bank. This approach implies conservative macroeconomic policies (policies of low debt, low budget deficit and low inflation) and, in this sense, coincides with the current government policy; however, the requirements are much more consistent and articulate institutional reforms.

As regards the business environment, these reforms are almost the same as those proposed by the Stolypin Club, but significantly extend the boundaries of these proposals. The expansion is that the 'liberal approach' considers bridging the budget deficit, curbing inflation and non-increase of the public debt to be the most important institutional prerequisites for an enabling investment environment. In this regard, as a key element of the programme, it is suggested that a new 'budget rule' be formulated as a way to overcome the dependency of the economy on fluctuations in export prices.

Special attention is also paid to the social welfare state reform, which currently cannot be built on the models developed in the early twentieth century for an industrial society. Here, the issues of the contemporary model of the welfare state, including pension reform, targeting social support, and changing patterns of health care and education, form an integral part of the reform programme. The peculiar particular feature of the 'liberal approach' is that the modern welfare state is regarded, not as a purely social phenomenon, but as a combination of social, fiscal and investment issues.

The institutional reforms in the non-economic area, primarily public administration and law enforcement, play a key role in the 'liberal approach'. The issues related to the effectiveness of the public services, judiciary system, police and army are important components of the modernization of the Russian economy. They are associated with improvement in the level of trust in society as a key element in investment promotion.

The 'liberal approach' is the most difficult to implement. It requires an integrated approach, simultaneously advancing in different directions. The complexity of its political positioning lies in the fact that it is ideologically closely linked to the course pursued by the government of Dmitry Medvedev, being little different from its programme called "The main activities of the Government" (Government RF 2015b). It differs in the suggestion of prompt, more coherent implementation of the proposed measures.

Liberal modernization is a complex (and complicated) project – both intellectually and politically. It does not offer easy solutions giving immediate results, although it does not require significant social compromises, as the proposed reforms are not socially painful. However, these reforms will not appeal to the popular vote (elections). The internal contradiction of these reforms is that, being inherently democratic, they implicitly assume a benign dictator (which none of their proponents would ever accept).

The implementation of this policy would be more feasible if the general public and the political elite believed that no hydrocarbon price recovery will occur in the foreseeable future.

## Notes

1 See: Sinelnikov-Murylev *et al.* 2014; Orlova and Egiev 2015.
2 See: Strategy 2013.
3 In 1976, when Jose Lopez Portillo became president of Mexico, the country had huge budget resources from the hike in oil prices. The new president, popular in the country and the world, assumed that all difficulties would be overcome, and the government's main job would be "to manage abundance". However, the result of his 6 years in power was a sharp rise in corruption and inefficiency, which made him one of the most unpopular leaders of Mexico in the twentieth century.
4 See: Reinhart and Rogoff 2009.
5 See: Friedman 1956; Bernanke 1984.
6 See: Evdokimova *et al.* 2013.
7 For more detail on the mechanisms of the changes, see: Idrisov *et al.* 2015.
8 See: Idrisov 2015; Idrisov *et al.* 2015.
9 See: Medvedev 2015: 20
10 In more detail: Idrisov and Sinelnikov-Murylev 2013.
11 The proposals of the Stolypin Club, published in autumn 2015, state "the proportion of domestic state debt in the total volume of debt should not go below 60% of GDP" (Stolypin Club 2015: 60).
12 See: Maleva 2015: 12–13.
13 See: Maleva 2015: 16–17.
14 See: Strategy 2013.
15 "The Main directions of the work of the government", last version approved in May 2015 (Government RF 2015a, 2015b).
16 See: Glazyev 2015: 8.
17 See: Glazyev 2015: 11.
18 "The macroeconomic achievements of the last 10 years were undermined by the focused operation, planned, calculated, and executed by American specialists to use cognitive weapons to destroy the Central Bank, whose leadership blindly followed the recommendations of the IMF" (Glazyev 2015: 21).
19 See: Stolypin Club 2015.
20 See: Stolypin Club 2015.
21 The discussion of this topic is analysed in detail in: Mau 2013: 361–9.
22 The traditional argument that released money will lead to a growth in goods, filling of the trade market and, therefore, to a brake on inflation did not hold up to criticism, even 100 years ago. "New masses of goods thrown on to the market at the end of the production cycle will not only be insufficient to satisfy the acute commodity hunger, but will create a situation even worse than before the issue of new money", wrote A. Vainshtein in 1927 (Kondratiev 1927: 6). Note that, in this context (state prices), "commodity hunger", or shortages, is a synonym for inflation.

## References

Bernanke, B.S. (1984). "Permanent income, liquidity, and expenditure on automobiles: Evidence from panel data", *Quarterly Journal of Economics*, vol. 99, no. 3.

Central Bank of the Russian Federation. (2014). "Guidelines for the state monetary policy for 2015 and the period 2016 and 2017." Available at: www.cbr.ru/publ/ondkp/on_2015 (2016-2017).pdf (accessed 4 August 2017).

Central Bank of the Russian Federation. (2015). "Guidelines for the state monetary policy for 2015 and the period 2016 and 2017." Available at: www.cbr.ru/publ/ondkp/on_2016 (2017-2018).pdf (accessed 4 August 2017).

Evdokimova, T., Zubarev, A.V., and Trunin, P.V. (2013). *Vliyaniye realnogo obmennogo kursa rublya na ekonomicheskuyu aktivnost' v Rossii* [The Impact of the Real Rouble Exchange Rate on the Economic Activity in Russia], Series Gaidar IEP, Vol. 165. Moscow: Gaidar Institute.

Friedman, M. (1956). *A Theory of the Consumption Function*. Princeton, NJ: Princeton University Press.

Glazyev, S. (2015). "The report on urgent measures to strengthen the economic security of Russia and the conclusion of the Russian economy on a trajectory of faster growth." Moscow: RAS.

Government RF (2015a). "On approval of the plan of priority measures for the sustainable development of economy and social stability in 2015."The decree of the government of the Russian Federation, dated 27 January 2015, no. 98 N-R (ed. 16 July 2015). Available at: www.rg.ru/2015/02/02/plan-dok.html (accessed 4 August 2017).

Government RF (2015b). "The main activities of the government of the Russian Federation for the period until 2018." Available at: http://government.ru/news/18119 (accessed 4 August 2017).

Idrisov, G. (2015). "Vyigravshiye i proigravshiye: posledstviya izmeneniya uslovij torgovli dlya rossiyskoj promaslannosti" [Winners and losers: Consequences of changes in the terms of trade for the Russian industry], *Ekonomicheskoe Razvitie Rossii*, no. 4, pp. 26–9.

Idrisov, G. Ponomarev, Yu., and Sinelnikov-Murylev, S. (2015). "Usloviya torgovli i ekonomicheskoye razvitiye sovremennoj Rossii" [Terms of trade and economic development of modern Russia], *Ekonomicheskaya Politika*, no. 3, pp. 7–37.

Idrisov, G. and Sinelnikov-Murylev, S.G. (2013). "Byudzhetnaya politika i ekonomicheskiy rost" [Budget policy and economic growth], *Voprosy Ekonomiki*, no. 8, pp. 35–59.

Kondratiev, N.D. (ed.) (1927). *Kon'yunktura narodnogo khozyaystva SSSR i mirovogo v 1925/26 g* [Basic Data of USSR National Economy and World Economy in 1925/26]. Moscow: NKF SSSR.

Maleva, T. (ed.) (2015). *2014–2015: Ekonomicheskiy krizis – sotsial'noye izmereniye* [2014–2015: Economic Crisis – Social Measurement]. Moscow: Delo.

Mau, V. (2013). *Reformy i dogmy: gosudarstvo i ekonomika v epohu vojn i revolyutsij (1861–1929)* [Reforms and Dogmas: State and economy in the era of reforms and revolutions (1861–1929)], 3rd edn. Moscow: Delo.

Medvedev, D. (2015). "A new reality: Russia and global challenges", *Journal of Russian Economics*, no. 1, (2), pp. 108–28.

Orlova, N. and Egiev, S. (2015). "Strukturnye faktory zamedleniya rosta rossiyskoj ekonomiki" [Structural Factors of the Russian Economic Slowdown], *Voprosy Ekonomiki*, no. 12, pp. 69–84.

Reinhart, C.M. and Rogoff, K.S. (2009). *This Time is Different: Eight centuries of financial folly*. Princeton, NJ: Princeton University Press.

Sinelnikov-Murylev, S., Drobyshevsky, S., and Kazakova, M. (2014). "Dekompozitsiya tempov rosta VVP Rossii v 1999–2014 godah" [Decomposition of GDP growth rates in Russia in 1999–2014]', *Ekonomicheskaya Politika*, no. 5, pp. 7–37.

Stolypin Club. (2015). "Ekonomika rosta" [The economy of growth (short version)], Moscow. Available at: www.finanz.ru/novosti/aktsii/ekonomika-rosta-stolypinskogo-kluba-1000872947 (accessed 4 August 2017).

Strategy. (2013). *Strategy-2020: New model of growth – new social policy*, 2 vols. Moscow: Delo.

# 19 New economic reality

## Lessons of stabilization and prospects of growth

By the beginning of 2017, the economic recession had effectively stopped, and material production sectors (industry and agriculture) and wholesale trade started positive trends back in 2016. This completed the anti-crisis policy period, and the objective to ensure economic growth was brought to the fore.

The anti-crisis policies of 2015 and 2016 deserve a separate analysis. Their measures and results are shaping the foundation for the country's further development, a new economic growth model. The lessons from this recent period are useful in terms of the opportunity to use the accumulated experience in the futuren crises.

From the start, the government's anti-crisis policy came under severe criticism from almost every possible direction. It was criticized for a rigid monetary policy aimed at decisively suppressing inflation, for insufficiently utilizing the US and EU experience with their powerful monetary and fiscal stimulation measures, and for the lack of measures to support various industries or deal with their inefficiency. This was augmented by criticism of the monetary authorities for maintaining high interest rates, insufficient business loans and tough measures to purge the banking system. All these criticisms were justified to a certain extent, as there can be no popular economic policy under economic crisis.

However, one cannot ignore at least two important positive features of the 2014–16 anti-crisis policy.

First, the government and the Bank of Russia avoided populist measures and the standard macroeconomic and institutional mistakes usually made by authorities under severe economic and political conditions, although nudged by many influential political and economic players. Although populist measures ensure short-term mitigation of the situation, they lead to large, long-term losses. It is the conflict between short-term results (in the form of economic growth) and medium-term goals (improved efficiency) that has posed the greatest danger for Russia's policy. The fetish for short-term growth rates could have led to populist measures with grave socio-economic consequences in the not-too-distant future.[1]

Second, it should be admitted that the actual situation has turned out to be considerably better over the past 2 years than was expected in late 2014. Moreover, despite the longer recession, it was better than in 2008 and 2009 in terms of most economic indicators, although the political and foreign economic environment was far more adverse (Table A.1).

Below is a list of certain vital components and outcomes from the anti-crisis policies of 2015–16, which are laying the foundation for future (post-crisis) economic growth.

*The country retained macroeconomic stability*, which is manifested primarily in the budget deficit, national debt and persistently decreasing inflation.

In 2016, the government returned to 3-year budgeting. Despite the symbolic nature of this step, it appears to be important for securing confidence in the economic policy. Equally important in this respect is the consistent implementation of the course towards reducing inflation to 4 per cent by the end of 2017.

In the budget adopted, an attempt was made to loosen the traditional tie between its income basis and changes in oil prices. The government recognized the futility of this connection and budgeted for a flat oil price of US$40 per barrel. This measure effectively introduced a new budget rule based on invariable expenses relative to oil price fluctuations.

Holding back expenses helps control the federal budget deficit and the extended government budget deficit, despite the substantial drop in income (even in nominal terms). The federal budget deficit was 2.4 per cent of the GDP in 2015 and 3.4 per cent at the end of 2016, compared with around 6 per cent in 2009 (or 3.4 per cent, 3.7 per cent and 6.3 per cent of the extended government budget, respectively). As for the ratio of the deficit to total federal budget expenses, almost 24 per cent of expenses were covered through deficit financing sources in 2009, compared with 12.6 per cent and 18.1 per cent in 2015 and 2016, respectively. The increase in the total federal budget deficit in 2015 and 2016 coincided with a decreasing oil and gas deficit (from 10.0 per cent to 9.4 per cent of the GDP). Thus, the government succeeded in controlling the deficit for both the federal budget and the overall budget system.

Russia remains a country with a national debt that is exceptionally low, at 13 per cent of GDP, and primarily in the national currency – 9 per cent. The regional budget situation is more complicated: over the past few years, it remained very tense, because, under crisis conditions, regional entities were required to perform their social obligations. Although the debt held against regional budgets is low (below 3 per cent of the GDP), the risk of an acute crisis remained quite real over the past few years. In 2016, the situation improved slightly, at least in three respects. First, a significant portion of commercial debt was restructured into budget debt, on more favourable terms for the regions. Second, almost all of the regional debt is now denominated in the national currency. Third, the debt owed by the regions began to decrease, although insignificantly, by 0.1 per cent of GDP in 2016.[2]

The government budget's dependency on the oil and gas sector is decreasing. The share of oil and gas revenues out of the total federal budget revenues is gradually decreasing, from 51 per cent in 2014, and 43 per cent in 2015, to about 36 per cent in 2016. Undoubtedly, this was conditioned, not so much by the diversification of the Russian economy's structure as by the falling global oil prices, which were not fully compensated for by the fall of the rouble against the dollar.

And the share of oil and gas revenues is falling against a backdrop of declining total federal budget revenues, even in nominal terms.

The Bank of Russia's inflation-targeting policy and a floating exchange rate was especially criticized by many politicians, business people and experts. At the same time, these hard decisions, made in the autumn of 2014, had significant consequences for macroeconomic stability in Russia.

By the end of 2016, inflation had reached 5.4 per cent, which was unprecedented for modern Russia. The government succeeded in retaining and even increasing international reserves: US$377.7 billion (up 2.5 per cent) as of 1 January 2017.

In 2016, capital flight has decreased substantially, from US$152.1 billion in 2014, to US$57.5 billion in 2015, and then to US$15.4 billion in 2016 (estimated by RF Central Bank). The outflow of private capital in 2015 and 2016 was, to a greater extent, related to the repayment of foreign debt by banks and corporations.

Accordingly, the country's total foreign debt was reduced. In 2015 and 2016, the foreign debt for state corporations decreased. For example, in 2015, the government's foreign debt, according to the extended definition,[3] decreased by 12.1 per cent to US$268.1 billion, and the foreign debt of government authorities decreased by 26.6 per cent to US$30.6 billion. The latter fact, however, is not a definitely positive phenomenon in terms of growth financing, as it resulted from financial sanctions.

After the acute crisis and devaluation in 2014, the current account condition improved, and its stability increased: the current account remained positive, and the outflow of capital stabilized quickly under a floating foreign exchange rate.[4]

Shaping the institutional framework for future economic growth, the Bank of Russia pursued consistent and stringent measures to revitalize the banking sector and to remove lending institutions from the market that did not meet the regulator's supervisory requirements. Ninety-seven banking licences were revoked in 2016, which is slightly more than in the preceding years (ninety-three licences were revoked in 2015, and eighty-six in 2014). Lending institutions whose licences were revoked in 2016 held RUB1.2 trillion in total assets, or 1.4 per cent of the total assets of the banking sector at the beginning of 2016 (RUB1.1 trillion, or 1.4 per cent, in 2015, and RUB0.4 trillion, or 0.8 per cent, in 2014, respectively).

This led to positive shifts in the bank's operations. Following a sharp reduction in profits in 2015, when the banking sector earned RUB192 billion, profits began to recover: the banking sector earned RUB930 billion in profits in 2016. However, the return on equity (11 per cent) in annual terms in 2016 was significantly lower than from 2011 to 2013 (17–19 per cent).

*Deposits by companies and households* were boosting the stability of the banking system and simultaneously laying the foundation for a resumption of economic growth.

Bank deposits grew in 2015. This is an important indicator, as the main source of investments for companies is their own resources. However, this trend changed in 2016, owing to an increase in the exchange rate of the rouble and a reduction in interest rates on deposits. From January to October 2016, the total deposits held by companies in the banking system decreased by RUB2.3 trillion, to RUB11.3 trillion as of 1 November 2016. These funds remain significant, despite the reduction from a 35-day cycle as of 1 January 2016, to a 28-day cycle as of 1 November 2016 (prior to 2014, the amount of term deposits did not exceed a 20-day cycle).

Similarly, in 2015 and 2016, a certain amount of growth was observed, followed by stabilization in the savings held with banks by households. The deposit growth rate was between 11 and 12 per cent in 2016. Rouble deposits rose by about 15 per cent whereas foreign exchange deposits barely changed: US$94.0 billion at the beginning of the year, and US$94.7 billion as of 1 November 2016 (a 0.8 per cent increase). The proportion of deposits held in foreign currencies decreased from 29.8 per cent as of 1 January 2016, to 25.7 per cent by the end of the year

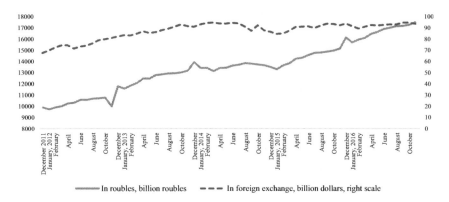

*Figure 19.1* The volume of bank deposits
Source: Central Bank of Russia, calculations by the IEP

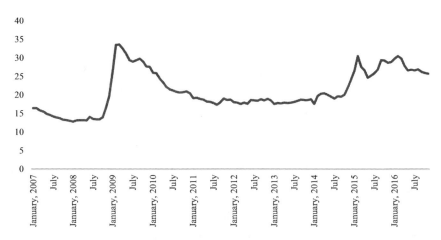

*Figure 19.2* The proportion of bank deposits in foreign exchange, per cent
Source: Central Bank of Russia, calculations by the IEP

(see Figures 19.1 and 19.2). The floating foreign exchange rate served as the means by which *no mass transfer of rouble deposits into foreign exchange occurred for the first time in post-communist Russia.*

## Employment

An important factor in ensuring social and political stability was the low level of unemployment, which, during the previous 2 years, was 5–6 per cent of the working-age population. On the one hand, the working-age population continued to decline, owing to people from quite a sizable generation retiring. On the other hand, the specific aspects of the Russian labour market contributed to the trend: the reduction in economic activity (crisis) was accompanied, not by decreased employment, but by a reduction in working hours and wages. Both factors are interrelated, because the demographic situation is forcing employers to maintain official employment and not rely on the open labour market (see Tables A.1 and A.4).

The biggest difficulties during the period of falling oil prices befell those industries that benefited the most from the Dutch disease – that is, primarily services (especially commerce) and construction. Their adaptation and recovery only began in 2016, which was reflected in the demand for consumer and mortgage loans. In these areas, there is a gradual positive trend, which is natural given the circumstances of a deflating consumer bubble characteristic of booming rental income periods.

## Mortgage loans

Following the mortgage boom in 2013 and 2014, when the housing loan debt grew by 31–32 per cent annually, and the annual disbursement of new loans reached RUB1.82 trillion, the amount of mortgage disbursements dropped sharply in 2015 (RUB1.17 trillion), but demand for mortgages rose by roughly 13 per cent in 2016 (from 1 November 2015 to 1 November 2016), to RUB1.5 trillion. As a result, the total housing loan debt held by individuals reached RUB4.4 trillion in 2016.

Overdue debt under those loans remained insignificant at 1.8 per cent of the total debt. The non-perfoming loan share was 1.2 per cent on rouble housing loans and over 30 per cent on foreign currency nominated loans, but the share of total housing loans held in foreign currencies did not exceed 2 per cent of the total housing loans (see Figures 19.3 and 19.4).

## Retail loans

The total debt under retail loans stopped decreasing at the end of 2016. The annual increase as of the end of November 2016 became positive (up 0.3 per cent), whereas the debt decreased by 7.3 per cent in 2015. The increase in housing loan debt means a corresponding reduction in consumer loan debt. The proportion of overdue debt

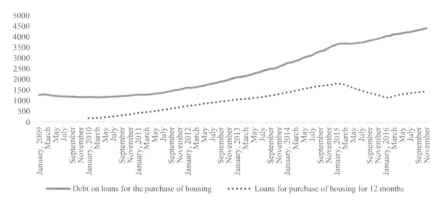

*Figure 19.3* The housing loan market indicators, RUB billion
*Source:* Central Bank of Russia, calculations by the IEP

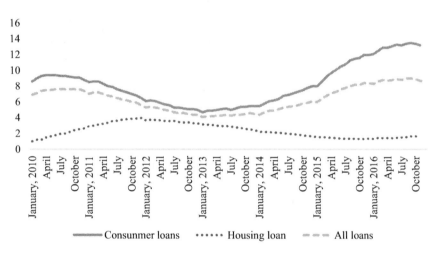

*Figure 19.4* The percentage of overdue loans in credits to individuals, per cent
*Source*: Central Bank of Russia, calculations by the IEP

reached its peak in August 2016 (9.0 per cent of all loans and 13.5 per cent of consumer loans), after which it began to slowly decline (to 8.6 per cent and 13.2 per cent, respectively).

The accumulated debt owed by Russian households was insignificant compared with developed market economies: slightly more than RUB11 trillion (13 per cent of GDP). However, taking into account the higher interest rates (the average annual cost of a performing bank loan was 16.4 per cent in 2016) and short maturities (according to the repayment schedule, the average term on retail loans is 44 months; the actual term, taking into account early repayments, is 18 months), the servicing of bank loans in Russia accounted for 10 per cent of disposable household income

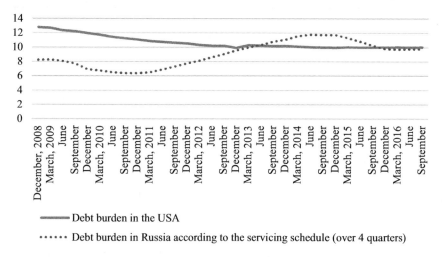

——— Debt burden in the USA

······ Debt burden in Russia according to the servicing schedule (over 4 quarters)

*Figure 19.5* The debt burden on the disposable income of the population in the Russian Federation and the United States, per cent

Source: Central Bank of Russia, Federal State Statistics Service, Federal Reserve, calculations by the IEP

in 2016, compared with the US, where retail loan debt is up to 78 per cent of GDP. In other words, the debt service burden for the average Russian is the same as that for the average American, whereas the relative amount of debt in Russia is six times lower. It should be noted that, over the past 2 years, the debt burden relative to income decreased: it peaked around 12 per cent of disposable income in 2014 (Figure 19.5).

## Diversification of Russian exports

In 2015 and 2016, there were controversial and simultaneously important shifts in the trends for Russian exports. The general trend is for declining exports at times when their structure is being diversified. This reduction is clear, given the decelerating global economy and growing geopolitical tension, resulting in declining demand for products and, respectively, declining prices. This also explains the diversification of exports, as the prices for fuel and energy products and metals fell significantly further than other product categories. As a result, beginning in 2014, the proportion of exports of fuel and energy products has decreased continuously (from 72 per cent in 2014 to below 60 per cent in 2016), whereas the share of other product categories has increased (agriculture, chemicals, light industry, textiles, machinery and equipment). The reduction in the total value of exports in non-energy industries progressed at a lower rate, and growth was observed in some industries, compared with the same period of the previous year, from January to September 2016 (see Tables 19.1 and 19.2). The volume of agricultural exports caught up with armament exports and even exceeded them.

Table 19.1 Changes in the breakdown of export and import products in Russia from 2014 to 2016, per cent of total

| EAEU TN VED (Commodity classification for foreign economic activity) code | Product category | Export 2014 | Export 2015 | Export 2016* | Import 2014 | Import 2015 | Import 2016 |
|---|---|---|---|---|---|---|---|
|  | Total | 100.0 | 100.0 | 100.0 | 100.0 | 100.0 | 100.0 |
| 01–24 | Food products and agricultural raw materials (except for textiles) | 3.8 | 4.7 | 6.0 | 13.9 | 14.6 | 13.7 |
| 25–27 | Mineral products | 70.4 | 63.8 | 59.2 | 2.6 | 2.7 | 1.8 |
| 27 | Fuel and energy products | 69.5 | 62.9 | 58.2 | 1.4 | 1.6 | 0.8 |
| 28–40 | Chemical industry products, rubber | 5.9 | 7.4 | 7.3 | 16.2 | 18.6 | 18.6 |
| 41–43 | Raw hides, furs and derivative products | 0.1 | 0.1 | 0.1 | 0.4 | 0.4 | 0.4 |
| 44–69 | Wood and paper products | 2.3 | 2.9 | 3.4 | 2.1 | 2.0 | 1.9 |
| 50–67 | Textiles, textile products and footwear | 0.2 | 0.3 | 0.3 | 5.7 | 5.9 | 6.0 |
| 71 | Precious stones, precious metals and derivative products | 2.4 | 2.3 | 3.1 | 0.4 | 0.3 | 0.2 |
| 72–83 | Metals and derivative products | 8.1 | 9.6 | 10.1 | 6.7 | 6.4 | 6.3 |
| 84–90 | Machinery, equipment and vehicles | 5.3 | 7.4 | 8.6 | 47.6 | 44.8 | 47.2 |
| 68–70, 91–97 | Other products | 1.4 | 1.6 | 1.9 | 4.4 | 4.2 | 3.9 |

Sources: Federal Custom Service of Russia (official website, Customs Statistics for Foreign Trade section, www.customs.ru/index.php?option=com_content&view=article&id=13858&Itemid=2095); calculations by the Russian Academy for Foreign Trade

Table 19.2 Dynamics of the cost of exports, 2012–16, US$ billion

| Year | 2012 | 2013 | 2014 | 2015 | 2016 |
|---|---|---|---|---|---|
| Food products and agricultural raw materials (except for textiles) (01–24) | 16.8 | 16.3 | 19.0 | 16.2 | 17.1 |
| Fuel and energy products (27) | 368.4 | 370.8 | 345.6 | 216.1 | 166.2 |
| Chemical industry products, rubber (28–40) | 32.1 | 30.8 | 29.2 | 25.4 | 20.8 |
| Light industry (41–49) | 10.7 | 11.6 | 12.0 | 10.2 | 10.1 |
| Textiles, textile products and footwear (50–67) | 0.8 | 0.9 | 1.1 | 0.9 | 0.9 |
| Metallurgy (71–83) | 58.3 | 55.1 | 52.3 | 40.8 | 37.7 |
| Machinery, equipment, and vehicles (84–90) | 26.6 | 28.8 | 26.5 | 25.4 | 24.4 |
| Other products (68–70, 91–97) | 5.6 | 6.6 | 7.0 | 5.5 | 5.5 |

Source: Federal Custom Service of Russia

218  *The Russian version of the global crisis*

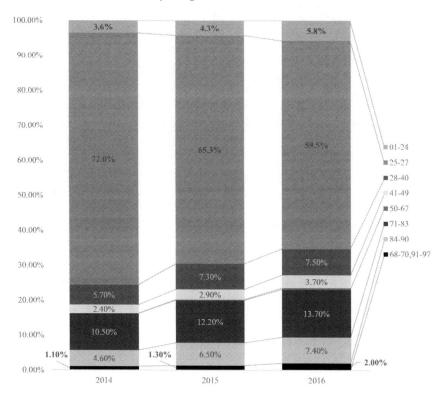

*Figure 19.6* Dynamics of the share of product categories in total exports of Russia
*Source*: Calculations by the authors, based on the data of the FCS of Russia

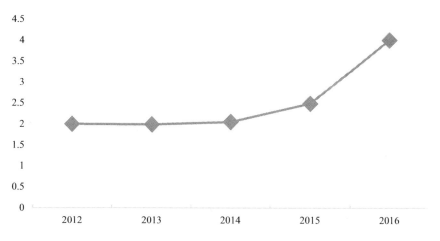

*Figure 19.7* The coefficient of the diversification of Russian exports
*Source*: Calculations based on FCS data

This resulted in diversification of Russian exports. The export diversification coefficient doubled from 2014 to 2016 (Figure 19.6).[5]

The dynamics of export reflect a problem typical of modern crises: an inconsistency between short-term and long-term economic growth objectives. The reduction in exports is undoubtedly an unpleasant phenomenon that negatively impacts current growth and budget opportunities. However, the diversification of exports is laying the foundation for stable economic trends and a stable budget system in the medium term. Of course, that depends on the government and businesses taking advantage of the evolving circumstances and ensuring the increasing competitiveness of non-commodity industries, without relying exclusively on the advantages of a low foreign exchange rate.[6]

## Economic policy priorities

Russia's economic policy faced two key challenges: economic growth and household well-being. These challenges are correlated, as the first leads to increased well-being, and the second generates demand for economic growth.

Solving these tasks is not simple, as Russia faces a structural crisis rather than a cyclical one. The end of the downturn does not automatically restore growth. Without special efforts to build a new growth model, the potential for growth will remain low, which means that the economy will hover around zero (or within statistical error). Unlike a recession, this may last long enough for the political elite to form a model suitable for modern challenges, with the respective impact on well-being and social stability.

The most serious challenge facing Russia is not that of overcoming the recession, but that of achieving economic growth. Of course, we mean sustainable, long-term growth accompanied by structural modernization, rather than the achievement of good-looking statistics. In the foreseeable future, Russia must strive for growth rates exceeding the world average (or somewhere between those of Germany and China).

This is not a trivial task and has no standard solutions, unlike macroeconomic stabilization. Solutions should be contingent upon the challenges of modern technological and social trends – both global and national. An answer to these challenges requires major institutional reforms in all spheres of society, not exclusively in the economic realm.

The following are key points for economic policy that can solve both issues:

Consistent disinflation, which is a natural basis for lowering interest rates and raising investment activity in Russia, will also guarantee social stability. Inflation must be brought down to a target of 4 per cent in 2018. A determination to reach this target would be very important politically, economically and socially.

Decisive disinflation now is not only necessary but possible. If oil prices stay at the present level, Russia will in fact get rid of the 'Dutch disease'. In previous years, attempts to reduce inflation were constrained by the risk of lowered competitiveness due to surplus (that is, not tied to the growth of labour productivity) strengthening of the rouble. Now, however, in the absence of significant increases in oil prices, these risks will not threaten the economy. It presents an additional stimulus for macroeconomic invigoration.

The effectiveness of budgetary policy is frequently brought up by Russian politicians and economists; however, the availability of cheap money over the last 10 years has not brought about the realization of these goals. There are four options here: budgetary manoeuvres, improvements in budgetary procedures, increases in the effectiveness of the budget network, and clarifications of the fiscal rules based on experience and current realities. Key here is the question of the influence of separate budget line items on economic growth.[7]

Over the past few years, the allocation of budget expenditures underwent negative changes. Expenditures that promote increasing reserves and the quality of factors of production (labour and capital), as well as the growth of total factor productivity (primarily investments in human capital and infrastructure), have not increased, and in some cases have decreased, relative to GDP. The share of non-productive expenses has grown. This structural shift limits the effectiveness of budget stimulation.[8]

The prospect of budget rule is a special problem. As oil prices are relatively low, the issue may not seem pertinent. However, it makes sense to discuss it. The fiscal rule of the 2000s, which called for rent income to be moved into sovereign funds, was a reaction to the Soviet experience of completely spending all rent income, making the country vulnerable to shocks from changes in economic conditions. The experience of 2009–12 demonstrated the serious drawbacks of this model: the presence of a 'safety cushion' is a disincentive to modernization. A crisis is a time that pushes you towards modernization, but a financial reserve allows you to continue in a *business as usual* mode.

We need to re-examine the very concept of using surplus income and, therefore, fiscal rules. Given the reality in Russia, it would be wise to have stricter guidelines defining the cut-off price for market revenues (setting it at a rather low level) and balancing the current budget (that is, the budget of repeating obligations) at the level of revenues that are most protected from the fluctuations of external factors. If there are additional rent revenues, they should be used for a development budget – that is, to finance expenses with a final time horizon. This model would allow more active investment in development when the market is good, and would not create the temptation to pour money into problems when there is a crisis.

Support for non-oil exports is currently another important priority. Import substitution became a fashionable topic. However, it is not the same as foisting low-quality domestic products on to people at a high price, especially when their producers are demanding financial aid from the budget. The Russian economy may benefit from import substitution, but the type that would be competitive in an open market. In other words, it is important to stimulate export-oriented import substitution. Support for non-oil exports and that for import substitution must go hand in hand.

Several conditions must be met for this to occur.

First, there should be no obstacles to non-oil exports. Yet, despite calls to stimulate exports, there was more talk about tariff and non-tariff restrictions. There were proposals to limit grain and metal exports. These could easily be followed by limits on chemical exports, and so on. The problem is understandable: under devaluation, exports become more attractive, which leads to problems with filling the domestic market. However, these complications (only potential in part, as demand within the country is also falling) should not be a reason to reject improvements in the structure of Russian exports. There are enough levers to supply the domestic market, without need to obstruct the foreign expansion of our producers.

Second, one should not create import offsets – artificial barriers to keep foreign competitors out of the Russian market. The present exchange rate is an adequate barrier to protect domestic manufacturers, although imported goods, paradoxically, could help price stability in a number of ways.

Third, it is important not to interfere with efforts by domestic companies to improve and restructure. This will be accompanied by a rationalization of employment, which, for all its pain, would be an element in modernization. Rationalization is important, both for export-oriented companies and for companies that are primarily focused on import substitution.

Attracting private investment (domestic and foreign) once again becomes a priority in economic policy at both the federal and regional levels. When rent revenues were high, this was less important, because the budget influx could compensate for gaps in the investment climate. Russia's improved position in the Doing Business ratings is an important benchmark. However, in today's geopolitical situation, its significance is extremely limited and conditional.

Authorities at all levels must orient themselves towards attracting investors, just as the authorities of Novgorod Oblast did in the 1990s and those of Kaluga or Ulyanovsk oblasts did within the last 15 years. This must be one of the key parameters in assessment of the effectiveness of regional administration, no less important than salaries in the budget sector.

Deregulation, protection of the rights of entrepreneurs and development of small and medium businesses are different but closely connected economic policy priorities. Legislation should be favourable for business, helping to attract entrepreneurs rather than repel them. Yet, even at the level of naming regulations, we can see a worsening attitude towards entrepreneurship. In the past, the law was called "On protecting the rights of companies and individual entrepreneurs when implementing state control (oversight) and municipal control" (26 December 2008, no. 294-FZ); now, the draft law is called "On federal, regional, and municipal control". The point is not in the name but in the practice, which is in no way favourable to business activity, despite the improved status of Russia in the Doing Business rating and the president's direct instructions "to lift restrictions on business maximally, freeing it from obtrusive oversight and control". In this regard, we should return to the approach in the Gref Programme, elaborated in 1999–2000, which outlined substantial simplifications in licensing and expanded the role of insurance.

A complex of measures stimulating competition must be elaborated. This is of particular importance in the current macroeconomic and geopolitical situation, when devaluation and sanctions limit access to competing goods and services in the domestic market. The policy of stimulating competition should be considered the equivalent of a policy limiting monopolies, which in some cases are in complete contradiction. Russia needs a competitive policy and not a "struggle against monopolies", which is often understood as curtailing those who have achieved market success.

The list of problems has not exhausted the modernization agenda during this crisis. Other important institutional and structural reforms are needed in human capital (education, health, pension system), which involves social, fiscal and investment factors. Russia needs new approaches to social policy, foreign economic activity and spatial development.

A key challenge for Russian economic development would be to create a mechanism to recover economic growth while avoiding populist scenarios. The way this issue is resolved will have a huge impact on the life of Russia in the post-global-crisis world.

## Notes

1 During the "acceleration" policy of 1986–9, increased growth rates were achieved through macroeconomic destabilization (sharp growth in the national debt and budget deficit), resulting in a decade-long period of stagnation, followed by another decade to return the economy to the pre-crisis level (for more, see: Mau, 2014: 22–4).
2 For more, see: Deryugin 2016.
3 The foreign debt of the public sector according to the extended definition covers the foreign debt owed by administrative government agencies, the central bank, banks and non-banking corporations, in which administrative government agencies and the Central Bank own, directly or indirectly, 50 per cent or more of the capital, or control them in another way.
4 The mechanism for adapting the Russian economy to the decreasing real exchange rate of the rouble was reviewed in: Drobyshevsky and Polbin 2016.
5 Calculation by G. Idrisov (RANEPA). The degree of Russian export diversification was calculated based on the diversification index used by the World Bank (the Herfindahl–Hirschman index). Available at: http://wits.worldbank.org/wits/wits/wits help/Content/Utilities/e1.trade_indicators.htm (accessed 5 August 2017).
6 See: Kadochnikov *et al.* 2016.
7 See: IMF 1995; Moreno-Dodson 2013.
8 See: Knobel and Sokolov 2012; Idrisov and Sinelnikov-Murylev 2013, 2014.

## References

Deryugin, A. (2016). "Regional'nye byudzhety: zatyagivayem poyasa" [Regional budgets: At the limit of possibilities], *Ekonomicheskoe Razvitie Rossii*, no. 12, pp. 70–5.

Drobyshevsky, S. and Polbin, A. (2016). "O roli plavayuursa rublya v stabilizatsii delovoj aktivnosti pri vnesneekonomicheskih shokah" [On the role of floating rouble in stabilizing business activity under foreign trade shocks], *Problemy Teorii i Praktiki Upravleniya*, no. 6, pp. 66–71.

Idrisov, G. and Sinelnikov-Murylev, S. (2013). "Byudzhetnaya politika i ekonomicheskiy rost" [Budget policy and economic growth], *Voprosy Ekonomiki*, no. 8, pp. 35–59.

Idrisov, G. and Sinelnikov-Murylev, S. (2014). "Formirovaniye predposylok dolgosrochnogo rosta: kak ih ponimat'?" [Forming sources for a long-run growth: How to understand?], *Voprosy Ekonomiki*, no. 3, pp. 4–20.

IMF. (1995). *Unproductive Public Expenditures: A pragmatic approach to policy analysis.* Prepared by K. Chu, S. Gupta, B. Clements, D. Hewitt, S. Lugaresi, J. Schiff, L. Schuknecht, and G. Schwartz. IMF Pamphlet Series, no. 48.

Kadochnikov, P., Knobel, A., and Sinelnikov-Murylev, S. (2016). "Otkrytost' rossijskoj ekonomiki kak istochnik ekonomicheskogo rosta" [Openness of the Russian economy as a source of economic growth], *Voprosy Ekonomiki*, no. 12, pp. 26–42.

Knobel, A. and Sokolov, I. (2012). "Otsenka byudzhetnoj politiki RF na srednesrochnuyu perspektivu" [Evaluation of Russia's budget policy in medium-term perspective], *Ekonomicheskoye rasvitie Rossii*, no. 12 (19), pp. 23–32.

Mau, V. (2014). "V ozhidanii novoj modeli rosta: sotsial'no-ekonomicheskoye razvitiye Rossii v 2013 godu" [Waiting for a new model of growth: Russia's social and economic development in 2013], *Voprosy Ekonomiki*, no. 2, pp. 4–32.

Moreno-Dodson, B. (ed.) (2013). *Is Fiscal Policy the Answer? A developing country perspective*. Washington, DC: The World Bank.

# Conclusion
## Medium-term economic policy priorities

The key objective of economic policy is to create conditions for sustainable growth in the medium term. The success criteria should be that growth rates exceed the world average and that they are accompanied by structural modernization of institutions. To do this, one should create a new growth model, based not so much on increasing production factors – labour and capital (as there are substantial internal and external constraints) – as on increasing the effectiveness of their use – that is, increasing the total factor productivity. It would essentially mean the transition from a model based on the stimulation of demand to an economy focused on stimulating supply.

What are the key elements of this model and, respectively, the objectives of economic policy?

*First*, there is preservation of a conservative (cautious) macroeconomic policy that includes maintaining the stability of the budget while reducing the budget load in the GDP, and lowering the dependency of the budget (and therefore the whole economy) on fluctuations in the external economic environment.

The existing structure of budgetary expenditures needs to be rationalized, and its efficiency needs to be improved. This task cannot be achieved through organizational measures such as introducing state programmes and thereby replacing some federal or departmental targeted programmes. The programme nature of the budget is only a form, which will not automatically bring new content.

One must implement the budget manoeuvre while selecting sectors of primary importance for economic growth. Based on theoretical works and the international experience of contemporary history, such budget expenditures should include investment in human capital and transport infrastructure.

The budgetary network requires restructuring and modernization. This task cannot be accomplished solely by the introduction of normative per capita financing and the abolition of inefficient budget institutions. First of all, executive authorities should decide on the prospects of specific state and municipal (government, budgetary, autonomous) agencies.[1]

Finally, in the face of high uncertainty in both political and economic conditions in Russia, it would be appropriate to form, along with the next annual budget, a 'contingency budget', in order to not lose time in developing a new budget in case of a dramatically deteriorating situation, but to be able immediately to offer its ready-made version to legislators.

*Second* is a consistent reduction in inflation. The transition to inflation targeting is the first step in this direction. Maintaining of inflation at 4 per cent level would be the most important factor in ensuring predictability in economic life and would also increase the affordability of commercial loans.

Disinflation helps to strengthen the position of the rouble as a regional reserve currency. The rouble has certain advantages that enable it to become a regional currency (first of all, the size of Russian economy, and the fact that bordering countries gravitate towards Russia), although there are significant limitations: the resource-based economy presupposes increased volatility in the exchange rate. Despite the devaluation problems of 2014–15, this task should not be withdrawn from the agenda. It would be appropriate to prepare a special programme (action plan) to strengthen the international position of the rouble.

*Third* is streamlining the economic situation in the regions, taking measures to limit increases in expenditure obligations and debts while increasing the involvement of regions in collecting taxes. It would be important to undertake a wide-ranging discussion of the principles of federalism, to expand the tax base and increase the collection rate of taxes within the responsibility of the regions and municipalities, and, on this basis, to provide conditions for the development of interregional competition for investors and businesses. This requires significant institutional measures to be taken.[2]

In formulating economic principles and policies, one should not take decisions that lead to increased costs. With all the importance of social development and the wages of state employees, ignoring competitive ability can negatively affect the willingness of investors to locate their production facilities in the country, that is, to invest in Russia.

*Fourth*, there is the use of the conditions that are prevailing owing to devaluation to stimulate the diversification of the national economy and exports. Devaluation offers opportunities for the development of national producers, for import substitution. This development requires, not only the withdrawal of foreign competitors, but also availability of investment resources and, consequently, the investment climate for increasing national production.

Import substitution cannot be reduced to the internal market being filled with domestic goods of lower quality and higher prices. Import substitution that is worthy of public support must be export-oriented, that is, it must offer products and services that are competitive, not only inside the country, but also in foreign markets.

*Fifth* – accordingly – stimulating competition is one of the institutional priorities. Its importance increases in the face of devaluation, which leads to a substantial limitation of competition from imported goods.

Russia needs serious institutional and ideological changes. The attention of antitrust authorities should be focused on maintaining competition and prevention of it being limited by administrative methods, instead of fighting against successful firms that gain marketable weight thanks to their effectiveness.

There is, therefore, a need for a significant reduction in the number of anti-trust cases under investigation, with attention being focused on those that are most prominent and economically significant; anti-monopoly policy should no longer be oriented towards individual businessmen and small and medium-sized businesses, or companies with a small market share; control over small and medium-sized firms should be reduced; and there should be a focus on counteracting monopolistic trends in large companies, which have lobbying power.

*Sixth* is the development of human capital – improvement of the efficiency of welfare state institutions. In a modern, post-industrial society, the principles of the welfare state, established at the turn of the nineteenth–twentieth centuries, demonstrate absolute inefficiency. It is pointless to invest big money in these sectors before their institutional modernization in line with the challenges of the twenty-first century.

A post-industrial welfare state will differ substantially from the traditional industrial one, and it is exactly today that its fundamental principles are being searched for. Even now, one can identify a number of its characteristic features, which include: the continuous and lifelong nature of provided services, where people learn and are treated throughout their lifetime; individualization – that is, the possibility for an individual to define his or her own trajectories and mechanisms of education and health care, choosing from a variety of offered educational and health-care services; globalization of services and international competition for customers, where education and health-care institutions compete, not with neighbouring schools and hospitals, and not even with relevant institutions in their country, but with institutions all over the world; privatization of social services, while the role of private expenditure on human capital development is increased, because private payments or co-payments are not only natural but also inevitable, as a result of the technological modernization of these sectors and growth of welfare; and the emergence of new technologies that are radically changing the nature of the services provided by these service sectors.

All these features help, not only to form the basis for the modernization of human capital sectors, but also to carry out the economic and political modernization of the entire country, including its technological base.

*Seventh*, there is reform of the labour market and enhancement of the territorial mobility of the workforce.

Measures should be taken to enhance the flexibility of labour legislation, which currently does not reflect the realities of the post-industrial era, and primarily the features of production in the face of dominating information technologies. Strict labour legislation and economic agents' weak discipline need to be abandoned, flexible labour laws need to be adopted, and strong discipline of market participants should be ensured. New forms of employment need to be brought into legislation, which will reflect the development of information technology. The measures to adjust labour legislation include: adjustment, in accordance with today's realities, of basic concepts of 'working time', 'business day', 'workplace', and so on; an increase in the flexibility of labour relations, simplifying recruitment and dismissal procedures – reducing the notice period of dismissal, thereby reducing the costs of dismissal, including the size of severance pay; significant expansion of the grounds for conclusion of fixed-term employment contracts, with possible complete repeal of open-term employment contracts with individuals;

simplification of procedures for changes to the terms of employment contracts and termination of employment contracts for economic reasons; change to the organization of working time: expansion of opportunities for flexible schedules, development of remote forms of employment, calls for workers on request, and so on; and simplification of HR record management, including cancellation of work record books.

Political pressure on the regions and businessmen to artificially maintain employment must be abandoned. Of course, the state must minimize the socio-political risks of workforce release. Such risks do exist, but they are being reduced owing to the demographic trend (reduction in the number of employed persons of working age).

In addition to reform of labour legislation, it is necessary to take measures to support interregional mobility. Its potential is not so great, and yet the state should stimulate the workforce to move to the points of economic growth, which can partly mitigate the effects of the reduction in the economically active population. To activate internal labour migration, it would be appropriate to create a single national database of vacancies; increase Russians' access to social and other services at the place of actual residence – especially where medical insurance is concerned; introduce registration with the tax authorities in the form of a simple notification, which should provide access to social benefits throughout the country; and develop affordable rental and corporate housing sectors.[3]

Measures should be taken to improve Russia's immigration attractiveness: a transition from the restrictive regulation of migration to differential; stimulation of 'settled' migration; and a policy to attract a highly skilled workforce (including stimulation of education and academic immigration and mobility). The most difficult is to stimulate the migration of a highly skilled workforce, but solving this task is much more important than discussing problems of illegal migration of unskilled workers.

*Eighth*: the stepping-up of efforts to integrate the Russian economy into the international division of labour must continue, despite all geopolitical complexities. Here, we have the following key areas: the formation of mechanisms of post-Soviet integration, participation in various regional free trade groupings, and the formation and protection of value chains generated by domestic business.

The most important is to develop and strengthen the EurAsian Economic Community. Post-Soviet integration can have a number of important implications. First, it expands the boundaries of the market and creates an important precedent of reintegration, which is open to other countries. Second, it promotes the international competitiveness of the rouble and becomes a step towards its transformation into a regional reserve currency. Third, apart from competition of products, it creates conditions for the competition of institutions and jurisdictions, and, although the institutions of the partner countries are not very attractive, the mere fact of competition will contribute to positive institutional changes.

Various formats and institutions of interaction within the framework of the Eastern Partnership, BRICS, and so on, are becoming more significant. However, these directions should not remove the tasks of interacting with the EU, despite all the difficulties associated with sanctions and other political complications.

Accession to the WTO has helped to diversify exports, although foreign sanctions play negative role in this respect and mitigate the role of WTO in international competetiveness. Of course, the state and business should take appropriate coordinated efforts, but additional chances to increase the activity of Russian companies in international production chains are emerging.

All this should aid Russia's search for new niches in the global division of labour through the diversification of raw-materials exports, stimulating exports of goods other than raw materials and the international cooperation of Russian firms. After all, successful modernization spurts over the last 50 years have been associated with export orientation.

*Ninth*, and finally, non-economic factors and institutions – the quality of law enforcement and the judicial system, the effectiveness of public administration – are critically important to economic growth. The key issue is undoubtedly the security of life and property as a precondition for any business.

From an economic point of view, the essence of the proposed measures can be defined as the policy of stimulating supply, in contrast to the policy of stimulating demand. Various countries, at different times, have given preference to one or other model of growth. Stimulating supply involves creating conditions favourable to the performance growth of domestic producers, including low inflation and low interest rates, the removal of institutional barriers to business, clear and transparent rules, and predictable and stable macroeconomics. In this situation, the state should undertake to develop the technical and social infrastructure, including effective financial markets, a flexible labour market and high-quality human capital.

## Notes

1 See: Klyachko and Sinelnikov-Murylev 2012.
2 In particular, one can benefit from the experience of those US states that underwent a series of defaults in the mid nineteenth century. In those days, many states were forbidden to adopt budgets with a deficit by the Constitution. This meant that the states could borrow money only for the implementation of specific projects, but not to cover the budget deficit. In other words, these states could borrow money in order to address some problem, but its repayment and servicing had to be included in the budget, which had to be balanced on these conditions (see: Henning and Kessler 2012).
3 See: Maleva 2011.

## References

Henning, C.R. and Kessler, M. (2012). "Byudgetno-nalogovy federalism: istorichesky opyt SSHA dlya Yevropeiskogo soyuza" [Fiscal federalism: US history for architects of Europe's fiscal union], *Ekonomicheskaya Politika*, no. 5.

Klyachko, T. and Sinelnikov-Murylev, S. (2012). "O normativah byudgetnogo finansirovaniya i regulirovaniya velichiny platy za obucheniye v gosudarstvennykh vuzakh" [About standards of budgetary funding and regulation of tuition fees in public universities], *Ekonomicheskaya Politika*, no. 6.

Maleva, T. (2011). "Rossiysky rynok truda: effektivnost zanyatosti ili sokrascheniye bezrabotitsy?" [Russian Labour Market: Effectiveness of Employment or Reduction in Unemployment?]. In *Modernization and Human Development. The UNDP Report on Human Development Capacity*. Moscow: UNDP.

# Appendix

Table A.1 Main economic indicators for the Russian Federation, 2007–16

| | 2007 | 2008 | 2009 | 2010 | 2011 | 2012 | 2013 | 2014 | 2015 | 2016 |
|---|---|---|---|---|---|---|---|---|---|---|
| *Macroeconomic indicators (growth in physical volume as percentage of the previous year)* | | | | | | | | | | |
| GDP | 8.5 | 5.2 | −7.8 | 4.5 | 4.3 | 3.5 | 1.3 | 0.7 | −2.8 | −0.2 |
| Industry | 6.8 | 0.6 | −10.7 | 7.3 | 5.0 | 3.4 | 0.4 | 1.7 | −0.8 | 1.3 |
| Agriculture | 3.3 | 10.8 | 1.4 | −11.3 | 23.0 | −4.8 | 5.8 | 3.5 | 2.6 | 4.8 |
| Construction | 18.2 | 12.8 | −13.2 | 5.0 | 5.1 | 2.5 | 0.1 | −2.3 | −4.8 | −4.3 |
| Wholesale trade | 9.5 | 5.4 | 2.0 | 3.0 | 4.4 | 3.6 | 0.7 | −3.6 | −10.0 | 2.6 |
| Retail trade | 16.1 | 13.7 | −5.1 | 6.5 | 7.1 | 6.3 | 3.9 | 2.7 | −10.0 | −4.6 |
| Retail consumption by household | 14.3 | 10.6 | −5.1 | 5.5 | 6.8 | 7.9 | 5.2 | 2.0 | −9.8 | −4.5 |
| Investments in fixed capital | 23.8 | 9.5 | −13.5 | 6.3 | 10.8 | 6.8 | 0.8 | −1.5 | −8.4 | −2.3 |
| Share of wages in GDP (methodology change in 2011) | 46.7 | 47.4 | 52.6 | 49.6 | 43.9 | 44.2 | 46.1 | 46.4 | 46.8 | 48.4 |
| Share of profits and mixed income within GDP (methodology change in 2011) | 34.1 | 32.6 | 30.8 | 32.7 | 41.8 | 41.4 | 40.0 | 38.9 | 43.1 | 41.7 |
| *Public finance and international reserves* | | | | | | | | | | |
| Surplus (+)/deficit (−) of the consolidated budget, % of GDP | 6.0 | 4.9 | −6.3 | −3.4 | 1.4 | 0.4 | −1.2 | −1.1 | −3.4 | −3.7 |
| Surplus (+)/deficit (−) of the federal budget, % of GDP | 5.4 | 4.1 | −6.0 | −3.9 | 0.7 | −0.1 | −0.4 | −0.5 | −2.4 | 3.4 |
| Oil and gas deficit of the federal budget, % of GDP | −3.3 | −6.5 | −13.7 | −12.2 | −9.3 | −10.5 | −10.4 | −10.1 | −9.4 | −9.1 |
| Russian domestic national debt (at year end, RUB billion) | 1,248.8 | 1,499.8 | 2,094.7 | 2,940.4 | 4,190.6 | 4,977.9 | 5,722.2 | 7,241.2 | 7,307.6 | 8,003.0 |
| Foreign national debt (Ministry of Finance data, US$ billion) | 44.9 | 40.6 | 37.6 | 40.0 | 35.8 | 50.8 | 55.8 | 54.4 | 50.0 | 51.2 |

| | | | | | | | | | | |
|---|---|---|---|---|---|---|---|---|---|---|
| Consolidated national debt (% of GDP) | 7.2 | 6.5 | 8.3 | 9.0 | 9.0 | 9.7 | 10.6 | 13.0 | 13.2 | 12.9 |
| Reserve Fund (2007 – Stabilization Fund), at year end, US$ billion | 156.81 | 137.09 | 60.52 | 25.44 | 25.21 | 62.08 | 87.38 | 87.91 | 49.95 | 16.03 |
| National Welfare Fund at year end, US$ billion | | 87.97 | 91.56 | 88.44 | 86.79 | 88.59 | 88.63 | 78.0 | 71.72 | 71.87 |
| International reserves at the Bank of Russia, year end | 478.8 | 427.1 | 439.0 | 479.4 | 498.6 | 537.6 | 509.6 | 385.5 | 368.4 | 377.7 |

### Labor market

| | | | | | | | | | | |
|---|---|---|---|---|---|---|---|---|---|---|
| Overall unemployment rate (ILO methodology), annual average, % | 6.0 | 6.2 | 8.3 | 7.3 | 6.5 | 5.5 | 5.5 | 5.2 | 5.6 | 5.5 |
| Average wages (RUB thousand/month) | 13.6 | 17.3 | 18.6 | 21.0 | 23.4 | 26.6 | 29.8 | 32.5 | 34.0 | 36.7 |
| Wages in real terms | 17.2 | 11.5 | −3.5 | 5.2 | 2.8 | 8.4 | 4.8 | 1.2 | −9.0 | −0.6 |
| Real disposable household income | 12.1 | 2.4 | 3.0 | 5.9 | 0.5 | 4.6 | 4.0 | −0.7 | −3.2 | −5.9 |
| Population with cash income below subsistence level, millions | 18.8 | 19.0 | 18.4 | 17.7 | 17.9 | 15.4 | 15.5 | 16.1 | 19.5 | 19.5 |

### Banking system

| | | | | | | | | | | |
|---|---|---|---|---|---|---|---|---|---|---|
| Number of active lending institutions at year end | 1,136 | 1,108 | 1,058 | 1,012 | 978 | 956 | 923 | 834 | 733 | 623 |
| Number of banking licences withdrawn during the year | 49 | 33 | 43 | 27 | 18 | 22 | 32 | 86 | 93 | 97 |
| Assets | 46.1 | 32.7 | 3.7 | 14.8 | 21.4 | 20.4 | 14.2 | 18.6 | −1.5 | 2.1 |
| Debt owed by domestic corporations (excluding banks) under bank loans | 52.4 | 28.6 | 0.0 | 9.6 | 22.8 | 15.5 | 11.6 | 12.7 | 5.0 | −0.1 |
| Debt owed by domestic individuals under bank loans | 58.3 | 31.2 | −11.7 | 14.4 | 35.5 | 39.1 | 27.7 | 11.6 | −7.3 | 0.7 |
| Share of overdue loans to domestic corporations, excluding banks | 0.9 | 2.2 | 6.0 | 5.5 | 4.8 | 4.6 | 4.1 | 4.1 | 6.0 | 6.1 |
| Share of overdue loans to individuals | 3.1 | 3.6 | 6.9 | 7.1 | 5.3 | 4.1 | 4.5 | 6.0 | 8.4 | 8.3 |
| Profit, RUB billion | 508 | 409 | 205 | 573 | 848 | 1,012 | 994 | 589 | 192 | 930 |

*Sources*: Federal State Statistics Service; Ministry of Finance; Central Bank of Russian Federation

Table A.2 GDP growth rates by years of leading developed and developing countries in 1990–2016, per cent

| | Share in world GDP (2016) | 1990 | 1991 | 1992 | 1993 | 1994 | 1995 | 1996 | 1997 | 1998 | 1999 | 2000 | 2001 | 2002 | 2003 | 2004 | 2005 | 2006 | 2007 | 2008 | 2009 | 2010 | 2011 | 2012 | 2013 | 2014 | 2015 | 2016* |
|---|---|---|---|---|---|---|---|---|---|---|---|---|---|---|---|---|---|---|---|---|---|---|---|---|---|---|---|---|
| The world, total | | 3.4 | 2.6 | 2.3 | 2.1 | 3.2 | 3.3 | 3.9 | 4.1 | 2.5 | 3.6 | 4.8 | 2.5 | 3.0 | 4.3 | 5.4 | 4.8 | 5.5 | 5.7 | 3.0 | −0.1 | 5.4 | 4.2 | 3.5 | 3.3 | 3.4 | 3.2 | 3.1 |
| Developed countries | 61.1 | 3.2 | 1.6 | 2.3 | 1.4 | 3.4 | 2.8 | 3.0 | 3.5 | 2.7 | 3.6 | 4.1 | 1.6 | 1.8 | 2.1 | 3.2 | 2.7 | 3.1 | 2.7 | 0.1 | −3.4 | 3.1 | 1.7 | 1.2 | 1.2 | 1.9 | 2.1 | 1.7 |
| Group of 7 | 46.9 | 2.9 | 1.2 | 2.1 | 1.3 | 3.1 | 2.4 | 2.7 | 3.3 | 2.7 | 3.2 | 3.7 | 1.3 | 1.3 | 1.9 | 2.9 | 2.5 | 2.6 | 2.1 | −0.3 | −3.8 | 2.9 | 1.6 | 1.4 | 1.3 | 1.7 | 1.9 | 1.5 |
| European Union, EU | 22.0 | 2.5 | 1.2 | 0.9 | −0.2 | 2.9 | 2.8 | 2.1 | 2.8 | 2.9 | 3.0 | 3.9 | 2.3 | 1.5 | 1.5 | 2.7 | 2.3 | 3.6 | 3.3 | 0.6 | −4.3 | 2.1 | 1.7 | −0.4 | 0.3 | 1.6 | 2.3 | 2.0 |
| USA | 38.9 | 1.9 | −0.1 | 3.6 | 4.1 | 1.8 | −0.3 | −2.8 | 2.5 | 1.6 | 2.2 | 1.7 | 2.4 | 2.6 | 1.9 | −0.1 | 3.6 | 4.1 | 1.8 | −0.3 | −2.8 | 2.5 | 1.6 | 2.2 | 1.7 | 2.4 | 2.6 | 1.6 |
| Japan | 6.3 | 5.6 | 3.3 | 0.8 | 2.8 | 1.7 | −1.1 | −5.4 | 4.2 | −0.1 | 1.5 | 2.0 | 0.3 | 1.2 | 5.6 | 3.3 | 0.8 | 2.8 | 1.7 | −1.1 | −5.4 | 4.2 | −0.1 | 1.5 | 2.0 | 0.3 | 1.2 | 1.0 |
| Germany | 4.6 | 5.3 | 5.1 | 1.9 | 3.0 | 3.3 | 1.1 | −5.6 | 4.1 | 3.7 | 0.5 | 0.5 | 1.6 | 1.7 | 5.3 | 5.1 | 1.9 | 3.0 | 3.3 | 1.1 | −5.6 | 4.1 | 3.7 | 0.5 | 0.5 | 1.6 | 1.7 | 1.8 |
| United Kingdom | 3.5 | 0.7 | −1.1 | 0.4 | 3.7 | 2.6 | −0.6 | −4.3 | 1.9 | 1.5 | 1.3 | 1.9 | 3.1 | 2.2 | 0.7 | −1.1 | 0.4 | 3.7 | 2.6 | −0.6 | −4.3 | 1.9 | 1.5 | 1.3 | 1.9 | 3.1 | 2.2 | 1.8 |
| France | 3.3 | 2.9 | 1.0 | 1.6 | 3.9 | 2.4 | 0.2 | −2.9 | 2.0 | 2.1 | 0.2 | 0.6 | 0.6 | 1.3 | 2.9 | 1.0 | 1.6 | 3.9 | 2.4 | 0.2 | −2.9 | 2.0 | 2.1 | 0.2 | 0.6 | 0.6 | 1.3 | 1.2 |
| Italy | 2.5 | 2.0 | 1.5 | 0.8 | 3.7 | 1.5 | −1.1 | −5.5 | 1.7 | 0.6 | −2.8 | −1.7 | 0.1 | 0.7 | 2.0 | 1.5 | 0.8 | 3.7 | 1.5 | −1.1 | −5.5 | 1.7 | 0.6 | −2.8 | −1.7 | 0.1 | 0.7 | 0.9 |
| Portugal | 0.3 | 4.0 | 4.4 | 1.1 | 3.8 | 2.5 | 0.2 | −3.0 | 1.9 | −1.8 | −4.0 | −1.1 | 0.9 | 1.5 | 4.0 | 4.4 | 1.1 | 3.8 | 2.5 | 0.2 | −3.0 | 1.9 | −1.8 | −4.0 | −1.1 | 0.9 | 1.5 | 1.4 |

| | | | | | | | | | | | | | | | | | | | | | | | | | | | |
|---|---|---|---|---|---|---|---|---|---|---|---|---|---|---|---|---|---|---|---|---|---|---|---|---|---|---|---|
| Ireland | 0.4 | 8.5 | 1.9 | 3.3 | 9.9 | 3.8 | −4.4 | −4.6 | 2.0 | 0.0 | −1.1 | 1.1 | 8.5 | 26.3 | 8.5 | 1.9 | 3.3 | 9.9 | 3.8 | −4.4 | −4.6 | 2.0 | 0.0 | −1.1 | 1.1 | 8.5 | 26.3 | 5.2 |
| Spain | 1.7 | 3.8 | 2.5 | 0.9 | 5.3 | 3.8 | 1.1 | −3.6 | 0.0 | −1.0 | −2.6 | −1.7 | 1.4 | 3.2 | 3.8 | 2.5 | 0.9 | 5.3 | 3.8 | 1.1 | −3.6 | 0.0 | −1.0 | −2.6 | −1.7 | 1.4 | 3.2 | 3.2 |
| Greece | 0.3 | 0.0 | 3.1 | 0.7 | 3.9 | 3.3 | −0.3 | −4.3 | −5.5 | −9.1 | −7.3 | −3.2 | 0.4 | −0.2 | 0.0 | 3.1 | 0.7 | 3.9 | 3.3 | −0.3 | −4.3 | −5.5 | −9.1 | −7.3 | −3.2 | 0.4 | −0.2 | 0.0 |
| Canada | 2.0 | 0.2 | −2.1 | 0.9 | 5.2 | 2.1 | 1.0 | −2.9 | 3.1 | 3.1 | 1.7 | 2.2 | 2.5 | 1.1 | 0.2 | −2.1 | 0.9 | 5.2 | 2.1 | 1.0 | −2.9 | 3.1 | 3.1 | 1.7 | 2.2 | 2.5 | 1.1 | 1.4 |
| Developing countries | 38.9 | 3.9 | 4.4 | 2.4 | 3.0 | 3.1 | 4.0 | 5.1 | 4.8 | 2.3 | 3.6 | 5.8 | 3.7 | 4.5 | 6.7 | 7.9 | 7.2 | 8.1 | 8.6 | 5.8 | 2.9 | 7.5 | 6.3 | 5.3 | 5.0 | 4.6 | 4.0 | 4.1 |
| China | 15.1 | 3.9 | 9.3 | 14.2 | 8.5 | 14.2 | 9.7 | 9.4 | 10.6 | 9.5 | 7.9 | 7.8 | 7.3 | 6.9 | 3.9 | 9.3 | 14.2 | 8.5 | 14.2 | 9.7 | 9.4 | 10.6 | 9.5 | 7.9 | 7.8 | 7.3 | 6.9 | 6.7 |
| India | 3.0 | 5.5 | 1.1 | 5.5 | 3.8 | 8.6 | 3.9 | 8.5 | 10.3 | 6.6 | 5.6 | 6.6 | 7.2 | 7.6 | 5.5 | 1.1 | 5.5 | 3.8 | 8.6 | 3.9 | 8.5 | 10.3 | 6.6 | 5.6 | 6.6 | 7.2 | 7.6 | 6.8 |
| Russia | 1.7 | −3.0 | −5.0 | −14.5 | 10.0 | 8.5 | 5.2 | −7.8 | 4.5 | 4.3 | 3.5 | 1.3 | 0.7 | −3.7 | −3.0 | −5.0 | −14.5 | 10.0 | 8.5 | 5.2 | −7.8 | 4.5 | 4.3 | 3.5 | 1.3 | 0.7 | −3.7 | −0.2 |
| Brazil | 2.4 | −3.1 | 1.5 | −0.5 | 4.1 | 6.1 | 5.1 | −0.1 | 7.5 | 3.9 | 1.9 | 3.0 | 0.1 | −3.8 | −3.1 | 1.5 | −0.5 | 4.1 | 6.1 | 5.1 | −0.1 | 7.5 | 3.9 | 1.9 | 3.0 | 0.1 | −3.8 | −3.6 |
| Indonesia | 1.3 | 9.0 | 8.9 | 7.2 | 4.9 | 6.3 | 6.0 | 4.6 | 6.2 | 6.2 | 6.0 | 5.6 | 5.0 | 4.8 | 9.0 | 8.9 | 7.2 | 4.9 | 6.3 | 6.0 | 4.6 | 6.2 | 6.2 | 6.0 | 5.6 | 5.0 | 4.8 | 5.0 |
| Mexico | 1.4 | 5.1 | 4.2 | 3.6 | 5.3 | 3.2 | 1.4 | −4.7 | 5.1 | 4.0 | 4.0 | 1.4 | 2.2 | 2.5 | 5.1 | 4.2 | 3.6 | 5.3 | 3.2 | 1.4 | −4.7 | 5.1 | 4.0 | 4.0 | 1.4 | 2.2 | 2.5 | 2.3 |
| South Korea | 1.9 | 9.3 | 9.7 | 5.8 | 8.8 | 5.5 | 2.8 | 0.7 | 6.5 | 3.7 | 2.3 | 2.9 | 3.3 | 2.6 | 9.3 | 9.7 | 5.8 | 8.8 | 5.5 | 2.8 | 0.7 | 6.5 | 3.7 | 2.3 | 2.9 | 3.3 | 2.6 | 2.8 |
| Saudi Arabia | 0.8 | 8.3 | 9.1 | 4.6 | 6.0 | 8.4 | 1.8 | 4.8 | 10.0 | 5.4 | 2.7 | 3.6 | 3.5 | 8.3 | 9.1 | 4.6 | 6.0 | 8.4 | 1.8 | 4.8 | 10.0 | 5.4 | 2.7 | 3.6 | 3.5 | 1.4 |
| South Africa | 0.4 | −0.3 | −1.0 | −2.1 | 4.2 | 5.4 | 3.2 | −1.5 | 3.0 | 3.3 | 2.2 | 2.3 | 1.6 | 1.3 | −0.3 | −1.0 | −2.1 | 4.2 | 5.4 | 3.2 | −1.5 | 3.0 | 3.3 | 2.2 | 2.3 | 1.6 | 1.3 | 0.3 |

*Note*: * From 1990 to 2015: data from The World Bank; 2016: data from the IMF

*Sources*: World Bank, IMF

Table A.3 The increase in output of industrial production in 2009–16 over 2008, per cent

|  | 2009 | 2010 | 2011 | 2012 | 2013 | 2014 | 2015 | 2016 |
|---|---|---|---|---|---|---|---|---|
| Index of industrial product | -10.7 | -4.2 | 0.6 | 4.0 | 4.4 | 6.2 | 2.6 | 3.7 |
| Mining | -2.8 | 0.9 | 2.7 | 3.7 | 4.9 | 6.4 | 6.7 | 9.3 |
| Extraction of fuel and energy minerals | -1.1 | 2.5 | 3.7 | 4.4 | 5.4 | 6.8 | 6.8 | 9.6 |
| Extraction of minerals. except fuel and energy | -16.1 | -12.0 | -6.2 | -3.0 | -0.8 | 0.8 | 3.1 | 3.9 |
| Manufacturing processes | -15.2 | -6.2 | 1.3 | 6.5 | 7.0 | 9.3 | 3.4 | 3.4 |
| Manufacture of food products, including drinks and tobacco | 0.3 | 3.5 | 7.6 | 12.0 | 12.6 | 15.4 | 17.8 | 20.6 |
| Textile and clothing manufacture | -16.1 | -8.7 | -8.0 | -7.3 | -3.4 | -5.8 | -16.8 | -12.4 |
| Manufacture of leather, leather goods and footwear | -1.5 | 18.1 | 24.8 | 22.5 | 17.1 | 13.8 | 0.8 | 6.0 |
| Pulp and paper industry; publishing and printing activities | -15.9 | -13.3 | -7.7 | -2.3 | -7.4 | -7.0 | -12.9 | -12.2 |
| Intermediate demand products | -12.2 | -1.9 | 2.2 | 5.9 | 6.4 | – | – | -6.1 |
| Wood processing and production of wood products | -23.1 | -12.8 | -3.9 | -7.6 | -0.2 | -5.5 | -8.7 | -6.1 |
| Manufacture of coke and refined petroleum products | -0.6 | 5.4 | 9.4 | 12.8 | 15.4 | 21.9 | 22.3 | 19.4 |
| Chemical production | -5.4 | 4.6 | 14.6 | 19.3 | 25.7 | 25.8 | 33.8 | 40.9 |
| Manufacture of rubber and plastic products | -12.9 | 8.4 | 20.7 | 36.2 | 44.2 | 55.0 | 49.3 | 57.3 |
| Metallurgical production and manufacture of finished metal products | -16.4 | -6.0 | 0.5 | 5.4 | 5.4 | 6.0 | -0.9 | -3.2 |
| Manufacture of vehicles and equipment | -33.2 | -23.1 | -14.5 | -12.2 | -15.2 | -21.8 | -30.5 | -27.8 |
| Manufacture of other non-metallic mineral products | -33.2 | -23.5 | -17.9 | -9.1 | -10.9 | -9.3 | -16.4 | -21.9 |
| Manufacture of machinery and equipment | -33.2 | -23.1 | -14.5 | -12.2 | -15.2 | -21.8 | -30.5 | -27.8 |
| Manufacture of electrical, electronic and optical equipment | -31.6 | -18.6 | -9.0 | -3.2 | -4.2 | -4.6 | -12.2 | -13.0 |
| Production and distribution of electricity, gas and water | -2.7 | -0.6 | -0.4 | 0.9 | -1.6 | -1.7 | -3.3 | -1.8 |
| *For reference* | | | | | | | | |
| Investments in fixed assets | -23.0 | -3.2 | 1.3 | -2.7 | -8.7 | -11.0 | -19.6 | -10.4 |
| Retail trade turnover | 4.7 | 18.4 | 37.0 | 53.4 | 69.9 | 89.0 | 97.5 | 4.7 |

*Source*: Federal State Statistics Service

Table A.4 The balanced financial result of the economy's enterprises in January–September 2012–16, RUB billion

| | 2012 | 2013 | 2014 | 2015 | 2016 | Growth 2016 to 2015, % |
|---|---|---|---|---|---|---|
| Total in the economy | 7,716.4 | 6,541.6 | 5,902.7 | 8,421.7 | 11,587.7 | 137.6 |
| Oil and gas sector | 1,833.5 | 1,707.1 | 2,648.6 | 2,653.1 | 2,186.0 | 82.4 |
| Extraction of fuel and energy minerals | 1,503.6 | 1,472.5 | 2,408.9 | 2,379.4 | 1,513.3 | 63.6 |
| Transportation by pipeline | 264.6 | 244.9 | 109.3 | 148.8 | 340.2 | 228.6 |
| Manufacture of coke and refined petroleum products | 754.4 | 555.1 | 279.1 | 450.1 | 513.4 | 114.1 |
| Processing production and extraction of other minerals | 2,161.8 | 1,617.4 | 936.9 | 2,179.5 | 3,479.4 | 159.6 |
| Production of consumer demand products | 296.8 | 290.3 | 281.6 | 412.7 | 501.7 | 121.6 |
| Production of intermediate demand products | 1,056.0 | 651.5 | 461.4 | 1,326.9 | 2,467.6 | 186.0 |
| Production of investment demand products | 185.4 | 185.5 | 49.6 | 98.0 | 256.2 | 261.4 |
| Production and distribution of electricity, gas and water | 201.4 | 129.3 | 164.1 | 235.7 | 706.6 | 299.8 |
| Building sector | 157.5 | 121.0 | 91.4 | 123.1 | 130.6 | 106.1 |
| Trade and repair | 1,837.2 | 1,849.3 | 1,406.8 | 2,075.1 | 2,306.4 | 111.1 |
| Transport (except pipeline) | 375.4 | 248.2 | 15.1 | 202.3 | 541.3 | 267.6 |
| Financial activities | 280.6 | 268.8 | 228.1 | 327.0 | 820.1 | 250.8 |
| Communication, research and development | 331.1 | 347.5 | 247.6 | 313.6 | 357.8 | 114.1 |
| The agricultural sector | 126.8 | 74.4 | 181.7 | 272.0 | 266.6 | 98.0 |

Sources: Federal State Statistics Service

*Table A.5* The share of expenditures on the social spheres of transport, housing and communal services in the total amount of expenditures of the consolidated regional budgets in 2005–16, per cent

|  | 2005 | 2006 | 2007 | 2008 | 2009 | 2010 | 2011 | 2012 | 2013 | 2014 | 2015 |
| --- | --- | --- | --- | --- | --- | --- | --- | --- | --- | --- | --- |
| Transport (including roads) and communal services | 22.9 | 23.4 | 25.3 | 26.4 | 22.1 | 20.5 | 20.9 | 21.9 | 21.9 | 21.4 | 21.0 |
| Social sphere (education, cultural, healthcare, sport, social policy) | 52.1 | 54.0 | 52.9 | 49.2 | 52.4 | 54.9 | 58.5 | 61.0 | 60.8 | 61.7 | 61.5 |

*Sources*: Federal Treasury, calculation of RANEPA

*Appendix* 239

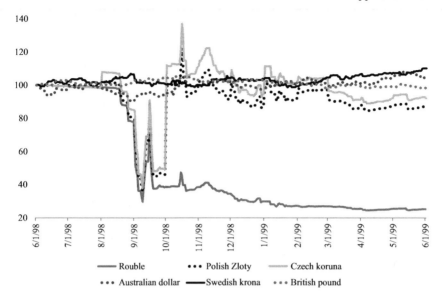

*Figure A.1* Exchange rate dynamics of a number of national currencies against the US dollar

*Sources*: Central Bank of Russian Federation, Federal Reserve

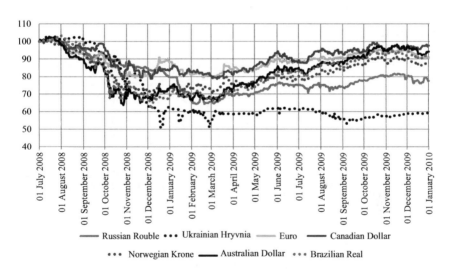

*Figure A.2* The dynamics of the rouble and the currencies of a number of countries in 2008–9 (1 July 2008 = 100)

*Sources*: Central Bank of Russian Federation, Federal Reserve

240  *Appendix*

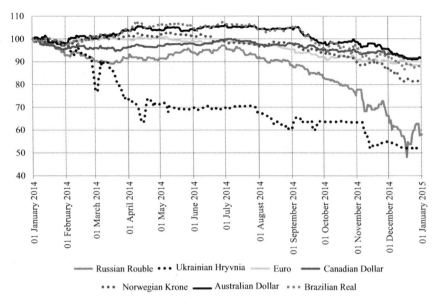

*Figure A.3* The dynamics of the rouble and the currencies of a number of countries in 2014 (1 July 2014 = 100)

*Sources*: Central Bank of Russian Federation, Federal Reserve

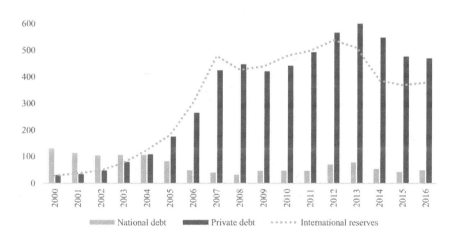

*Figure A.4* Russia's external debt and international reserves

*Source*: Central Bank of Russian Federation

Appendix 241

*Figure A.5* Oil prices for 46 years, dollars/barrel
*Source*: IMF

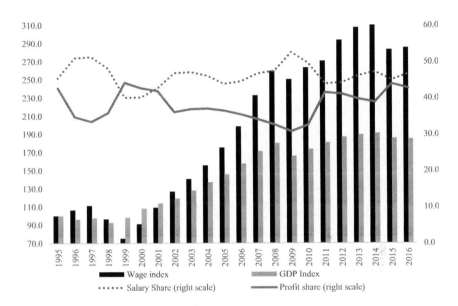

*Figure A.6* Dynamics of wages and profit in GDP (1995–2016)
*Source*: Federal State Statistics Service

# References

Acemoglu, D., Yegorov, G., and Sonin, K. (2013). "A political theory of populism", *Quarterly Journal of Economics*, vol. 128, no. 2, pp. 771–805.

Aftalion, F. (1990). *The French Revolution: An economic interpretation*. Cambridge, UK: Cambridge University Press.

Arkhipov, S., Anisimova, L., Batkibekov, S., Drobyshevsky, S., Drobyshevskaya, T., Izryadnova, O., Kadochnikov, P., Kochetkova, O., Lugovoi, O., Mau, V., Stupin, V., Trunin, I., Shardrin, A., Shatalov, S., Radygin, A., Bobylev, Yu., Logacheva, T., Serova, E., Khramova, I., Kralova, N., Tikhonova, T., Volovik, N., Leonova, N., Prikhodko, S., Ilyukhina, E., Mikhailov, L., Sycheva, L., Timofeev, E., Rozdetsvenskaia, I., Shishkin, S., Kolosnitsyn, I., and Sinelnikov, S. (2000). *Russian economy in 1999: Trends and prospects*. Issue 21. Moscow: IET.

Ashley, M. (1962). *Financial and Commercial Policy under the Cromwellian Protectorate*. London: Frank Cass.

Åslund, A. (1995) *How Russia Became a Market Economy*. Washington, DC: The Brookings Institution.

Åslund, A. (2002). *Building Capitalism*. Cambridge, UK: Cambridge University Press.

Bauman, Z.A. (1997). "Post-Modern Revolution?" In Frentzel-Zagorska, J., *From a One-Party State to Democracy*, 1st edn. Amsterdam: Rodopi.

Bazarov, V. (2014). *Izbrannye proizvedeniya* [Selected works], 2 vols. Moscow: Delo.

Bernanke, B.S. (1984). "Permanent income, liquidity, and expenditure on automobiles: Evidence from panel data", *Quarterly Journal of Economics*, vol. 99, no. 3.

Brinton, C. (1965). *The Anatomy of Revolution*. New York: Vintage Books.

Brutskus, B.D. (1922). "Problemy narodnogo khoziaistva pri sotsialisticheskom stroie" [Problems of national economy under the socialist system], *Economist*, no. 1–3.

Brzezinski, Z. (2009). "The group of two that could change the world", *The Financial Times*, 14 January. Available at: www.ft.com/content/d99369b8-e178-11dd-afa0-0000779fd2ac (accessed 1 August 2017).

Burdekin, R.C.K. and Burkett, P. (1996). *Distributional Conflict and Inflation*. London: Macmillan.

Burke, E. (1986). *Reflections on the Revolution in France*. London: Penguin Books.

Central Bank of the Russian Federation. (2014). "Guidelines for the state monetary policy for 2015 and the period 2016 and 2017." Available at: www.cbr.ru/publ/ondkp/on_2015 (2016-2017).pdf (accessed 4 August 2017).

Central Bank of the Russian Federation. (2015). "Guidelines for the state monetary policy for 2015 and the period 2016 and 2017." Available at: www.cbr.ru/publ/ondkp/on_2016 (2017-2018).pdf (accessed 4 August 2017).

Centre for Economic Conjuncture (1998a). Business activity of basic industrial enterprises of Russia in November 1998. Moscow: Center for Economic Conjuncture, 1998.

Centre for Economic Conjuncture (1998b). Industrial production dynamics. Preliminary results of 1998. Conjunctural assessment for 1999 (according to the reporting data for January-November 1998). Moscow: Center for Economic Conjuncture, 1998.

Centre for Economic Conjuncture (1998c). Industrial production intensity indices (January 1990–October 1998). Moscow: Centre for Economic Conjuncture, 1998.

Centre for Strategic Studies of the Bank of Moscow. (2010) "Development of the banking system of Russia in 2010–2011. On the way to 'cheap money'."

Crouzet, F. (1990). *Britain Ascendant: Comparative Studies in Franco-British Economic History*. Cambridge, UK: Cambridge University Press.

Crouzet, F. (1996). "France". In *The Industrial Revolution in National Context: Europe and the USA*, pp. 36–63. Eds M. Teich and R. Porter. Cambridge, UK: Cambridge University Press.

Dalin, S.A. (1983). *Inflyatsiya v epokhi sotsial'nykh revolyutsiy* [Inflation in the Period of Social Revolution]. Moscow: Nauka.

Deryugin, A. (2016). "Regional'nye byudzhety: zatyagivayem poyasa" [Regional budgets: At the limit of possibilities], *Ekonomicheskoe Razvitie Rossii*, no. 12, pp. 70–5.

De Tocqueville, A. (1997). *Staryj poryadok i revolyutsiya* [The Old Regime and the Revolution]. Moscow: Moscow Philosophical Foundation.

Di Tella, R. and Rotemberg, J.J. (2016). "Populism and the return of the 'paranoid style': Some evidence and a simple model of demand for incompetence as insurance against elite betrayal." Harvard Business School Working Paper 17–056. Cambridge, MA: Harvard Business School.

Dornbusch, R. and Edwards, S. (1990). *Macroeconomic Populism*. Amsterdam: Elsevier Science.

Dornbusch, R. and Edwards, S. (eds) (1991). *The Macroeconomics of Populism in Latin America*. Chicago, IL, and London: University of Chicago Press.

Drezen, A. (1996). "The political economy of delayed reform", *The Journal of Policy Reform*, no. 1, pp. 25–46.

Drobyshevsky, S. and Polbin, A. (2016). "O roli plavayuursa rublya v stabilizatsii delovoj aktivnosti pri vnesneekonomicheskih shokah" [On the role of floating rouble in stabilizing business activity under foreign trade shocks], *Problemy Teorii i Praktiki Upravleniya*, no. 6, pp. 66–71.

Dunn, J. (1989). *Modern Revolutions*. 2nd edn. Cambridge, UK, and New York: Cambridge University Press.

*Economist, The*. (2008). "Inflation's back", *The Economist*, 22 May, p. 17. Available at: www.economist.com/node/11409414 (accessed 2 August 2017).

*Economist, The*. (2012). "Europe's Achilles heel", *The Economist*, 12 May.

El-Erian, M. (2010). *Navigating the New Normal in Industrial Countries*. Washington, DC: Per Jacobson Foundation.

Erlich, A. (1960). *The Soviet Industrialization Debate, 1924–1928*. Cambridge, MT: Harvard University Press.

Evdokimova, T., Zubarev, A.V., and Trunin, P.V. (2013). *Vliyaniye realnogo obmennogo kursa rublya na ekonomicheskuyu aktivnost' v Rossii* [The Impact of the Real Rouble Exchange Rate on the Economic Activity in Russia], Series Gaidar IEP, Vol. 165. Moscow: Gaidar Institute.

Falkner, S.A. (1919). *Bumazhnye den'gi frantsuzskoj revolyutsii (1789–1797)* [Paper Money in the French Revolution (1789–1797)]. Moscow: Editorial & Publishing Department of VSNKh.

## References

Ferguson, N. (2008). "Geopolitical consequences of the credit crunch", *The Washington Post*, 21 September.

Ferguson, N. (2008). *The Ascent of Money: A financial history of the world*. New York: Penguin.

Fisher, S., Sahay, R., and Vegh, C.A. (1996). "Stabilization and growth in transition economies. The early experience", *Journal of Economic Perspectives*, vol. 10, no. 2, pp. 45–66.

Freeland, Ch. (2009). "Lunch with the FT: Larry Summers", *The Financial Times*, 11 July. Available at: www.ft.com/content/6ac06592-6ce0-11de-af56-00144feabdc0 (accessed 1 August 2017).

Freinkman, L. and Dashkeev, V. (2008). "Rossiya v 2007 g.: riski zamedleniya ekonomicheskogo rosta na fone sohranyauscheisya institutsionalnoy stagnatsii" [Russia in 2007: Risks of slowing economic growth against the background of institutional stagnation]. *Voprosy Ekonomiki*, no. 4, pp. 75–93.

Friedman, M. (1956). *A Theory of the Consumption Function*. Princeton, NJ: Princeton University Press.

Fukuyama, F. (1989). "The end of history?", *The National Interest*, Summer 1989.

Gaidar, Ye. (1995). *Gosudarstvo i evolutsiya* [State and Evolution]. Moscow: Eurasia.

Gaidar, Ye. (1996). *Dni porazhenij i pobed* [Days of Defeat and Victory]. Moscow: Vagrius.

Gaidar, Ye. (1997). "Power and property: A Russian divorce", *Izvestia*, 1 October.

Gaidar, Ye. (ed.) (1998). *Ekonomika perekhodnogo perioda: ocherki ekonomicheskoj politiki postkommunisticheskoj Rossii. 1992–1997* [Economics of Transition: Essays on the economic policies of post-communist Russia. 1992–1997]. Moscow: IET.

Gerschenkron, A. (1962). *Economic Backwardness in Historical Perspective: A book of essays*. Cambridge, MA: Belknap Press.

Glazyev, S. (2015). "The report on urgent measures to strengthen the economic security of Russia and the conclusion of the Russian economy on a trajectory of faster growth." Moscow: RAS.

Goldstone, J.A. (1991). *Revolution and Rebellion in the Early Modern World*. Berkeley & Los Angeles, CA: University of California Press.

Government RF (1998). Resolution of the Government of the Russian Federation, dated 21 October 1998, no. 1226.

Government RF (2015a). "On approval of the plan of priority measures for the sustainable development of economy and social stability in 2015."The decree of the government of the Russian Federation, dated 27 January 2015, no. 98 N-R (ed. 16 July 2015). Available at: www.rg.ru/2015/02/02/plan-dok.html (accessed 4 August 2017).

Government RF (2015b). "The main activities of the government of the Russian Federation for the period until 2018." Available at: http://government.ru/news/18119 (accessed 4 August 2017).

Greenspan, A. (2007). *The Age of Turbulence: Adventures in a New World*. London: Penguin.

Henning, C.R. and Kessler, M. (2012). "Byudgetno-nalogovy federalism: istorichesky opyt SSHA dlya Yevropeiskogo soyuza" [Fiscal federalism: US history for architects of Europe's fiscal union], *Ekonomicheskaya Politika*, no. 5.

Hirschmann, A. (2010). *Ritorika reaktsii: izvrascheniye, tschetnost', opasnost'* [The Rhetoric of Reaction: Perversity, futility, jeopardy]. Moscow: HSE Publishing.

Huntington, S.P. (1968) *Political Order in Changing Societies*. New Haven, CT: Yale University Press.

Huntington, S.P. (1991) *The Third Wave: Democratization in the late twentieth century*. Norman, OK, and London: University of Oklahoma Press.

Idrisov, G. (2015). "Vyigravshiye i proigravshiye: posledstviya izmeneniya uslovij torgovli dlya rossiyskoj promaslannosti" [Winners and losers: Consequences of changes in the terms of trade for the Russian industry], *Ekonomicheskoe Razvitie Rossii*, no. 4, pp. 26–9.

Idrisov, G. and Sinelnikov-Murylev, S. (2013). "Byudzhetnaya politika i ekonomicheskiy rost" [Budget Policy and Economic Growth], *Voprosy Ekonomiki*, no. 8, pp. 35–59.

Idrisov, G. and Sinelnikov-Murylev, S. (2014). "Formirovaniye predposylok dolgosrochnogo rosta: kak ih ponimat'?" [Forming sources for a long-run growth: How to understand?], *Voprosy Ekonomiki*, no. 3, pp. 4–20.

Idrisov, G. Ponomarev, Yu., and Sinelnikov-Murylev, S. (2015). "Usloviya torgovli i ekonomicheskoye razvitiye sovremennoj Rossii" [Terms of trade and economic development of modern Russia], *Ekonomicheskaya Politika*, no. 3, pp. 7–37.

Illarionov, A. (ed.) (1997). *Rossiya v menyajuschemsya mire* [Russia in the Changing World]. Moscow: IEA.

IMF. (1995). *Unproductive Public Expenditures: A pragmatic approach to policy analysis*. Prepared by K. Chu, S. Gupta, B. Clements, D. Hewitt, S. Lugaresi, J. Schiff, L. Schuknecht and G. Schwartz. IMF Pamphlet Series, no. 48.

IMF. (2016). "Gross domestic product." Available at: http://data.imf.org/regular.aspx?key=60998124 (accessed November 2016).

Kadochnikov, P. and Ptashkina, M. (2014). "Liberalizatsiya vneshnej torgovli v Kitaye: otvet na vyzovy nachala 1990h godov" [Liberalization of foreign trade in China: Responding to challenges of the early 1990s], *Ekonomicheskaya Politika*, no. 6, pp. 103–13.

Kadochnikov, P. Knobel, A., and Sinelnikov-Murylev, S. (2016). "Otkrytost' rossijskoj ekonomiki kak istochnik ekonomicheskogo rosta" [Openness of the Russian economy as a source of economic growth], *Voprosy Ekonomiki*, no. 12, pp. 26–42.

Kay, J. (2009). "Why 'too big to fail' is too much for us to take", *The Financial Times*, 27 May.

Kissinger, H. (2011). *On China*. New York: Penguin.

Klyachko, T. and Sinelnikov-Murylev, S. (2012). "O normativah byudgetnogo finansirovaniya i regulirovaniya velichiny platy za obucheniye v gosudarstvennykh vuzakh" [About standards of budgetary funding and regulation of tuition fees in public universities], *Ekonomicheskaya Politika*, no. 6.

Knobel, A. and Sokolov, I. (2012). "Otsenka byudzhetnoj politiki RF na srednesrochnuyu perspektivu" [Evaluation of Russia's budget policy in medium-term perspective], *Ekonomicheskoye rasvitie Rossii*, no. 12 (19), pp. 23–32.

Kondratiev, N. (1925). "Bol'shiye tsikly konjunktury" [The major cycles of the conjuncture], *Voprosy konjunktury*, vol. 1, no. 1, pp. 28–79.

Kondratiev, N.D. (ed.) (1927). *Kon'yunktura narodnogo khozyaystva SSSR i mirovogo v 1925/26 g* [Basic Data of USSR National Economy and World Economy in 1925/26]. Moscow: NKF SSSR.

Kornai, J. (1980). *Economics of Shortage*, Vol. 2. Amsterdam: North Holland Publishing.

Lipset, S.M. (1960). *Political Man. The social basis of politics*. New York: Doubleday.

Maleva, T. (2011). "Rossiysky rynok truda: effektivnost zanyatosti ili sokrascheniye bezrabotitsy?" [Russian Labour Market: Effectiveness of Employment or Reduction in Unemployment?]. In *Modernization and Human Development. The UNDP Report on Human Development Capacity*. Moscow: UNDP.

# References 247

Maleva, T. (ed.) (2015). *2014–2015: Ekonomicheskiy krizis – sotsial'noye izmereniye* [2014–2015: Economic Crisis – Social Measurement]. Moscow: Delo.

Malle, S. (1994) "Privatizatsiya v Rossii: osobennosti, tseli, deystvuyuschiye litsa" [Privatization in Russia: Peculiarities, goals, and agents], *Voprosy Ekonomiki*, no. 3.

Mau, V. (1997). "Stabilization, elections, and perspectives of economic growth", *Problems of Economic Transition*, vol. 40, no. 4, pp. 5–26.

Mau, V. (1999). *Ekonomicheskaia reforma: skvoz' prizmu konstitutsii I politiki* [Economic Reform: Through the Prism of the Constitution and Politics]. Moscow: Ad Marginem.

Mau, V. (2001). *Ekonomika i revolyutsia: uroki istorii* [Economy and Revolution: Lessons of history]. *Voprosy Ekonomiki*. No. 1.

Mau, V. (2002). "Post-communist Russia in post-industrial world: Elements of catching-up policy", *Voprosy Ekonomiki*, no. 7.

Mau, V. (2008). "Russia's economic policy in 2007: Successes and risks", *Voprosy Ekonomiki*, no. 2, pp. 4–25.

Mau, V. (2010). "Global crisis: Experience of the past and challenges of the future", *Herald of Europe*, no. 7, pp. 31–42.

Mau, V. (2013). *Reformy i dogmy: gosudarstvo i ekonomika v epohu vojn i revolyutsij (1861–1929)* [Reforms and Dogmas: State and economy in the era of reforms and revolutions (1861–1929)], 3rd edn. Moscow: Delo.

Mau, V. (2014). "V ozhidanii novoj modeli rosta: sotsial'no-ekonomicheskoye razvitiye Rossii v 2013 godu" [Waiting for a new model of growth: Russia's social and economic development in 2013], *Voprosy Ekonomiki*, no. 2, pp. 4–32.

Mau, V. (2016). "Between crises and sanctions: Economic policy of the Russian Federation", *Post-Soviet Affairs*, vol. 32, no. 4, pp. 350–77.

Mau, V. and Kuzminov, Ya. (eds) (2013). *Strategy-2020: New Model of Growth – New Social Policy*, 2 vols. Moscow: Delo.

Medvedev, D. (2015). "A new reality: Russia and global challenges", *Journal of Russian Economics*, no. 1, (2), pp. 108–28.

Ministry of Finance of the Russian Federation. (2016a). "Internal debt." Available at: http://minfin.ru/ru/perfomance/public_debt/internal/structure/total/ (accessed September 2016).

Ministry of Finance of Russian Federation. (2016b). "External debt." Available at: www.gks.ru/wps/wcm/connect/rosstat_main/rosstat/ru/statistics/publications/catalog/doc_11387 17651859 (acccessed November 2016).

Moreno-Dodson, B. (ed.) (2013). *Is Fiscal Policy the Answer? A developing country perspective*. Washington, DC: The World Bank.

Mudde, C. and Kaltwasser, C.R. (2011). "Voices of the peoples: Populism in Europe and Latin America compared", *Kellog Institute Working Paper*, Issue 378.

North, D. (1997). *Instituty, institutsional'nye izmeneniya I funktsionirovanie ekonomiki* [Institutions, Institutional Change and Economic Performance]. Moscow: Economic Book Foundation Nachala.

Novozhilov, V. (1926). "Nedostatok tovarov" [Shortage of goods], *Finance Bulletin*, no. 2.

OECD. (2016). "Gross domestic product (GDP)." Available at: https://data.oecd.org/gdp/gross-domestic-product-gdp.htm (accessed October 2016].

Ofer, G. (1987). "Soviet economic growth (1928–1985)", *Journal of Economic Literature*, vol. xxv, no. 4, pp. 1767–833.

Orlova, N. and Egiev, S. (2015). "Strukturnye faktory zamedleniya rosta rossiyskoj ekonomiki" [Structural Factors of the Russian Economic Slowdown], *Voprosy Ekonomiki*, no. 12, pp. 69–84.

Pappe, Y.S. (ed.) (1997). *Finansovo-promyshlennye gruppy i konglomeraty v ekonomike i politike sovremennoi Rossii* [Financial and Industrial Groups and Conglomerates in the Economy and Politics of Modern Russia]. Moscow: Center for Political Technologies.

Peretz, E. (1927). *Dnevnik (1880–1883)* [Diary (1880–1883)]. Moscow, Leningrad: Gosizdat.

Pierce, A. (2008). "The Queen asks why no one saw the credit crunch coming", *The Telegraph*, 5 November. Available at: www.telegraph.co.uk/news/uknews/the royalfamily/3386353/The-Queen-asks-why-no-one-saw-the-credit-crunch-coming.html (accessed 27 July 2017).

Piketty, T. (2015). *Capital in the Twenty-First Century*. Moscow: Ad Marginem Press.

Politi, J. (2014). "Berlin has no right to lecture, says Renzi", *The Financial Times*, 3 October.

Putin, V. (2009). Speech at Davos meeting, 29 January. Available at: www.vesti.ru/doc.html?id=246949 (accessed 4 August 2017).

Reinhart, C.M. and Rogoff, K.S. (2008). "This time is different: A panoramic view of eight centuries of financial crises." Working paper 13882, National Bureau of Economic Research. Available at: www.nber.org/papers/w13882.pdf (accessed 1 August 2017).

Reinhart, C.M. and Rogoff, K.S. (2009). *This Time Is Different: Eight centuries of financial folly*. Princeton, NJ: Princeton University Press.

Rodrik, D. (2008). "The death of the globalization consensus." Project Syndicate, 11 July. Available at: www.project-syndicate.org/commentary/rodrik21 (accessed 1 August 2017).

Rogoff, K. (2008). "America goes from teacher to student." Project Syndicate, 4 February. Available at: www.project-syndicate.org/commentary/rogoff39 (accessed 1 August 2017).

Rosser, J.B. and Rosser, M.V. (1997). "Schumpeterian evolutionary dynamics and the collapse of Soviet-block socialism", *Review of Political Economy*, vol. 9, no. 2, pp. 211–23.

Rosstat. (2014). *Delovaya aktivnost' organizatsij v Rossii* [Business activity of entities in Russia]. Available at: www.gks.ru/bgd/free/b04_03/isswww.exe/stg/d04/264.htm (accessed 4 August 2017).

Rosstat. (2016a). "Budget salary arrears. Data on eight sectors: Industry, construction, transport, agriculture, education, health, science and art." Available at: www.gks.ru/bgd/regl/B03_36/IssWWW.exe/Stg/d020/i020420r.htm (accessed October 2016).

Rosstat. (2016b). "The number of strikes." Available at: www.fedstat.ru/indicator/33477 (accessed October 2016).

Russian–European Centre for Economic Policy, The. (1995). *An Overview of Russia's Economy*, no. 1, pp. 49–50, 204.

Saborowski, C., Sanya, S., Weisfeld, H, and Yepez, J. (2014). "Effectiveness of capital outflow restrictions." Washington, DC: International Monetery Fund.

Sachs, J.D. (1989). *Developing Country Debt and the World Economy*. Chicago, IL: University of Chicago Press.

Say, J.B. and Bastiat, F. (2000). Say, J.B., *Traktat po politicheskoj ekonomii* [A Treatise on Political Economy]. Bastiat, F., *Ekonomicheskiye sofizmy. Ekonomicheskiye garmonii* [Economic sophisms. Economic harmonies]. Moscow: Delo.

Scholars of the Department of Economics of the RAS (1998). "Open letter of scholars of the Department of Economics of the RAS to the president of the Russian Federation, the Federal Assembly and the government of the Russian Federation", *Economics & Life*, no. 37.

Shleifer, A. and Treisman, D. (2000). *Without a Map. Political tactics and economic reform in Russia*. Cambridge, MA, and London: MIT Press.

Shuvalov, I. (2010). "Rossiya na puti modernizatsii" [Russia on the path of modernization], *Ekonomicheskaya Politika*, no. 1.
Sinelnikov-Murylev, S., Drobyshevsky, S., and Kazakova, M. (2014). "Dekompozitsiya tempov rosta VVP Rossii v 1999–2014 godah" [Decomposition of GDP growth rates in Russia in 1999–2014], *Ekonomicheskaya Politika*, no. 5, pp. 7–37.
Skocpol, Th. (1979). *States and Social Revolutions*. Cambridge, UK: Cambridge University Press.
Smith, A. (1977). *An Inquiry into the Nature and Causes of the Wealth of Nations*. Chicago, IL: University of Chicago Press.
Stalin, I. (1951). *Sobraniye sochinenij* [Collected Works], Vol. 13. Moscow: Gospolitizdat.
Stalin, I. (1997). *Sobraniye sochinenij* [Collected Works], Vol. 16. Moscow: Pisatel.
Starodubrovskaya, I. and Mau, V. (2001a). *Velikie Revolutsii ot Kromvelya do Putina* [Great Revolutions. From Cromwell to Putin]. Moscow: Vagrius.
Starodubrovskaya, I. and Mau, V. (2001b). *The Challenge of Revolution: Contemporary Russia in historical perspective*. Oxford, UK: Oxford University Press.
State Statistics Committee of Russia. (1994). *The Russian Federation in Figures in 1993*, p. 32.
State Statistics Committee of Russia. (1999). *Statistical Yearbook of Russia*, p. 290.
State Statistics Committee of Russia. (2002). *Statistical Yearbook of Russia*, p. 334.
Stolypin Club. (2015). "Ekonomika rosta" [The economy of growth (short version)], Moscow. Available at: www.finanz.ru/novosti/aktsii/ekonomika-rosta-stolypinskogo-kluba-1000872947 (accessed 4 August 2017).
Strategy. (2013). *Strategy-2020: New model of growth – new social policy*, 2 vols. Moscow: Delo.
Summers, L. (2014). "Reflections on the new 'Secular Stagnation hypothesis'." Vox, CERP's Policy Portal, 30 October. Available at: http://voxeu.org/article/larry-summers-secular-stagnation (accessed 2 August 2017).
Taylor, J. (2009). "Exploding debt threatens America", *The Financial Times*, 27 May.
Teulings, C. and Baldwin, R. (eds) (2014). "Secular stagnation: Facts, causes and cures." London: Centre for Economic Policy Research Press. Available at: http://voxeu.org/content/secular-stagnation-facts-causes-and-cures (accessed 2 August 2017).
Thornhill, J.A. (2008). "A year of chocolate box politics", *The Financial Times*, 24 December.
Tilly, Ch. (1993). *European Revolutions, 1492–1992*. Oxford, UK: Blackwell.
Ulyukaev, A. (2009). "Rossiya i novaya ekonomicheskaya realnost'" [Russia and new macroeconomic reality]. In *X International Scientific Conference on Development of Economy and Society*. Moscow: Higher School of Economics Publishing House.
Vanhanen, T. (1968). *Prospects for Democracy: A study of 172 countries*. London & New York: Routledge.
Vedev, A. and Kosarev, A. (2012). "Nekotorye kolichestvennye otsenki vozdejstviya institutsionalnyh ogranichenij na ekonomicheskij rost v Rossii" [Some quantitative estimates of the impact of institutional constraints on economic growth in Russia], *Ekonomicheskaya Politika*, no. 1.
Williamson, J. (1990). "What Washington means by policy reform". In J. Williamson (ed.). *Latin American Readjustment: How Much Has Happened*, 1st edn. Washington, DC: Peterson Institute for International Economics.
Witte, S. (1900). "O polozhenii nashej promyshlennosti. Vsepoddaneyshij doklad ministra finansov. Fevral 1900" [On the condition of our industry. The most loyal report of the minister of finance. February 1900]. In S. Witte (2006). *Collected Works and Documentary Materials*, Vol. 4, Book 1. Moscow: Nauka.

World Bank, The. (1996). *From Plan to Market*. Washington, DC: Oxford University Press.
World Bank, The. (1997). *The State in a Changing World*. Washington, DC: Oxford University Press.
World Bank, The. (2014). *Confidence Crisis Exposes Economic Weakness. Russian Economic Report*. No. 31.
Yudaeva, K. and Godunova, M. (2009). "Lessons of crisis for Russia: Macroeconomic policy", *Economicheskaya Politika*, no. 6, pp. 30–41.

# Index (persons)

Alexander II Nikolayevich (Romanov) (17 [29] April 1818–1 [13] March 1881) — Russian emperor (1855–81); launched "Great Reforms", including the abolition of serfdom (19 February 1861); assassinated by terrorists. **18**

Bazarov, Vladimir Alexandrovich (real surname Rudnev; 27 July (8 August) 1874–16 September 1939) — Russian philosopher and economist, social democrat; author of Russian translation of *Das Kapital* by Karl Marx; active participant in economic debates in the 1920s; in 1921–30, one of the leading economists in the State Planning Commission (Gosplan). **159, 203**

Bonaparte Napoleon I (15 August 1769–5 May 1821) — French general; emperor of France, 1804–15. **24**

Brown, James Gordon (b. 20 February 1951) — British politician, member of Parliament (Labour; from 1983), seventy-fourth prime minister of Great Britain (2007–10). **105**

Bukharin, Nikolai Ivanovich (27 September (9 October) 1888–15 March 1938) — Soviet statesman and Communist Party leader; member of the Central Committee of the Party (1917–34), candidate member of the Central Committee of the CPSU(b) (1934–7); full member of the USSR Academy of Sciences (1929). **159**

Camdessus, Michel (b. 1 May 1933) — French economist, managing director of the IMF, 1987–2000. **56**

Carter Jr., James Earl "Jimmy" (b. 1 October 1924) — Thirty-ninth president of the United States (1977–81); Democrat; Nobel Peace Laureate in 2002. **102**

252  *Index (persons)*

| | |
|---|---|
| Chernomyrdin, Viktor Stepanovich (9 April 1938–3 November 2010) | Russian statesman, minister of the Gas Industry of the USSR (1985–9), founder and first president of Gazprom Corporation; chairman of the government of the Russian Federation (1992–8); Russian ambassador in Ukraine (2001–9). **16, 55, 60, 68, 69, 71, 89** |
| Chubais, Anatoly Borisovich (b. 16 June 1955) | Head of the State Property Committee, responsible for the first stage of privatization in post-communist Russia (1991–3); first deputy chairman of the government of the Russian Federation in 1997–8, minister of finance (1997), head of the presidential administration of the Russian Federation in 1997–8; chairman of the board of JSC Rusnano since 2011. **53, 55, 57, 58, 68, 70** |
| De Talleyrand-Perigord, Charles Maurice (2 February 1754– 17 May 1838) | French politician and diplomat, minister of foreign affairs (1797–9, 1799–1807, 1814–15). **16** |
| De Tocqueville, Alexis-Charles-Henri Clerel (29 July 1805– 16 April 1859) | French political philosopher, politician, leader of the Conservative Party of Order, minister of foreign affairs of France (1849); political theorist. **21** |
| Dubinin, Sergey Konstantinovich (b. 10 December 1950) | Russian economist; governor of the Central Bank of Russia (1995–8); chairman of the supervisory board of VTB Bank. **57** |
| Fedorov, Boris Grigorievich (13 February 1958–20 November 2008) | Financier, businessman and investor; minister of finance of the Russian Federation (1990, 1993–4); deputy chairman of the government of the Russian Federation (1992–4, 1998); director of the State Tax Service of the Russian Federation (1998). **57** |
| Friedman, Milton (31 July 1912– 16 November 2006) | American economist, Nobel Prize Laureate, 1976. **101** |
| Fukuyama, Yoshihiro Francis (b. 27 October 1952) | American philosopher, political scientist; SENIOR researcher of the Center for Democracy, Development and the Rule of Law at Stanford |

Index (persons)   253

| | |
|---|---|
| | University; author of many books, including *The End of History and the Last Man* (1992). **17** |
| Gaidar, Yegor Timurovich (19 March 1956–16 December 2009) | Russian state and political figure, economist; first deputy chairman of the government of the Russian Federation (1992, 1993); acting chairman of the government of the Russian Federation (1992); in December 1991, launched complex post-communist reforms in Russia. **34, 75** |
| Gerashchenko, Viktor Vladimirovich (b. 21 December 1937) | Russian banker, financier; headed the country's central bank three times – State Bank of the USSR (1989–91) and Central Bank of Russia (1992–4, 1998–2002). **74, 78** |
| Ginzburg, Abram Moiseyevich (8 September 1878–30 December 1937) | Revolutionary, economist, publicist; from 1929, the deputy chairman of the Institute of Industrial and Economic Research of VSNKh (Supreme Soviet of the National Economy); member of RANION (Russian Association of Social Science Institutes). **159** |
| Gustov, Vadim Anatolievich (b. 26 December 1948) | Member of the Federation Council of the Federal Assembly of the Russian Federation; governor of the Leningrad Region (1996–8); first deputy chairman of the government of Russia (1998–9). **74** |
| Hollande, François Gerard Georges Nicolas (b. 12 August 1954) | President of France (2012–17); the first secretary of the Socialist Party of France in 1997–2008. **114** |
| Hoover, Herbert Clarke (10 August 1874–20 October 1964) | Thirty-first president of the United States (1929–33); Republican. **95** |
| Huntington, Samuel Phillips (18 April 1927–24 December 2008) | American researcher and analyst, social philosopher and political scientist; founder of the leading US political magazine, *Foreign Relations*. **43, 44** |
| Keynes, John Maynard (5 June 1883–21 April 1946) | The most influential economist of the twentieth century; one of the founders of modern macroeconomics. **101** |

## Index (persons)

| | |
|---|---|
| Kiriyenko, Sergey Vladilenovich (b. 26 July 1962) | Chairman of the government of the Russian Federation (1998); director general of the State Atomic Energy Corporation Rosatom (2005–16); since 2016, first deputy head of the administration of the president of the Russian Federation. **57–60, 64, 68–71, 73, 75, 80, 81, 89** |
| Kokovtsov, Vladimir Nikolayevich (6(18) April 1853–29 January 1943) | Minister of finance in 1904–5 and 1906–14, chairman of the Council of Ministers of the Russian Empire in 1911–14, Count (from 30 January 1914). **18, 172** |
| Kondratiev, Nikolai Dmitrievich (4(16) March 1892–17 September 1938) | Russian economist; active participant in economic debates in the 1920s; developed the theory of economic cycles, known as "Kondratiev waves"; director of the Conjuncture Institute of Narkomfin (1920–28). **98, 159, 203** |
| Kudrin, Alexey Leonidovich (b. 12 October 1960) | Minister of finance of the Russian Federation (2000–11); dean of the Faculty of Liberal Arts and Sciences of St Petersburg State University; chairman of the board of trustees of the Gaidar Institute of Economic Policy; since 2016, chairman of the Council of the Center for Strategic Research. **172, 204** |
| Kuibyshev, Valerian Vladimirovich (25 May (6 June) 1888–25 January 1935) | Revolutionary, Communist Party and political figure; chairman of the USSR Coluncil for National Economy (de facto Ministry of Industry in 1926–30), chairman of the State Planning Committee (Gosplan, 1930–4), deputy chairman of the Council of People's Commissars (USSR Government, 1923–35). **159** |
| Kulik, Gennady Vasilievich (20 January 1935) | Russian statesman, member of the State Duma; deputy chairman of the government of the Russian Federation (1998–9). **74** |

Index (persons) 255

| | |
|---|---|
| Lvov, Dmitry Semenovich (2 February 1930–6 July 2007) | Russian economist, academician-secretary of the Department of Economics of the Russian Academy of Sciences (1996–2002). **75** |
| Makarov, Nikolai Pavlovich (20 December 1886–1 October 1980) | Russian economist, professor; in 1924–30, dean of the Faculty of Economics of the Timiryazev Moscow Agricultural Academy. **159, 203** |
| Maslyukov, Yuri Dmitrievich (30 September 1937–1 April 2010) | Soviet and Russian statesman, member of the Politburo of the CPSU Central Committee (1989–90), first deputy chairman of the Council of Ministers of the USSR (1988–91), first deputy chairman of the government of the Russian Federation (1998–9). **74, 77, 79** |
| Medvedev, Dmitry Anatolyevich (b. 14 September 1965) | Chairman of the government of the Russian Federation (since 8 May 2012); president of the Russian Federation (2008–12). **195, 204** |
| Mellon, Andrew William (24 March 1855–27 August 1937) | American banker, businessman, US secretary of the treasury under Presidents W. Harding, K. Coolidge and G. Hoover (1921–32). **95** |
| Morgan Jr, John Pierpont "Jack" (7 September 1867–13 March 1943) | American banker. **93** |
| Nemtsov, Boris Yefimovich (9 October 1959–27 February 2015) | Russian statesman; first deputy chairman of the government (1997–8); deputy of the State Duma (1999–2003); governor of the Nizhny Novgorod Region (1991–7). **55, 68, 70** |
| Nixon, Richard Milhous (9 January 1913–22 April 1994) | Thirty-seventh president of the United States (1969–74), thirty-sixth vice-president of the United States (1953–61). **95, 101** |
| Preobrazhensky, Yevgeny Alexeyevich (15(28) February 1886–13 July 1937) | Revolutionary activist, Soviet economist and sociologist. **159** |
| Primakov, Yevgeny Maximovich (29 October 1929–26 June 2015) | Soviet and Russian politician and state figure; chairman of the Council of the |

256  *Index (persons)*

|   |   |
|---|---|
|   | Union of the Supreme Soviet of the USSR (1989–90); director of the Foreign Intelligence Service of Russia (1991–6); foreign minister of the Russian Federation (1996–8); chairman of the government of the Russian Federation (1998–9) and president of the Chamber of Commerce and Industry of Russia (2001–11). **36, 74–8, 80–2, 84, 88, 89** |
| Putin, Vladimir Vladimirovich (b. 7 October 1952) | President of the Russian Federation (2000–8 and since 2012); chairman of the government of the Russian Federation (1999–2000, 2008–12), secretary of the Security Council (1999), director of the Federal Security Service (1998–9). **89, 148, 182, 197** |
| Reagan, Ronald Wilson (6 February 1911–5 June 2004) | Fortieth president of the United States (1981–9), Republican; Thirty-third governor of the State of California (1967–75). **173** |
| Shanin, L.G. | Economist, head of the Financial and Economic Administration of the People's Commissariat of Finance in the 1920s. **159** |
| Sokolnikov, Grigory Yakovlevich (Hirsch Yankelevich Brilliant, 3 August 1888–21 May 1939) | Soviet statesman; people's commissar (minister) for Finance of Russia (1922–3) and of the USSR (1923–6); author of monetary reform of 1922. **159, 172** |
| Stalin, Joseph Vissarionovich (real surname Dzhugashvili, 9(21) December 1879–5 March 1953) | General secretary of the Central Committee of the CPSU(b) (1922–53); chairman of the Council of Ministers of the USSR (1946–53). **10, 20, 159** |
| Steinbruck, Peer (b. 10 January 1947) | German politician; from 2002 to 2005, he held the post of prime minister of the Federal State of North Rhine-Westphalia; in 2005–9, he was German finance minister and vice-chairman of the SPD (Social Democrats). **102** |
| Stepashin, Sergey Vadimovich (b. 2 March 1952) | Russian state and political figure; director of the Federal Security Service |

of the Russian Federation (1994–5); minister of justice of the Russian Federation (1997–8); minister of internal affairs of the Russian Federation (1998–9); chairman of the government of the Russian Federation (May–August 1999); deputy of the State Duma (1999–2000); chairman of the Accounts Chamber of the Russian Federation (2000–13). **84, 89**

| | |
|---|---|
| Stolypin, Petr Arkadevich (2(14) April 1862–5(18) September 1911) | Statesman the Russian Empire; minister of home affairs (1906–11), prime minister (1906–11); assasinated by terrorist. **18** |
| Summers, Lawrence Henry (b. 30 November 1954) | American economist, director of the National Economic Council (20 January 2009–December 2010), US secretary of the treasury (1999–2001). **97** |
| Thatcher, Margaret Hilda, Baroness Thatcher, née Roberts (13 October 1925–8 April 2013) | Seventy-first prime minister of Great Britain (1979–90). **173** |
| Vainshtein, Albert Lvovoich (3 February 1892–15 April 1970) | Soviet economist, statistician and bibliographer; one of the founders of the Russian school of economic and mathematical analysis and cliometrics. **205** |
| Volcker, Paul Adolph (b. 5 September 1927) | American economist; US deputy minister of finance (1969–74); president of the Federal Reserve Bank of New York (1975–9) and chairman of the board of the Federal Reserve System of the United States (1979–87). **95, 102** |
| Vyshnegradsky, Ivan Alexeyevich (20 December 1831 (1 January 1832)–25 March (6 April) 1985) | Russian scientist and statesman; minister of finance (1887–92). **18** |
| Witte, Sergey Yulievich (17(29) June 1849–28 February (13 March) 1915) | Russian statesman; minister of finance (1892–1903); chairman of the Committee of Ministers (1903–6); chairman of the Council of Ministers (1905–6); successfully introduced the "gold standard" in Russia (1897); member of the State Council from 1903. **18, 19, 172** |

## Index (persons)

Xiaoping, Deng (22 August 1904–19 February 1997) — Chinese politician and reformer; actual leader of China from the late 1970s to the early 1990s. **181**

Yeltsin, Boris Nikolayevich (1 February 1931–23 April 2007) — Russian politician and statesman; first president of the Russian Federation (1991–9); head of the government of the Russian Federation (1991–2). **53, 58, 67, 68, 73, 74**

# Index

acceleration (*uskorenie*) 160, 161, 172, 178, 222
agrarian society 16
agriculture 18, 49, 67, 81, 159, 203, 209, 215, 232
anti-crisis policy 6, 8, 58, 59, 73, 80, 94, 96, 105, 126–30, 177, 178, 192, 193, 209, 210
anti-inflationism 33, 34, 130
anti-trust authorities 226
Avtovaz 144

balance of payments 49, 53, 121, 122, 138, 140; account of 49, 139
Bank of Russia *see* Central Bank of Russian Federation
bankruptcy 2, 34, 65, 74, 105, 106
banks, banking sector: deposits 51, 60, 101, 104, 123, 125, 169, 190, 211–13; restructuring 83
barter 85
Bear Stearns 105
'big state' 131
braking mechanism 169, 170
BRICS (Brazil, Russia, India, China, South Africa) 162, 201, 228
budget 9, 25, 49, 56, 57, 64, 70, 75, 80, 96, 129, 134, 140, 144, 148, 150, 162, 167, 174, 183, 193, 210, 225; debt 197, 210; deficit 40, 49, 55, 73, 76, 83, 110, 117, 135, 141, 196–9, 204, 229; expenditures 23, 49, 75, 94, 134, 138, 149, 150, 184, 196, 220, 225; rule 167, 180, 184, 188, 189, 204, 210; sequestering 196; subsidies 34, 201; surplus 55, 75, 134
budgetary policy 6, 56, 65, 158, 196, 220
'business as usual' 128, 131, 142, 180, 184, 189
business environment 22, 151, 204

capital 19, 151; inflow 42, 122, 138; markets 112, 149, 179; outflow 83, 107, 138, 148, 155, 168, 178, 179, 190, 198, 211
catch-up industrialization 149, 181
Central Bank of Russian Federation 38, 54, 169, 180, 181, 202, 209
central planning 173
Citibank 105
commodity exchange 113
Commonwealth of Independent States (CIS) 38
communities (*obshchinas*) 18, 20
competitiveness 22, 32, 81, 150, 153, 174, 178, 181, 182, 195, 219
consumer lending 164, 175
consumer market 74, 195
consumer prices 60
corruption 23, 138, 143, 153
Council of Federation 71
country risks 140, 179
crass Keynesianism 94, 102, 126, 182
creative class 152, 157
credit default swap (CDS) 98
credit model of consumption 155, 165
credit rating 43, 53, 56
crisis: budget 23, 32, 42, 64, 65; in the communist system 20; dotcom 110; economic 3, 23, 31, 40, 74, 93, 94, 121, 127, 148, 203; financial 23, 32, 42, 49, 53–89, 94, 134; fiscal 23, 53, 82, 167; of the growth model 169, 187; of industrialism 26; non-payments 24, 33, 66, 73; structural 2, 9, 94–6, 162, 172, 173, 182, 187, 188, 219; transformational 2, 7
currency board 75
currency corridor 54
customs 40, 142, 153
Customs Union 81, 141, 148

## 260  Index

Davos Forum 77, 79, 182
debt: budget 197, 210; commercial 105, 124, 197; corporate 123, 136; external (foreign) 23, 24, 49–51, 69, 123, 172, 198, 211, 222; internal (domestic) 23, 24, 50, 51, 60, 70; national (sovereign, state) 7, 24, 50, 54–6, 58, 59, 69, 124, 134, 136, 155, 173, 196, 197, 202, 210; regional 71, 168, 174, 210; servicing 50, 51, 56, 69, 123, 175, 197, 203, 229; short 83
default 23, 24, 68, 83, 122
defence industry 50, 201
deflationary shock 101
deglobalization 113
deindustrialization 3
delayed stabilization 33
demand 74, 78, 102, 126, 128, 129, 143, 144, 149, 164, 169, 170, 174, 183, 193, 194, 200, 229; constraints 33; domestic 113, 146, 155, 187
demand-side economics 109, 143, 149
devaluation 54, 55, 58–60, 65, 59, 73, 77, 125, 168, 169, 178, 179, 194, 195, 226
dirigisme 34, 77, 96, 105, 131
disinflation 33, 168, 219, 226
Doing Business rating 152, 154, 180, 221
domestic market 18, 51, 70, 73, 125, 170, 192, 195, 221
Dow Jones Industrial Average 53
'Dutch disease' 7, 193, 194, 213, 219

economic downturn 1, 173, 178
economic growth 1, 7, 9, 10, 42, 49, 96, 97, 106, 110, 111, 112, 116, 121, 133, 143, 145, 147, 155, 162, 169, 171, 172, 184, 200, 202–4, 209, 219, 229
emerging markets 53, 70, 102, 110, 148
employment 2, 96, 106, 141, 157, 163, 175, 180, 183, 192, 213, 227, 228
'end of history' 17
energy: companies 66, 110; market 113; prices 65, 111, 113, 121, 123, 131, 135, 143, 160
English Civil War 21
equilibrium market 33
Eurasian Economic Community (EurAsEC) 228
Euro-Asian Economic Union 145, 201
European Central Bank 191
European Union (EU) 102, 107, 145, 155, 169

exchange rate 54, 57, 61, 75, 125, 130, 140, 180, 221; fixed 75–7, 82; floating 60, 188, 193, 197, 211, 213; risk 54, 190; stabilization 49, 81
exit strategy 9, 152, 157
expenditures: non-productive 196; productive 196
export sectors 76, 194
external financial markets 178

Federal Commission for Securities 57
Federal Reserve System of the United States 70, 93, 191
Federal Treasury 167
fiscal balance 149
fiscal policy 49, 55, 80, 102, 112
'fiscal rule' 172, 220
Fitch IBCA 56
free traders 21

G20 9, 127, 136, 168
Gaidar Institute for Economic Policy 183
Gazprombank 198
Gazprom 58, 66, 80
GKO, Government Short-Term Commitment (*Gosudarstvennoye Kratkosrochnoye Obyazatyelstvo*) 51, 53, 54, 5860, 70, 175
Gosplan 203
Government of the Russian Federation 20, 23–5, 30, 32–4, 36, 42, 43, 55–60, 64, 68–71, 74, 7880, 84, 89, 129, 134, 141–2, 193, 195–7, 204, 209–10
Great Depression 93, 102
gross domestic product (GDP) 9, 18, 63, 127, 128, 134, 144, 169, 170, 187, 189, 193–4; per capita 17, 44, 104

household income 84, 214
human capital 114, 115, 145, 160, 188, 196, 222, 227
hyperinflation 25, 79, 84

Imperial Bank 59
import substitution 84, 139, 168, 169, 194, 195, 220, 226
income tax 58, 162, 263
industrialization 18–20, 113, 181, 189
industrial society 3, 20, 29, 94, 114, 115, 204
inequality 96, 116, 200
inflation 6, 24, 25, 33–6, 42, 60, 69, 75, 112, 136, 137, 150, 168, 174, 183, 192, 203, 205, 226

inflationism 33, 35, 65, 76–80
inflation targeting 112, 140, 145, 162, 168, 180, 193, 211
institutional risks 175
International Monetary Fund (IMF) 53, 56–70
interventionism 101
investments: climate 148, 151, 158, 170, 202; direct 79, 125, 138, 147; foreign 94, 121, 155, 179, 195; state 201
Izborsk Club 200, 201

jobless recovery 140, 141
joint-stock companies 19

Keynesianism 93, 95, 96, 101, 102, 109
Kondratiev cycles 10, 98, 201

labour market 96, 140, 141, 144, 163, 170, 199, 213, 227
labour productivity 94, 114, 134, 164, 170, 172, 219
laissez-faire 117
Lehman Brothers 105, 182
liberalism 17, 29, 96, 104, 109, 117
liberalization 6, 33, 34, 75, 78, 94, 111, 200
liberal modernization 209

margin calls 59, 123, 124
market environment 34
'middle income trap' 171
mineral resources 50
Ministry of Finance 58, 70, 73, 75, 159, 184
monetarism 96, 201
monetary policy 33, 34, 38, 40, 49, 57, 59, 60, 75, 96, 103, 111, 125, 126, 130, 150, 168, 172, 191, 197, 209
Moody's 56
moral hazard 123, 124
mortgage loans 150, 213
Moscow Interbank Currency Exchange (MICEX) 60

natural monopolies 168, 202
natural order 17
neo-liberalism 95, 109
net interest income 199
'new industrialism' 113
'new normality' 111
Nord Stream gas pipeline 9
Norilsk Nickel 67

OFZ, Federal Loan Obligations (*Obligatsyi Federal'novo Zaima*) 51, 53–5, 58–60
oil prices 9, 11, 30, 49, 60, 111, 127, 131, 152, 162, 167, 178, 183, 189, 210, 219
oligarchs 31, 74
Organization for Economic Cooperation and Development (OECD) 145

Paris Club 56
pension system 115, 222
*perestroika* 23, 41, 160
'political rent' 35, 36
polycentricity of power 31
population 114, 158; working-age 11, 96, 151, 158, 183, 192, 199
populism 33, 38–41, 65, 76, 79, 80, 103, 104, 107, 147, 182, 200, 209, 222
post-communist development 20, 29
post-industrial society 7, 26, 29, 145, 227
private sector 20, 35, 175
privatization 3, 17, 23–5, 33–6, 41–5, 66, 67, 76, 79, 94, 105, 123, 142, 145
privatization programme 44
production: decline in 44, 94; growth 85, 86
productivity 8, 79, 98, 143, 151, 163, 170, 174, 183, 192, 220, 225
profit repatriation 54
property: private 45, 79, 104, 105, 173; state 42
protectionism 22, 34, 78, 195, 202
purchasing power parity 150

quantitative easing 111, 182, 201, 202

RAO UES of Russia 57, 66
rate: credit rate 183; interest rate 1, 36, 54–8, 78, 102, 111, 116, 144, 145, 155, 168, 180–2, 191, 196, 197, 219, 229; key rate 197, 202; nominal rate 191; policy rate 38, 54, 101, 102, 130, 182, 197, 199; refinancing rate 183
real disposable income 164
real sector 80, 101, 123, 129, 130
real wages 86, 164
recession 10, 11, 78, 96, 101, 102, 104, 110, 115, 121, 128, 155, 162, 169, 178, 182
recovery growth 170
reindustrialization 97, 113
reserve currency 95, 102, 112, 126, 145, 226, 228
reserve fund 137, 199

resource-based economy 226
restrictive monetary policy 75
retail loans 198, 213–15
retail turnover 164
return on equity 211
revolution: in England 16, 22, 26; in France 16, 17, 21, 26; in Russia 18, 20
Rosneft 57, 67, 71, 142, 179
Rosselkhozbank 198
RTS-1 index 53, 55, 57–9, 61, 73
RusHydro 142
Russian Academy of Sciences 75, 76
Russian Railways 142

Sakhalin-2 project 37
sanctions 2, 3, 5, 10, 68, 177–80, 181, 183, 187, 189, 191, 203, 211, 222, 228, 229
savings 8, 19, 49, 51, 84, 110, 113, 115, 125, 158, 181, 197–9, 203, 212
Sberbank 81, 142
SBS-Agro Bank 59
separatist regions 31
small business 73, 105, 126, 142
social insurance 115
special economic zone 142
Stabilization Fund 7, 150
stagflation 9, 93, 95, 102, 103, 112, 126, 128, 168, 173, 174, 182
State Duma 6, 40, 57–9, 64, 65, 71, 74, 76, 78, 147

stock market 73, 88, 122–4, 128, 138, 147
Stolypin club 200–2, 204
Strategy 2020 148, 187, 200
strike 5, 68, 84, 86
structural modernization 97, 144, 148, 180, 189, 219, 225
supply-side economics 109, 143, 144
Supreme Soviet 37–40
surplus value 163
sustainable growth 94, 104, 155, 225
Svyazinvest 53, 58, 67

Tokobank 57
transaction costs 22, 32, 45

unemployment 74, 93, 96, 102, 110, 126, 127, 141, 157, 163, 175, 199, 213

value added tax (VAT) 163
VEB (Russian Development Bank) 125
Vneshtorgbank (VTB) 142, 198

wage arrears 56, 85, 86
"Washington consensus" 97, 116
welfare 76, 152, 185
welfare state 97, 114, 115, 204, 227
World Trade Organization (WTO) 141, 145, 148, 229

zero lower bound 116